# TOWARD
# A MARXIST
# THEORY OF
# NATIONALISM

# TOWARD
# A MARXIST
# THEORY OF
# NATIONALISM

## Horace B. Davis

Monthly Review Press
New York and London

*Library of Congress Cataloging in Publication Data*
Davis, Horace Bancroft, 1898-
   Toward a Marxist theory of nationalism.
   Includes bibliographical references.
   1. Nationalism and socialism. I. Title.
HX550.N3D33     320.5         77-91740
ISBN 0-85345-441-8

Monthly Review Press
62 West 14th Street, New York, N.Y. 10011
47 Red Lion Street, London WC1R 4PF

Manufactured in the United States of America

10  9  8  7  6  5  4  3  2  1

# Contents

# Foreword

Since there are many serious books on nationalism by writers acceptable to the Establishment, it may seem to some that there is no need for a specifically Marxist book. The raison d'être of the present volume is primarily that the questions a Marxist seeks to answer are not those that especially interest the Establishment.

Neither Marx nor Lenin got very far in the development and presentation of a systematic political theory, and their followers also have bypassed the field. "In no other area of the human sciences has the neglect been so marked," remarks Ralph Miliband. Yet for both Lenin and Marx the theory of the state, and specifically of nationalism, appeared as very important. Marx in the 1840s projected a book on the nation, and Lenin during World War 1 actually set to work to write a book on this same topic but was diverted by other matters. The result is that both men's writings in the field have to do with particular situations; broad generalizations, applicable to the whole range of the subject, tend to be lacking. For both Marxist and bourgeois writers on nationalism, European models constantly intrude. Thus in attempting to treat the subject from a general (global) point of view we are in a sense breaking new ground.

Materials for a systematic study are readily available. There is a vast and growing volume of writings on nationalism and the nation by Marxists as well as non-Marxists, and I do not pretend to have read, much less analyzed, more than a fraction of the literature. My selection of materials will seem arbitrary to some. If my admittedly partial and limited analysis throws light on the general subject, I will be satisfied.

I shall not confine my discussions to Marxists and would-be Marxists. The ideas of non-Marxist scholars are often lacking in logic, *according to their own lights,* and I shall feel free to show wherein I think they have gone astray.

I wish to express appreciation to those scholars who have made available unpublished writings of their own, such as Martin Klein and William Mandel. Very many others have contributed their advice and assistance and to all my thanks are due. The Louis M. Rabinowitz Foundation financed a trip to Europe, and the staffs of numerous libraries have greatly assisted the project.

# 1

## Introduction

Marxists profess to be internationalists, and yet everywhere we find Marxists acting as nationalists.[1] This orientation is sometimes of advantage to the long-run interests of the social revolution, sometimes not. Yet the attempts to fit nationalism into Marxist theory have so far been few and unsatisfactory. As Régis Debray has remarked:

> The near-silence of European Marxists on the question of nationalism will one day be seen as the most costly and ruinous of all historical omissions. Such people work in a vacuum.—Letter of Régis Debray (1969)

In Marxist theory, it has usually been assumed that the interests of class predominate, and that the form of economic organization (the relations of production) exercises a determining influence on the course of events. Perhaps for this reason, too little attention has been paid to a movement which is basically political and cultural. Social classes need to be analyzed afresh when the environment is different from that of nineteenth-century Europe. And the part played by nationalist motives in the social upheavals of the twentieth century has to be brought into focus and related to other movements. We can never allow ourselves to forget Sun Yat-sen's dictum that nationalism is one of the three great movements of the day (along with democracy and socialism).

In this chapter we shall state the problem and define our terms. There follows a discussion of the all-important problem of the ethics of nationalism. We then analyze the ideas of Stalin and Lenin on the national question, and trace the attempts of the Soviet Union to deal with the problem, during the revolution and since. A discussion follows on the experience of Yugoslavia and China. We then trace the relation of nationalism to social revolution in some Latin American countries, and summarize the theoretical contributions of Frantz Fanon and Amilcar Cabral with relation to the African scene. Along the way we shall have examined the relation of the several social classes to revolutionary socialism and nationalism.

## DEFINITION OF THE TERM

The experience and even the definition of nationalism have varied from time to time and from place to place. The attempt to bring together all of nationalism's manifestations has sometimes seemed an impossible task.[2] As Rosa Luxemburg said, the terms "national state" and "nationalism" are in themselves empty husks, into which all historical epochs and class relations pour their special material content (see Luxemburg, 1928:294). But nationalism has a common essence whose specific nature we must try to find.

If we include as nationalism all examples of resistance to alien domination,[3] we must decide that nationalism has always been with us, since such resistance goes back beyond the dawn of recorded history. Successful resistance to alien domination created certain states in Europe at the beginning of the modern period; one thinks immediately of the Dutch and English states. But were they nations? Not if we think of the nation as being comprised of the people rather than the rulers, and permeated by a feeling of national unity and national mission. In that sense, nationalism dates from no earlier than the eighteenth century.

Another attempt to classify types of nationalism distinguishes four main patterns, each of which has been especially characteristic of some one part of the world, which have appeared in more or less chronological order. These have been:

1. The nationalism of people with a long experience of concurrent development of state power and national consciousness, with citizenship determining nationality (Western Europe);

2. The nationalism of countries without a political experience of long duration but with a common language and a common self-image (Italy and Germany);

3. The nationalism of countries such as those of southeastern Europe, without a common political experience of long duration and often without an ethnically homogeneous territory, in which the religion of historical association is usually an important determinant of national consciousness; and

4. The nationalism of anticolonialism and of the drive for "modernity," generally associated with the Third World but manifest also in southeastern Europe. (Stoianovich, 1974:450).

This classification may be useful in a broad sense but it is far from exhaustive and contains overlapping categories, as is immediately obvious when we try to apply it: Is anticolonialism necessarily associated with the drive for modernity? Do India-Pakistan belong in the third category or the fourth? Where does Canada fit in? In categories one and four, the state has been the chief builder of the nation, whereas in categories two and three it is rather the other way round: but any reasonable consideration tells us that state and nation build each other.

The social communications school (Karl Deutsch et al.) defines nationalism in terms of social communication, meaning primarily the mass media: when there are no media, the prerequisites of nationalism are lacking by definition. This approach has the advantage of reducing the task of analysis to manageable proportions. The only question then is whether it has been reduced too far. Must we exclude all illiterate societies? Was there no mass nationalism in Tito's Yugoslavia, Mao's China, or Cabral's Guiné?

Another kind of arbitrary limitation of the field has been characteristic of some Marxists since Lenin's day: that of being willing to consider nationalism only if it results from the action of the bourgeoisie. Lenin chose to limit his field in this way; but even if we took his word for it that Poland and Ireland were not examples of modern nationalism (though Marx thought they were), we would simply not be able to handle the problem of nationalism in much of the Third World today if we discussed only the kind that emanates from a bourgeoisie.[4]

Some authors use the concept "nation" in different ways, depending on the area to which they are referring. As Karl Kautsky once explained:

> In Western Europe . . . the population of a state is designated as the nation. In this sense, for example, we speak of a Belgian nation (although Belgium is bilingual). The further east we go in Europe, the more numerous are the portions of the population in a state that do not wish to belong to it, that constitute national communities of their own within it. They too are called "nations" or "nationalities." It would be advisable to use only the latter term for them. (Kautsky, 1929, II:441)

Discussions of the nation would no doubt have gained in clarity if Kautsky's suggestion had been taken long ago. But it was not. Thus, Stalin in his 1913 essay "Marxism and the National Question" and Lenin in most of his writings made no distinction between nation and nationality.[5] Engels did make such a distinction, but it had little impact; his entire concept of the nationalities of southeastern Europe as nonviable social groups doomed to absorption and extinction had been abandoned by the turn of the century.

Not all of the language groupings in a multilingual state merit the designation of nationalities, even in eastern Europe. Some are too small. Others may reflect no desire on the part of the people to be considered as separate nationalities. In the absence of that, it is best to think of them simply as ethnic groups.

But when a group of people does evince a desire to be considered a nation, does that mean that they are a nation? To some this has indeed been thought of as the sole requisite to nationhood. At the time of World War I, it was said that "a nation exists when its component parts believe it to be a nation." Earlier the great French scholar Ernest Renan had referred to the nation as a "corporate soul."

A moment's thought will show the inadequacy of this approach. For one thing, it offers no means of distinguishing the nation from the tribe. But the two are really quite different, even if Indian tribes were once referred to as "nations." The members of the tribe are bound together by ties of consanguinity, those of the nation, by ties of territoriality. A nation has to have a location in space. The Jews of tsarist Russia made great efforts to be considered a nation, but it was not until they established themselves in Israel that such recognition was generally granted. The Gypsies may apply for recognition by the United Nations, but they are unlikely to succeed unless and until they are denomadized. (Hungary has taken steps to bring about such denomadization. The Soviet Union has been working on the same problem since 1926.)

A nation must also have a certain minimum size. Jamaica is a nation, but Anguilla is not. And finally, a nation must have a certain integration, or interdependence. Feudal society was poor material for nation-building because it was so decentralized.

Other prerequisites for the existence of a nation have been offered in profusion, but they will be found on examination to be redundant, or simply erroneous.[6] If the people of a nation live together, it seems unnecessary to specify that they have a common economic life. They may have a common history and a "national character," but they may not; Pakistan was not a historical entity, and the recently emerged African nations often took the borders set for them by the European powers, even when these cut across linguistic and historical lines. Wiatr says that a people are not a nation unless they are organized as a separate political state (Wiatr, 1969). This is indeed a peculiar point of view coming from a Pole: were the Poles not a nationality during the long period when there was no Polish state?

The new emphasis on the state as the measure and substance of the nation corresponds to the rise to statehood of many formerly subservient peoples, namely, the colonials. The United Nations is an organization of political states. But the nation is still far from coterminous with the state; nations may be built up within or outside of (in opposition to) existing state structures, now as formerly. It is only necessary to refer to the national movements of Biafra and Bangladesh to remind ourselves that the failure to distinguish adequately between state and nation is quite wrong.

Some Marxists, including Stalin and especially Karl Kautsky, included a common language as one characteristic feature of a nation. It is of course true that language is often, perhaps usually, associated with nationality; but this is by no means a universal combination. For most large nations and many medium and small ones have more than one language. Switzerland has five languages, of which three (German,

French, and Italian) are official, but it is a nation, however much its unity may have been strained during both world wars. And of course the same language may be spoken by more than one nation.

Usually it has been assumed that people will choose to be united with others speaking the same language, if only to form a stronger power unit, but the plebiscites conducted after World War I furnished some examples of people voting to join a nation that spoke a different language (Cobban, 1969:69-70).

Another assumption that has been challenged is that small peoples always wish their language to be preserved. It is clear that in Marxist theory at least, if the decision to abandon a language is to be made, it should be made by the people speaking that language and not by any outside authority.

We find then that a nation always has (1) a specified territory; (2) a certain minimum size; (3) some integration (centralization, inter-dependence); and (4) a consciousness of itself as a nation. The first and the fourth points are the key ones: a specified territory and national consciousness.

## HOW NATIONS ARE FORMED

While economics had obviously much to do with the formation of nations, the reasons for setting up such bodies have been primarily political. The nation-state is the favored form, under modern conditions, for organizing political life, resisting aggression, and increasing the power of the (territorial) group in various ways. From the point of view of traditional free-trade economics, the nation-state is a monstrosity; but for the purposes which people, including Marxists, have in mind today, the nation-state is ineluctable—we cannot do without it.

Nations are formed primarily in three ways.

First, they may be formed from states. The French state, the English state, the Dutch, the Spanish, and other European states that were in existence at the dawn of the modern era, all evolved into nations, some sooner than others. It would be a mistake to describe as nations the Dutch at the time they won their independence from Spain, or the English in the time of Queen Elizabeth; but the nation was clearly there in embryo, and it emerged full-fledged in most European countries in the wake of the Napoleonic wars.

Second, nations are formed in struggle against foreign oppression. The experience of shaking off European domination has made nations out of very many colonies that previously had little or no national consciousness.

The Poles are an interesting case because they had a state and were in the process of becoming a nation precisely at the time of the Third Partition in 1792. Thereafter the Polish nation was solidified in conflict, punctuated by repeated uprisings, and finally emerged as a recognized state in 1919.

The third way in which nations are formed is by first attaining cultural solidarity and then political expression of that solidarity. The succession states of the Dual Empire rose to national consciousness while still in subjection to Austria and Hungary. Italy and Germany are of course classical examples of countries whose cultural unification preceded the political.

The origin of nations is often confused with the origin of states. This confusion is to be expected when the terms "nation" and "state" are used interchangeably, as they commonly are. Some scholars do not make this distinction clear.[7]

The circumstances under which nationalist *movements* arise are very varied. The first mass nationalist organization in Indonesia, known as "Sarekat Islam" or "Islamic Union," grew out of a movement for religious reform. Starting before World War I, this Safari purism sought to "purify" the Moslem religion, much as the Puritans had sought to purify the Church of England in the seventeenth century. The movement struck deep roots in the population; it developed just after World War I into a crusade for political and economic revolution as well. It adopted an economic program that had been suggested by the Communist International. Thereafter, in 1921, it split into scriptural and Marxist wings, the latter evolving shortly into the Indonesian Communist Party. A similar sequence could be observed a little later in Morocco, where the 1930 Kutlat al-'Amal al-Watani, the National Action Bloc, a mass nationalist organization, grew out of the scriptural movement (Geertz, 1968:73, 84). In Algeria, in the early 1950s, the religious reform movement known as the "Badissia" after its leader got support both in the cities and among the peasants, especially the middle peasants; it was one of the two main sources of Algerian nationalism (Wolf, 1969:228-230ff.).

In earlier historical epochs, when cultures changed only slowly, peoples in a racially or culturally mixed society might live side by side for 500 or 1,000 years without amalgamating but without internecine warfare either. India and Guatemala are among the many good examples. But in the modern period, rapidly increasing ease of communication and the growth of interregional trade create strong pressures for the formation of a unitary state where this does not already exist. The central government may deliberately accentuate this pressure, as the Soviet Union is doing today.

Of course, such pressures may be counterproductive, especially where the central government is engaging in domination or exploitation, or even where it is not sufficiently solicitous of the (quite natural) local sentiment of the areas in question. And even a solicitude for local feelings may not prevent the rise of separatist sentiment if the area is undergoing a political or economic crisis (as we shall see in detail in our discussions of Yugoslavia).

It is not necessarily the case that the rise of nationalism is preceded by domination and exploitation or is the outgrowth of a crisis. Scotch and Welsh nationalists have alleged that they were politically or economically dominated, but this claim is hard to take seriously. Their respective nationalist movements, starting as cultural phenomena pure and simple, have still come to enroll a considerable proportion of the electorate, and are a factor in national elections.

In France also, the Brittany Liberation Front has been clamoring for more attention to be paid to the Breton (Gaelic) language, and early in 1974 emissaries of this group blew up a 630-foot transmitting tower in order to attract the attention of the world to their claims.

Usually the grievances of the mobilizing masses are more tangible than mere neglect. It is interesting to see how Establishment scholars, who avoid discussions of exploitation, handle this question. Karl Deutsch points out that there have been periods in European history when the intellectuals, the educated groups at the top, professed essentially the same culture, while the population at the bottom was not at all similar in the different areas. Civilization then was like a layer cake, with the greatest assimilation at the top, little or none at the bottom (Deutsch, 1953:170-72).

However, at a certain point in time the people at the bottom are mobilized for political organization; a Marxist might be permitted to say that they were called upon to resist exploitation. The distinctive national characteristics then become of political importance. The reason, according to Deutsch, has been a failure of assimilation. Now see in what clear, forthright language Deutsch conveys the crucial idea that nationalism arises out of a protest against discrimination and exploitation:

> The intensity and appeal of nationalism in a world of sharply differentiated income and living standards perhaps may tend to be *inversely proportional to the barriers to mobility between nations and classes, and strictly proportional to the barriers against cultural assimilation, and to the extent of the economic and prestige differences between classes, cultures and regions.* (ibid.: 180)

And what is the remedy that Deutsch suggests to a power elite confronted with such a protest? He proposes that assimilation be advanced; then the people in power can continue to retain their power:

> Knitting the population together in an ever tighter network of communication and complementarity based on the ever broader and more thorough participation of the masses of the populace . . . is sound power politics. (ibid.:184)

If this prescription is taken at face value, it can only mean that the "people at the top" are being advised to grant full rights and full facilities for advancement to all of the masses at the bottom, regardless of race, creed, or color. In other words, Deutsch sympathizes with the aspirations of the politically mobilizing masses. He does not however offer them any advice as to what they should do if the people at the top do not follow his recommendations.

Under modern conditions, the mere fact of cultural or racial differences in a population may be thought of as constituting an invitation to nationalism. The nation is so much a part of the European culture that Tom Nairn (1974) opened a discussion of Scotch nationalism by inquiring why there had *not* been Scotch nationalism until recently. Black nationalism in the United States has been endemic since early in the nineteenth century (see H. B. Davis in Cohen, 1974). The writer recalls a conversation he had in 1919, long before the fruition of

African nationalist aspirations, with an American black who had been fighting in France and was on his way home. The soldier expressed a desire to go back sometime to visit Egypt and see what the people there had done in the past. He referred to them as "my people." I thought at the time that he came from Egyptian ancestry, but reflection showed that this was unlikely. His ancestors more probably came from the Guinea Coast. He was thinking of *Africa* as his home; the achievements of the ancient Egyptians were also his. In retrospect this chance conversation seems especially interesting because the Garvey movement had not yet started in the United States. Thus, the nationalist organizer may be thought of as one who articulates a sentiment that has lain dormant. Theodore G. Vincent says of Marcus Garvey that his "objective was to give blacks a consciousness of the nationhood which already existed" (1971:22).

But a nation does not create itself; it has to be built. The time required to create a national consciousness is often underestimated by hasty politicians and military men. Take the case of Vietnam. In the northern half of that country, when the French, breaking their pledges, had reassumed control after World War II, the Vietnamese leaders were outraged and set about to organize a resistance movement. The military under Vo Nguyen Giap were ready to move; but on the advice of Ho Chi Minh they delayed for a period of years, while a painstaking campaign was conducted at the grassroots. When the peasants were fully indoctrinated—in this case, not only for nationalism but for socialism—the military operations were started, with what results the world knows.

Small ethnic groups, even when culturally self-conscious, do not always generate lasting nationalist consciousness, of course. In fact, we are tempted to say that this is the typical experience; a small ethnic group in contact with a large, aggressive nation may gradually be absorbed without leaving a trace.

Is humanity the poorer when this happens? The disappearance of an ethnic group is not the same as the disappearance of the constituent members of the group; they go on reproducing and may eventually contribute as much as anybody to the larger group that has absorbed them. But in the cases which especially interest us, the members of the minority group are dominated and exploited, both before and after the loss of the separate culture. To put an end to such domination is today the aim of the typical nationalist movement, which then acquires status in the eyes of Marxists.

It is true that Marxists have sometimes stressed the contributions, actual or potential, of smaller nationalities to world culture as the reason why they as Marxists stand up for the rights of such nationalities. Stalin did this in the period when he could still have some claim to be considered a Marxist (Stalin, 1942). But that, we repeat, is not really the point. Contributions to world science, or world culture in general, have a larger audience from the start when made in a language that is widely used. Ideas that are valid in one language can become available in others. There is no reason to think that a great writer would be deprived of an audience if that writer was not able to use his or her native idiom.

What is at stake in such cases—and it is no small matter—is the right of small ethnic groups to be entertained or edified in their own language, and this idea implies that they should be educated in that language and know something of its literature. Their culture will be "consolidated," to use Lenin's term.

Russians and other Marxists have sometimes been criticized for insisting too strongly on the linguistic and cultural rights of smaller nationalities. It is far better—far more in the spirit of Lenin—to err in this direction than to move in the other direction and fall into the trap of assimilationism, which is only a step removed from outright imperialism.[8] This is not to say that Communists in a country such as India should spend their time trying to build up linguistic groups into nationalities. This procedure can be justified in Marxist terms when, and only when, it is a contribution to freeing such groups from exploitation and domination by other cultural groups.

## MEASURING NATIONALISM

There is no accepted technique for measuring scientifically the extent and intensity of nationalist sentiment. Yet the need for making such measurement has been evident to policy-makers for some time. It seems to be especially difficult for the imperialist mentality to accept the idea that ordinary people may be passionately loyal to a socialist fatherland.

During the Vietnam war, the Establishment at Washington recognized that if the morale of the National Liberation Front (NLF) continued high, it would be practically impossible for the United States to subdue the Vietnamese people, north or south.

In mid-1964, the RAND Corporation, a research outfit financed primarily by the government, was commissioned to study the question: Who are the Vietcong and what motivates them? In charge of the project was Joseph J. Zasloff, a professor of political science at the University of Pittsburgh, who was a RAND consultant. He built up a staff who conducted interviews with over a hundred people from the liberated areas: prisoners, defectors, refugees, "anyone we could get ahold of." The data were analyzed with rare objectivity and while they were not all internally consistent, they did seem to point in a single direction. At least that was the conclusion of Zasloff and his associates, who presented their report late in 1964. They found that the anti-government guerrillas in the south represented an authentic national liberation movement.

They found—and this finding is of primary importance for our purposes—that there were many poor peasants who were fully aware of the issues and were very vocal in their aspirations for education, economic opportunity, equality, and justice for themselves and especially for their children. They looked on themselves as the legitimate rulers of an independent Vietnam; and on people put in power by foreigners as usurpers. They were, in a word, highly conscious nationalists, albeit illiterate ones. Bombing, it was thought, would have little effect on their morale, which was high.

Their nationalism was reinforced by their sense of social grievance. As security in the countryside deteriorated after 1960, and the influence of the NLF spread, the peasants with means fled to the province towns and Saigon, leaving the poorer elements as almost the sole inhabitants of the countryside. "The poor came under the control of the Front, and the war became in a real sense a class war" (Landau, 1972:33; direct quote from the Zasloff report, made available to the public early in 1972).

The findings of Zasloff, presented in summary form late in 1964, were not to the taste of the men around Lyndon Johnson. Zasloff returned to his university chair. But that was not the end of the affair. Another "scholar," a man of a different stripe, was to keep the project alive, collect more material, reinterpret the original interviews, and come up with a set of conclusions opposed to those of Zasloff. The new researcher was a professional anti-Sovieteer by the name of Leon Goure.

Goure had contacts that Zasloff had lacked. He peddled his findings, to the effect that NLF morale was deteriorating, to high circles in Washington—to Secretary Robert McNamara, to W. W. Rostow, to McGeorge Bundy. Goure's belief that "enemy" morale would ebb with increasing applications of force became the officially accepted doctrine in Washington.

Goure did not claim to be doing scientific research. He himself said later: "We didn't do research studies. You designed the questions to get the needed input." But his findings were accepted and endorsed by the highest level in the RAND Corporation and were not seriously challenged in Washington. The result was a stinging defeat for the United States and its whole policy of pacification. President Johnson in his famous "resignation" speech admitted that he had been unable even with the massive use of force to break the morale of the "Vietcong."

Another, very telling, illustration of failure to measure nationalist sentiment was the estimate of the psychology of the Cuban people in the early years of the Castro regime. If President Kennedy, Professor Schlesinger, and the top brass who planned the U.S.-sponsored invasion of Cuba had been better informed, they might have been spared the embarrassing defeat of the Bay of Pigs.

Surely, then, the development of techniques of measuring nationalism is important. But the imperialists, French and American, have not only failed to develop an acceptable technique of measuring nationalism, they have shown themselves completely unable to understand its workings. This failure constitutes an important reason why they have not developed an effective tactic to counter it.

The French in the last years of the Algerian War of Independence (1956–1963) developed a strategy of herding the Algerian peasants into concentration camps. This move was intended as an answer to Mao Tse-tung's proposition that the guerrillas are like fish that swim in the water, the water being the general population, the peasants. If the water is drained away, reasoned the French imperialist, the fish must die (Bennoune, 1973:47; quoting the French government report of December 1960).

Actually, when the Algerian peasants were collected into concentration camps, the effect was to unify them still further into a common effort. Local differences among them were swiftly overcome as all became ever more conscious of the joint effort they were engaged in. The concentration camp tactic, which was imitated by the U.S. imperialists in South Vietnam, was the very opposite of the tactic of "divide and rule." Its results were counterproductive, in terms of what the imperialists sought to accomplish. If the peasants had not been nationalists before, they would surely become so now. And indeed the inmates of the camps devised ways of communicating with the National Liberation Front and maintained their morale under heavy pressure until the battle—in this case the battle for the minds of the population—was won.

The study of the national question, suffused as it is with emotion and subjective judgments, is difficult at best. But the obstacles to be overcome before a really scientific study can be undertaken are greater than is generally realized because the basic data are suspect.

Even analyses of nationality based on census figures tend to be unreliable. In the U.S. Census of 1960, some five million members of minority groups were "omitted" from the tabulations; and ten years later the methods of collecting census data were still faulty. It is certain that the number of Puerto Ricans in the United States was greatly understated. We do not only refer to the criticism made by a leading member of the Puerto Rican community, that second and third generation Puerto Ricans who still considered themselves as belonging to their ancestral habitat should have been listed as Puerto Ricans rather than Americans. The fact that census forms were distributed by mail, that they could not be read by many of the (Spanish-speaking or illiterate) recipients (who may not even have received them), the presence of an attitude of suspicion toward all questionnaires, the absence of any concerted attempt to overcome this attitude, and the mobility of people which made it hard for them to receive mail—these and other factors added up to an unreliable head count in this area.

It has long been a commonplace among sociologists that counting the people of a given nationality is a problem beset with special difficulties. Florian Znaniecki reports on a 1934–1935 investigation of the inhabitants of the marshy Pripet area, in what was then part of Poland. The peasants were told, presumably on the basis of the language they spoke, that they were White Ruthenians. It was news to them. Nearly half of them did not know that such a nationality existed (Znaniecki, 1952:82).

Sometimes the illiterate peasants are not as backward as they may seem. Even in remote communities, people knew what government collected taxes from them and called on them for military service. They were accustomed to regard emissaries from the central government with well-founded suspicion.

Stories of how people change their nationalities are not any the less true for being old. Often quoted is an East European informant who said of a certain border village that the people changed their nationalities according to who was asking the question, or according to their economic interests or those of the head of the village.

In Yugoslavia the government, in an effort to bury old animosities between Serbs and Croatians, sought at one time to get people to think of themselves not as members of either of these groups, but as Yugoslavs. This well-intentioned move was attacked as a political ploy intended to injure those who did not answer in a certain way; it had to be abandoned.

Lenin was well aware that statistics are often a trap for the unwary. Yet when he set out—as he did—to write a book on the nationality problem, he began with a *statistical* discussion of the "Historical Background to National Movements." Unfortunately he got no farther than a demonstration that the West European imperialist countries and the United States and Japan were relatively homogeneous, while the East European countries had by and large a multinational composition (Lenin, CW, XXVIII:271-77).

## WHAT IS INTERNATIONALISM?

Internationalism, in the original Marxist sense, is incompatible with the conventional kind of nationalism, which consists in defending and advancing the national interests of a particular country. But since the socialist states are all forced to play international politics, with all the hypocrisies that that involves, they often find themselves supporting reactionary groups in the countries that are their political alllies. The first case on record was that of Lenin with regard to Turkey. Even stranger on the face of things, but perfectly intelligible nevertheless, were the rapprochements of Stalin and Hitler, or Mao and Yahya Khan.

Marxist internationalism has been, then, an affair of individuals or groups. The bearers of such internationalism are typically writers and publicists; but they may also be members of a fighting group such as the International Brigade in the Spanish War of 1935–1939. When socialist *governments* present themselves as bearers of proletarian internationalism, they must expect to be greeted with cynical reserve.

Internationalism, in the original Marxist sense, is quite compatible with support of anti-imperialist national liberation movements, especially if these are socialist oriented. The Romanians have recently proclaimed that the pursuit of national interests is "true internationalism," and, taken in context, this statement is not at all unreasonable (see King, 1973:253).

We submit that the term "internationalism" should be reserved for acts and policies that aid the international socialist revolution, and that employing it in any other sense is obfuscation, if not nationalism in disguise.

Should Marxists then abandon the attempt to be internationalists?

Yes, if they put the interests of their own country first, as heads of state must always do. But for those who are not part of the machinery of government of some socialist state, the case is different. Marxist theory must still be internationalist, even when particular socialist states are not. Internationalism, correctly understood and interpreted, is of the essence of Marxism.

Deutscher had this to say in a 1964 lecture:

> Socialists must be internationalists even if their working classes are not; socialists must also understand the nationalism of the masses, but only in the way in which a doctor understands the weakness or the illness of his patient. Socialists should be aware of that nationalism, but like nurses, they should wash their hands twenty times over whenever they approach an area of the labor movement infected by it. (Deutscher, 1971:110-11)

And Deutscher concluded: "Internationalism remains the vital principle of a new world" (ibid.:112).

If this proposition is intended to show that Marxists should support socialist revolutions everywhere, it is strictly orthodox by pre-1914 standards. But if it is intended to imply that socialist states should give diplomatic help to such revolutions, it is based on a misconception. Socialist states, in the first enthusiasm about their own revolutions, have sometimes sought to expand their experiences: the Soviet Union to Europe, and Cuba to Latin America. But when it became evident that this was not going to work, the socialist states in question adopted a policy of stabilization. Revolutions in other countries were not only not supported, they might even be condemned.

In early Marxist theory this problem was glossed over. It was believed that the revolution would take place simultaneously in the leading countries, and that socialist governments would not have national interests as against one another. In practice, however, socialist states decidedly do have national interests even against one another, and these invariably take precedence over the interests of other countries or movements.[9]

Let us take a quick look at some of the socialist revolutions in the making in the period since 1917, to determine whether the success of such revolutions was the prime consideration of the leading socialist country of the time.

With regard to Spain in the 1930s, it was not generally realized in the West how close the country had been to a socialist revolution. After the attempted Franco coup, the working class hit back with devastating force. As a Soviet historian later put it:

> July-August 1936 saw settled, in fact, the basic problems of the revolution, those of political power and ownership of the instruments and means of production. Local authority passed, in practice, into the hands of the armed proletariat. Also into their hands, and to a lesser extent into those of the peasants, passed all the instruments and means of production belonging to the capitalists and landowners. A large part of the bourgeoisie and of its state machine was liquidated on the territory held by the Republic. (Quoted in Claudín, 1975:224.)

At the end of August, representatives of the Anarcho-Syndicalist CNT are said to have met with representatives of the Marxist-Socialist UGT— these being the two leading workers' organizations in the country—and worked out a plan to set up a governing junta under Largo Caballero, a Left Socialist. The junta would include representatives of the Communist and Socialist parties and of the FAI, the anarchist political group, as well as of the CNT and UGT, but the bourgeois Republicans would be excluded.

The plan was laid before Soviet ambassador Rosenberg, who would have none of it. He suggested instead that the bourgeois Republican parties be included, and this was presently done; Largo Caballero was Prime Minister, but the workers' republic was dead (Claudín, 1975: n.59). In the labor movement, regional and doctrinal differences reasserted themselves, the Loyalist forces were weakened and split, and the victory of the Fascists was complete.

Stalin, as is well known, was not consulted about the formation of Tito's army in Yugoslavia in 1940. Stalin tried repeatedly to get Tito to join with Mihailovich, who was slaughtering Croatians in complete opposition to Tito's policies of national concord; later Stalin sought to have Tito recognize the government of King Peter in London, at a time when even the British had forsaken that government-in-exile. The British in the end had to persuade Stalin to accept Tito as the legitimate head of the Yugoslav government. It was Tito, not Stalin, who turned the international war into a civil war in Yugoslavia.

Kim Il Sung was organizing a very broad united front in Korea during the period before World War II, when word came through from the Comintern to set up a Communist party. Kim politely disregarded the instructions, and his form of organization proved to be successful in accomplishing its purposes, which were to carry out the socialist revolution.[10] Ho Chi Minh would not have carried the war to the French in Vietnam if he had followed the instructions from the Soviet Union, which in this instance coincided with the policies of the Communist Party of France.

Fidel Castro eventually made a united front with the Communist-led workers in the Cuban unions, but only at the end, just before the victorious march on Havana. The Cuban Communist Party was in good standing with the Soviet Union, which had approved, in effect, its policy of keeping the peace with Batista, even of cooperating with him. Castro eventually replaced the leadership of the Party and in effect absorbed it into the 26th of July Movement (see Halperin, 1972:204, 222).

With regard to Greece, just after World War II, Stalin was more loyal to his bargain with Churchill and Roosevelt (at Yalta) than he was to the international socialist revolution. Not only did Stalin not encourage the Greek Communist guerrillas to stage a revolution which would be at the same time nationalist and socialist, but when it appeared that they might succeed anyway, with Yugoslav help, Stalin turned the Greek Communists against the Yugoslavs and destroyed the basis of cooperation between them without which the Greek guerrilla war could not succeed (Djilas, 1969 statement). The Greeks apparently did not realize that Stalin, in his effort to protect the accord with Churchill and thus safeguard the Soviet Union, was prepared, even determined, to hand them back to the monarchy.

An example from recent history of a social revolution that was crushed with socialist countries' complicity is that of Indonesia. As recounted by David Horowitz, the policy favored in 1964–1965 for the Communist Party of Indonesia (PKI), by both the Chinese and the Russians, was that of keeping the peace and collaborating with the national bourgeoisie. But there were economic grievances. The peasants were land hungry. A law on agrarian reform, passed in 1960 under President Sukarno, was badly applied. So the peasant unions themselves began to divide the land of large proprietors. The Muslim parties and the Indonesian Nationalist Party (conservative) threatened to withdraw from the liberal coalition and to cause the fall of the government. The PKI, instead of leading the peasants, attempted to hold them back, as the Communist Party of China had done in China in 1927. In the fall of 1965, the proprietors moved to recover their land, and the landless peasants were mercilessly butchered; it is estimated that half a million "Communists" were killed.

The reactionary generals went on to seize state power, and later the Chinese, who had made up the bulk of the small trading element, were expelled from Indonesia in a body. The generals used Russian-supplied arms for their coup. Indeed, the Kremlin is said to have continued its aid to the generals after the coup, and to have defended the new counter-revolutionary dictatorship as much as a year later, on the ground that it was collaborating with the Soviet Union, and following an "anti-imperialist and anti-colonialist policy" (Horowitz, 1969: 212-14; based on *Le Monde*, Feb. 18, 1967, and *Avanti*, Dec. 17, 1966).

We do not argue that a socialist country *always* betrays socialist revolutions. That would be ridiculous. When it does not cost anything to do so, and when aid to such a revolution coincides with the interests of the established socialist country, that socialist country typically expresses sympathy for the success of a socialist revolution abroad; and aid is forthcoming. Thus both the Soviet Union and People's China came to the aid of socialist Vietnam in the 1960s, in spite of their sharp differences on other questions, because both had an interest in heading off the expansion of the United States onto the mainland of Asia. And the Soviet Union gave invaluable aid to Castro's Cuba at a time when there was no other way to salvage socialism on that island. Such aid need not of course be altruistic, and the granting of it may partake of the nature of adventurism, as the Chinese said was the case with the Soviet aid to Cuba in the missile crisis of 1962.

It might seem that the bad blood currently existing between the two leading socialist powers would enhance the possibility of a struggling new socialist state getting *some* kind of foreign aid. But this does not follow necessarily. China and the Soviet Union joined in aiding Vietnam; they might join in disregarding the interests of some would-be socialist state elsewhere, if their respective national interests so dictated. The revolutionary socialist uprising in Sri Lanka in 1971 found the Soviet Union and People's China both backing the established government (Halliday, 1971:56, 86, 91). This was not a Marxist position.[11]


## THE RATIONALITY OF NATIONALISM


Some Marxists today profess to regard nationalism as an irrational superstition. This attitude is a survival of the days when Marxists were dedicated exclusively to proletarian internationalism, and looked on nationalism as interfering with the class struggle. In these days when proletarian internationalism is dead, the national liberation movement is the most logical if not the only means of fighting colonial and semicolonial oppression, and all Marxists must perforce agree that such oppression must be fought. For the Marxist, then, nationalism is sometimes clearly rational.

In nineteenth-century Europe, nationalism was reasonable from the point of view of the bourgeoisie who were its main purveyors, as Lenin pointed out. Nationalism guaranteed the native bourgeoisie the internal market, and furnished them a means of protecting their interests abroad. The nationalism that led to the unification of Germany and Italy was clearly of advantage to their respective bourgeoisies.

Marxists granted these advantages, but still deplored the overgrowth of nationalism, which not only tended to damp down the class struggle but was bound up with militarism, war, and high taxes. Marxists also argued that economic nationalism fostered monopoly at home and thus was unreasonable from the point of view of workers as consumers. If Marxists' economics had been more up to date, they would no doubt have argued that nationalism in the form of imperialism perverted economic development in the colonies and betrayed the interests of the colonial proletariat.

There are few fields in which error is so rampant as in the evaluation of the part played by nationalism in historic events and of the motives for such nationalism. We content ourselves with one or two examples.

The Spanish-American War was presented to the American people as a crusade to free the Cuban people from Spanish domination—in other words, to support Cuban nationalism. Needless to say, this was not the main motivation of the Americans who made the war. Another popular explanation of the origins of the war was that it was made by the jingoistic press, certainly an oversimplified statement of the case. More sophisticated was the idea that the war was brought on in order to rescue the United States from an incipient depression; some even generalized this explanation and contended that when people are employed and prosperous they cease to be jingos! (see Schirmer, 1972: 47; and on the real causes of the war, see Schirmer, passim).

Such simplistic explanations and irrelevant appeals to the nationalist (patriotic) motive might be considered foreign to Marxist analysis; but Marxists are by no means immune to this kind of tactic.

When Yugoslavia was in economic difficulties in 1971, and Croatian students were following the lead of those in France and Germany and advancing anarchist "internationalist" solutions, it was President Tito who called on the loyal Croatian students to put down this kind of internationalism. Tito's speech was taken as a green light for the revival of Croatian nationalism, not only by the students to whom it was addressed but eventually by demagogues within and without the Yugoslav Communist Party, the League of Communists. The movement got completely out of hand.

Marxists therefore do well to think twice before appealing to nationalist motives. Consider the propaganda of the Communist Party of Germany, which in the period 1919–1933, under the direction of the Communist International, tended to blame Germany's woes on the Versailles Treaty. The Nazis of course also took this line, and so later the German Communists were in a poor position. The Communists should have challenged the Nazis on the ground that the real cause of the crisis was the capitalist system.

Socialist states are in great danger of substituting nationalism for socialism as their main goal. The containment of irrational nationalist passions becomes a number one priority in this era when a false step might be fatal to all civilization.

We are confronted with a dilemma: whether to consider nationalism a rationalist, secular, modern movement, or whether to emphasize the more distinctively national elements, many of which are frankly atavistic and irrelevant to modern conditions. The modernist emphasis would lead to an international culture in which national elements would tend to fade out; this was exactly the fate predicted for nationalism by an internationalist such as Karl Kautsky.

The philosopher Ernest Gellner has argued that this opposition is not a problem. Ultimately, he says, the nationalist movements invariably contain both elements:

> . . . a genuine modernism and a more or less spurious concern for local culture, or rather the re-employment of what had been a traditional culture for the enrichment and the trappings of a new education-rooted way of life, and for the provision of the defining differentiae of a new political unit. By the twentieth century, the dilemma hardly bothers anyone; the philosopher-kings of the "underdeveloped" world all act as westernizers, and all talk like *narodniks*. (Gellner, 1964:171)

Actually the situation is more complicated than Gellner indicates. The nationalist leaders of the twentieth century have to be in favor of development, and in that sense perhaps they are all Westernizers, but some, for instance Gandhi, have been far from a nationalist approach to some important problems. This is not to say that they have necessarily been insincere. And surely not all nationalists talk like *narodniks*. There are some who make only the barest obeisance toward populist aims. Others use the populist lingo but turn out to be apologists for imperialism, like Haya de la Torre in Peru, or simply careerists, while still others, and not the least important, are true Marxist social revolutionaries.

The opposition between the two approaches to nationalism is real enough, and is not always bridged in the individual, in spite of the well-known capacity of the human mind for entertaining mutually exclusive ideas at the same time. Very frequently encountered is the competition in the nationalist movement between the two types of leadership, the modern and the traditional, with first one and then the other attaining hegemony. The one that wins out in the end is the modernizing, Westernizing element, but it may be only after a protracted struggle.

Nationalism, then, is not in itself irrational, but it may be irrationally applied. Atavistic nationalism cannot be condemned out of hand; when considered as part of a movement for a people to regain its pride and self-respect, it has a constructive aspect. But belligerent, aggressive, chauvinistic nationalism is a menace and thus irrational from the point of view of humanity as a whole.


## CLASS ATTITUDES TO NATIONALISM

It has been customary to assume that particular social classes would take particular attitudes to nationalism in their respective countries. Before World War I the left wing of organized labor was internationalist-minded, and wanted to believe that this attitude characterized the whole working class. When World War I showed the hollowness of this assumption, many adopted the opposite point of view, and came to look on labor as "naturally" nationalistic.

Others have attributed nationalist sentiments to the lower middle class and the land-owning peasantry. Chalmers Johnson, whose ideas we shall consider a little later, makes this assumption with regard to the peasantry in two important countries. Some students, noting that the Nazis carried many rural districts in the election of 1932 in Germany, somewhat hastily attributed this result to the inbred nationalism of the peasants.

Rudolf Heberle decided to test this assumption. He made a careful study of the provinces of Schleswig and Holstein, in the north of Germany bordering on Denmark. His problem was: What had turned the peasants in Schleswig-Holstein from parties of moderate reform (the Social Democrats got 44 percent of the vote in 1903) to a majority of votes for the Nazis: 51 percent of the total Schleswig-Holstein vote in 1932, with some rural districts going almost solidly for the Nazis. Heberle found in effect that the reason for the shift was the economic crisis that began in 1929.

The Landvolk movement had arisen when debtors reacted, sometimes violently, against mortgage foreclosures. When this group went to pieces, the remnants joined the Nazis. The inroads of Nazi Nationalsozialistische Deutsche Arbeiterpartei (NSDAP) propaganda in the rural areas coincided roughly with the beginning of the depression (Heberle, 1970:26, 32, 56, 71).

The Nazis offered the peasants a variety of nostrums for their economic ills. Most of these were found also in the platforms of other parties. The NSDAP was different in that it sought total power and demanded total dedication. The psychology of the area was not at all that of a war of revenge against France; if anything, the peasants remained anti-Prussian and rather in favor of international conciliation and a new federative European order (ibid.:84, 122).

Of course, there were other factors in the Nazi successes. The NSDAP emphasized regional and rural culture (folk dances, and so forth). The peasants were also antiurban, and the Nazis learned to play on their prejudices. Indeed, the Nazi "line" was officially very propeasant; farmers were to be regarded as the privileged class (*der erste Stand*). Later, after the Nazis came into power, the policy of enforced entailment of middle-sized peasant properties gave the government a stranglehold on the villages, which, with government control of prices, gave the government a fairly effective technique for holding the peasants in line behind the regime. Hitler cajoled and praised the peasants (Friedrich, 1937:724, 730-31). But nationalism was the least part of the picture in the German rural areas.

It is clear that it was the economic crisis of capitalism and not nationalist propaganda that turned the German peasants, and the

German people in general, to the Nazis. The extreme demagogy of the propaganda, promising a complete revamping of society, came at a time when the collapse of the old order was apparent. For a variety of reasons the choice of the German people fell on the Nazis rather than on the Communists.

The great revolutionary leaders, such as Lenin and Mao, have employed a flexible policy toward all classes, including some, such as the middle peasants, who were not predisposed to favor socialism. In their approach to these classes, the major leaders have used nationalist and anti-imperialist appeals, but without surrendering the leadership of the movement to antisocialist elements, as revisionist socialist and later Communist party leaders have done repeatedly. True Leninists and Maoists have showed a real concern to convince their opponents.

The strong insistence on class analysis in the writings of both Lenin and Mao often blinds their would-be followers to the actual history of the policies followed by both. Neither the Russian nor the Chinese Revolution could have succeeded if the leaders had been doctrinaire and had insisted in practice on any particular analysis of the psychology of specified classes.

An appropriate analysis of particular countries and geographic areas will enable us to dispose of certain of these false theories of the relations of class and nationalism, and to substitute a more realistic approach.

# 2

## The Ethics of Nationalism

Aggressive imperialists customarily take a high moral line in describing their actions. They talk glibly of the "civilizing mission" and of "development" when their real motive for aggression is quite different. Thus Gladstone, writing to Queen Victoria to suggest that England might not be able to grab off colonies in all parts of the world at once, said that the time had come when England would have to stop "righting wrongs" in certain parts of the world. And Theodore Roosevelt, asserting the hegemony of the United States in Latin America, wrote to Congress in 1909 that "chronic wrong-doing ... may in America, as elsewhere, ultimately require intervention by some civilised nation" (Emerson, 1960:403).

We propose to submit this easy assumption, that one's own country is always right, to a searching examination. In order to do so, we must go back to the very beginning of nationalism, to the eighteenth century.

In the middle of the eighteenth century, before the term "nationalism" came into general use, Rousseau defined patriotism in such a way as to make it coincide with ethical behavior. In his theory, the goal and sanction of political activity was not the aggrandizement of the state but the welfare of the population, as determined by the General Will.

The individual, to Rousseau, had a duty to contribute to the formation of the General Will (thus democracy was tied in with the idea of patriotism) and a corresponding duty to abide by the General Will once that had been established. Rousseau deliberately labeled this ethical duty "patriotism," appealing to an emotion-laden motive as sanction for what was essentially ethical behavior. Patriotism was presently identified with nationalism. The association of democracy with nationalism was reinforced.when the French Revolution was threatened by invaders.

The nationalism of the Enlightenment was by and large rational rather than emotional, in spite of the overtones of Rousseau's "patriotism." But another kind of nationalism grew up at the end of the eighteenth century. It was based on culture and tradition and into it, too, Rousseau's thought entered. Rousseau had developed the antithesis between the primitive and the artificial, with the former getting the more favorable treatment. This idea was picked up and applied to the nation by early German romantic nationalists such as Herder and Fichte. The nation, they said, was a work of nature, and therefore, something sacred, eternal, organic, carrying a deeper justification than the works of men (Kohn, 1944:381, 351-52). This idea of the nation as preceding the state and eventually leading to its formation is very distinctly European; it has no relevance to the problems of newly formed nations such as most of those in Africa, where the state preceded the nation and conditioned its whole existence.

The nationalism of Herder and Fichte was tolerant of other nationalisms; it was liberal politically. As Herder put it:

> If each of these nations were to remain in its place, one might look on the earth as a garden where this national human plant would bloom one here and one there, where this species of animal here and that one there carries on its own business each according to its instincts and character. (Herder, 1909:84; author's translation).

Whether in the form of Herder's tradition and emotion or of Enlightenment rationalism, nationalism spread through Europe. In every country professed nationalists were the leading apostles of the doctrine of popular sovereignty, and they deduced from it the practice of political democracy and the right to self-determination. This was an anti-imperialist doctrine, and it was used to much effect in the countries seeking to free themselves from the domination of the French who had conquered most of Europe under the slogan of liberty, equality, and fraternity.

The term "nationalism" came to be used in three different senses, and the ethical question is quite different in each use. Nationalism may mean the effort to advance the fortunes of one's own nation, especially at the expense of others. In this use, there is no thought of the welfare of humanity, and ethics in that sense are excluded from the discussion unless expressly introduced.

Second, nationalism may be used in the sense of working for the welfare of the collectivity (the nation). It is then strictly an ethical term; in fact Rousseau's "patriotism" was in effect identical with ethics, at least on the domestic level. The third use of the term makes it almost synonymous with territorial integration on the national scale. "Nationalism" is counterposed to localism or regionalism on the one hand and internationalism on the other.[1] Let us discuss briefly the implications of this third usage. We shall then be able to return to the first one, which is the one that mainly concerns us in this chapter.

In *The Communist Manifesto* Marx and Engels show how, with the growing centralization and integration of industry, the local struggles of the workers give way gradually to national struggles. The class struggle appears.[2] In these passages Marx and Engels were not trying to show that the proletariat had adopted nationalism. The workers were not fighting for the interests of the national bourgeoisie against other national bourgeoisies; they were fighting for their interests as a class, on a national scale. Roman Rosdolsky has shown how the distortion in the meaning of "national" in these passages has been used to make out that nationalism was part of the philosophy of Marx and Engels (Rosdolsky, 1965:330-37, esp. 334). But Marx and Engels were not nationalists.

But integration may refer to the bridging of class differences, as when various social classes are drawn into a common action that overcomes class hostility at least temporarily. This kind of integration is just as moral or immoral as the purpose for which it is secured. National integration in wartime is as moral as the war, neither more nor less (see Sklar, 1967:2). From the Marxist standpoint, the struggle against national oppression has to be considered in its relation to the struggle against capitalism and for socialism. If "national unity" conflicts with the liberation of the working class, it should no doubt be opposed, to that extent. As Georges Haupt puts it:

> National unity is not an end in itself: it is only an instrumental value, to the degree that its achievement permits the working class to concentrate on its true class interests. (Haupt, *et al.*, 1974:13; author's translation)

Nationalism is not a thing, even an abstract thing, but a process, an implement. Minogue has called it a political style of action (Minogue, 1967). Indeed, the nation has been called a "struggle group"; citizens struggle not *for* the nation, but *through* the nation, for something which they, as individuals, desire (Allport, 1933:160). In saying this we do not of course imply that the individuals will themselves enjoy the fruits of the collective action; indeed, they may be dead before the end is achieved, if it is.

This makes clear how ridiculous is the demand, made for example by Albert Memmi, that the Left take a position on nationalism, for or against (Memmi, 1968:70). One does not take a position for or against a hammer, or a can opener, or any other implement. When used for murder, the hammer is no doubt a weapon; when used for building a house, it is a constructive tool. Nationalism considered as the vindication of a particular culture is morally neutral; considered as a movement against national oppression, it has a positive moral content; considered as the vehicle of aggression, it is morally indefensible.

Lenin long ago warned against universal endorsement of nationalist movements *per se,* since a particular nationalist movement may be led by elements interested not only in liberation from a foreign yoke but in suppressing and subverting the movement for social justice (socialism) within the country in question. The only scientific approach is to examine the issues and social classes involved, and their relation to the whole international scene before making a judgment.

For example, the defense of the French Revolution might seem to have been an action on behalf of human freedom and welfare; but how soon did the home of revolution become the base of operations for an aggressor (Napoleon)! The movements that in turn sought successfully to get rid of that aggressor were by and large democratic movements, and it was at this time, in the early nineteenth century, that the legend about the "natural" association of nationalism and democracy had its origin. But, at the very same time, the colonial aristocracy in Mexico was engaged in throwing off the Spanish yoke, not in the interests of democracy but for precisely the opposite reason: to preserve their privileges and head off a popular movement that a liberalized Spanish government might have assisted. "The movement for independence which had begun with demands for social reform ended in the maintenance of élite power" (Wolf, 1969:9). We are reminded how Europocentric our historical generalizations have often been.

Nationalism of the aggressive, imperialist type, associated in the early period with the name of Napoleon and later with those of Bismarck, Wilhelm II, Hitler, and Mussolini, was immoral. But we are getting ahead of our story. There have been many attempts to demonstrate that in advancing the interests of one's own nation, one is acting morally. Nationalism, it is asserted, is associated with democracy or with a special state morality. Conversely, smaller but influential schools of thought have condemned nationalism as a menace, for a variety of reasons. We will consider these arguments in turn.

## NATIONALISM AND DEMOCRACY

The proposition that nationalism "tends" to be associated with democracy (Hans Kohn's phrasing) has been a favorite idea of liberals. It is perhaps thought that the favorable connotations of democracy will rub off on nationalism—morality by association. So, it becomes a matter of some interest for us to establish (1) whether democracy and nationalism do indeed tend to be associated; and (2) whether such association, where it does occur, makes nationalism ethical or more nearly ethical. We are thinking now not of the "patriotism" described by Rousseau, which was ethical by definition, but of nationalism as it came to be known in the late eighteenth and early nineteenth centuries and subsequently.

A nationalist movement is ethical and democratic as long as it fights seriously for the rights of the underdog. But in this day and age this must mean that nationalism, in order to be ethical, must be anticapitalist and anti-imperialist. As pointed out so well by Régis Debray, nationalism must involve revolutionary socialism and socialism must involve revolutionary nationalism. It is not possible to think of one without the other.

The idea that nationalism "tends" to be associated with democracy would be more convincing if its proponents could get together on their use of terms and the time periods to which they are referring. Thus Hans Kohn, who describes democracy as "the inherent form of political organization characteristic of nationalism," thinks that nationalism lost its democratic associations around 1870, while Hans Morgenthau found that nationalism had an "essentially democratic" orientation until 1919 (Kohn, 1929:8; Morgenthau, 1961:188-89). Proponents of this point of view have a disconcerting way of redefining nationalism as they go, in such a way that if it is not democratic it is not nationalism. Also, both of the authors just cited qualify their generalizations almost out of existence (Kohn, 1954:26; Kohn, 1944:329-30; Symmons-Somonolewicz, 1968:49; Morgenthau, 1961). It is distressing that Kohn did not stick to the idea he expressed in 1954, that "nationalism is in itself neither good nor bad" (Kohn, 1954:22).

In some parts of the world, such as in Japan and the Middle East, there was never any special connection between nationalism and (capitalist) democracy. In Africa, when a wave of nationalist liberation movements had resulted in setting up literally dozens of new states in the 1960s, these were all endowed with parliamentary institutions of the Western democratic type. The subsequent wave of military coups showed how flimsy was the democratic base on which these new states had been erected. By 1975, French-trained army officers were ruling the Central African Republic, Chad, Dahomey, the Malagasy Republic, Mali, Niger, the Republic of the Congo, and Upper Volta.

The European nationalist rivalry that culminated in the rush to acquire colonies after 1870 and especially after 1880 does not strengthen the case for associating nationalism and democracy. Imperialism is not democratic; quite the contrary. Democracy, such as it was, stopped at the water's edge. Imperialists and their spokesmen commonly forget, or fail to mention, the main purpose of imperialist occupation of a foreign country, namely, the use of the local population as a source of surplus value for the imperialists. When it became evident that the European powers would not be able indefinitely to continue to dominate the rest of the world, some of them took steps to introduce a kind of self-government that would ensure the continuation of the economic privileges that were the real reason for colonization in the first place. If then the subjugated peoples did not at once adopt this supposedly "democratic" machinery of government, they can hardly be blamed for "not understanding" what democracy was all about.

The identification of nationalism and democracy which was made in the early nineteenth century now appears to have been little more than a coincidence. Nationalism may be and often is associated with democratic and also with socialist movements.[3] But even if the association had been much closer and more consistent, we could still not say that the association was "natural" or that it represented a constant historical tendency. Of course, national liberation movements are democratic insofar as they fight against alien domination; but this is only one kind of nationalism, and such movements themselves are not necessarily popularly controlled, much less socialist.

We see then that the attempt to justify nationalism on the grounds of its supposed association with democracy breaks down. But there is a much more sweeping claim on behalf of nationalism which we must now examine. Certain writers have maintained that nationalism is itself the expression of the highest morality.

## IS THERE A SPECIAL "STATE" MORALITY?

William McDougall would have us believe that nationalism is a tremendous and worldwide moral force. In his view, we should "seek in patriotism (nationalism) that reinforcement of character which is falsely declared to be the peculiar property of religion." McDougall maintains that the citizen's obligations to the political unit—city, state, or nation—"for national defense, for patriotic self-sacrifice, for loyalty to fellow-citizens . . . and to national . . . institutions" are moral obligations. He cites Hegel as a moral philosopher who took this point of view. He contrasts "national" systems of ethics with "universal" systems of ethics that have regard to the welfare of humanity as a whole; and he calls for a synthesis of the two (McDougall, 1934:240f.).

But can we accept this moral code attributed to Hegel, according to which "a man's conduct is right or moral in so far as he obeys the State, serves it, promotes its welfare, plays a part as a faithful cog in the great machine"? (ibid.:241-242). How can the state's interests be included in a universal system of ethics, when the state is concerned primarily, if not exclusively, with maintaining and advancing its own power?

Support of the state, in Hegel's system, was ethical only if the state in question was the embodiment of reason; and even the Prussian state, which he was popularly supposed to have held up as a model, did not meet that test, in Hegel's view. Indeed, contrary to the usual opinion, Hegel was not a nationalist, even though some of his followers, for instance, McDougall, have tried to use his philosophy as a justification for nationalism (Hertz, 1944:410).

McDougall defines ethical acts in terms of the motives of the people performing the acts. This procedure is logically indefensible. It is true that others, such as Josiah Royce, have sought to build an ethical system around the loyalty of the individual to something outside himself or herself (Royce, 1908). But that effort failed, as must any system of ethics that does not take the individual's *acts* as the measure of ethical behavior.

The attempt to lift the state above the canons of "ordinary" morality is nothing less than an effort to justify Machiavellianism in moral terms. Not even Machiavelli was so audacious.

Let us pursue a little further the implications of this argument. In deciding what his or her moral obligations are, the individual relies heavily on what may be called the "public conscience." After all, the argument goes, no individual can make a conscience alone; he or she always needs to do so in conjunction with society (Green, 1890:351).[4] The public conscience tells the individual to act in such a way as to promote or preserve national solidarity, especially in times of crisis, and to sacrifice his or her own good (and, in extreme cases, life) to the good of the nation (Royal Institute, 1939:319).

Nationalism thus appears as the expression of an absolute, exclusive devotion to one's own country. It is a sentiment of extended selfishness parading as the highest morality (Braunthal in Whitaker, 1961:192). We all recall how John Foster Dulles insisted that all nations ought to take the side of the United States in the Cold War; even neutralism he condemned as immoral.

There is no such thing as a system of nationalist ethics. The ends and aims of the state may be completely nefarious from the point of view of humanity as a whole; but humanity's is the only point of view that we can accept as ethical. There is one moral law, not two or many (Sampson, 1965:1f.).

The individual in performing a patriotic duty may indeed rise to heights of self-sacrifice. But his or her behavior is ethical, in the sense indicated, only if the welfare of humanity is served by whatever aim of the nation it is helping to advance.

We do not at all maintain that the majority of humans, or even any considerable part, are governed by ethical considerations in their actions on international issues. Even the rather obvious moral issue raised by the Vietnam war did not result in the jails being overcrowded with conscientious objectors in the United States, any more than the Algerian war did in France.

The ordinary citizen is interested primarily in power for his or her group—in this case, the nation. This point of view is well summed up by the title of an article on the CIA in a popular magazine: "I'm Glad the CIA is Immoral" (see Braden, 1967; see Hirsch, 1974). As a correspondent of the *New York Times* pointed out, with special reference to President Nixon's intervention on behalf of Lieutenant Calley:

> It is only a handful of people who at any time have bothered themselves with moral issues. The "ordinary" man is a tribal, vindictive and bloody-minded individual, and if he had his way we (Americans) would long ago have dropped atomic bombs on Russia, China and Hanoi. (Cohen, 1961)[5]

Yet—such are the ironies of history—it was precisely this "handful" whom the American colonists had in mind in 1776 when they addressed the Declaration of Independence to "the opinion of mankind"; and it is this handful to whom we now appeal rather than to the vast majority who care nothing for ethics in the international field.

There are those who try to absolve the ordinary citizen from responsibility for the oppressions involved in imperialism. The citizen of the imperialist country, it is said, does not know what is going on; he or she has nothing to do with it.[6] J. R. Seeley once made the statement that the British Empire was acquired in a fit of absence of mind.

It is not usually pointed out that people who argue this way are making a frontal attack on the whole concept of democracy. If the citizen is not responsible for what his or her government does, then how can it be called a democratic government?

But the most sophisticated attempt on record to make the pursuit of power appear as moral was no doubt that of Friedrich Meinecke (1862–1954), who has been called the most distinguished German historian of this century (Sterling, 1958:viii). Meinecke's ideas have come into renewed prominence in the United States, whose use of power was compared by the Swedish Prime Minister in 1973 to that of the Nazis (to President Nixon's acute discomfiture).

Meinecke thought that the statesman was fated to be continually torn between the injunction to be powerful and the injunction to be good (ibid.:31). He could not have been more wrong. The statesman follows to the best of his ability the injunction to make his nation powerful; otherwise he soon ceases to be a statesman. Meinecke was no apologist for Nazism. Far from it: he was uncompromisingly hostile to the Nazi regime. But he did posit a special "state morality" apart from general morality, and gave the weight of his authority, with heavy qualifications to be sure, to the doctrine of "my country right or wrong."[7]

He was challenged, of course. A fellow countryman and fellow historian, Alfred von Martin, wrote in 1946 with special reference to Meinecke's ideas: "There exists no *salus publica* apart from *justitia,* which is always supranational" (Kohn, 1944:105). And ironically, Meinecke, whose doctrines are today being revived by the imperialists, was himself an anti-imperialist. He glorified the nation partly because he thought it provided a barrier *against* imperialism, as indeed we see today in the wars of national liberation. And while his admonitions to statesmen to follow "God's law" were fated to go unheeded, he himself gave an example of moral toughness in the way he stood up to the Nazis.

Meinecke in his basic philosophy was not an isolated figure; indeed, he may be said to have typified the German philosophical attitude of his time.[8] The same philosophy was also widespread in the Anglo-Saxon countries. McDougall's outspoken cynicism gave expression to the philosophy that was actuating most of the sanctimonious defenders of nationalism.

It may be questioned whether the "moralism" of a Dulles had any effect in lining up public support for his aggressive policies, any more than the similar hypocrisies of Gladstone did in Victorian England.[9] The openly and avowedly aggressive aims of Hitler and Mussolini won quite as widespread support, within their respective countries, as long as they were winning; indeed, it was France, fighting a defensive war, that came apart at the seams in World War II. In World War I all the countries involved tried to show that they were fighting for some moral issue, but nobody was really fooled except those who wanted to be. Nearly everybody relied on the "public conscience," meaning that the individual surrendered his or her moral judgments to the state. Even those who recognized that "my country right or wrong" was an immoral doctrine still practiced it, and nationalists still do so, until the country begins to lose.[10]

Membership in a particular national group is sometimes represented as being in itself fine or admirable. But being (say) an Englishman could be admirable only if the individual had *chosen* his or her country in preference to all others. John Stuart Mill did make this ridiculous assumption [11] and he was echoed by Renan, who spoke of the nation as "a day-by-day plebiscite" (Renan, 1882:27). The last word on this vagary of political science was furnished by W. S. Gilbert in the song "He Is an Englishman" in *H.M.S. Pinafore* (1878).[12]

"Belonging" does fill a psychological need. In these days when the traditional institutions such as the family and the village community are breaking down all over the world, there are many who turn to the nation as a kind of refuge, to give their lives a broader meaning and purpose (Handlin, 1950:170). Other groups, such as racial ones, fill the same need. Some who become radicals get their sense of "belonging" from the movement, which indeed has morality among its objectives. Sometimes the individual shifts from one group to another in search of the one that best satisfies his or her particular need; some may revert to religion, most likely of a new kind.

But belonging is not in itself an ethical good, any more than is loyalty or nationality. Everything depends on what the group in question is up to. If it is doing no more than going through certain ritual observances, it has no special claim to ethical consideration. If the race or the nation is engaged in a struggle for equality, the people who participate in such a struggle are acting ethically. If, having won freedom from exploitation or discrimination for themselves, they go on to dominate others, their affiliation turns them from ethical to un-ethical behavior—unless of course they are urgently endeavoring to change the unethical behavior of their group.

But if nationalism is not necessarily good, either by definition or by association, and if being a member of a nation does not constitute by itself a meritorious action, what are we to think of those who have maintained that on the contrary nationalism is evil, or a menace to mankind?

## NATIONALISM AS A MENACE

Nationalism is a menace, according to thinkers of the anarchist school, because it involves the use of power, and to use power in social relations is wrong.

One of the early writers who mistrusted power and thought of it as evil was the German historian Jakob Burckhardt (1818–1897). However Burckhardt was not entirely consistent in his point of view; not all the results of power were bad. Speaking of Alexander the Great, he said: "It is always fortunate when a higher culture, a more gifted people, vanquishes a lesser culture, a less gifted one" (Kohn, 1954:150-53). P. J. Proudhon opposed the national unification of Germany and Italy because he felt it would lead to the growth of new large states, and he was opposed to the emergence of new concentrations of power because he, in his anarchist philosophy, believed any exercise of power to be bad (see Davis, 1967).

We shall not go extensively into the arguments for and against the use of power. However in view of the recent widespread reaction against all authority, especially on the part of the young, we will point out that much of the opposition is based on a misconception. A good example of a writer who seems to us to be the victim of such a misconception is R. V. Sampson, whose book *Equality and Power* appeared in England in 1965.[13] Sampson states flatly that power is the opposite of morality: "To the extent that the forces of power prevail over the forces of love, domination and subjection characterise human relations" (Sampson, 1965:2).

If Sampson, and before him Tolstoy (whom he quotes and in general follows), were right, then all attempts to improve things by political means are wrong, immoral; and Sampson so states (ibid.:16f).[14]

Ethical behavior has been possible in the past because sanctions were imposed on those who acted contrary to group norms. If we reject any resort to power, we are rejecting group activity as such; we are asking that people cease to behave as human beings.[15]

Power over other people may be exercised for or against the interests of the group; if against, then we call the system despotism, or class domination, or imperialism, as the case may be. The blank spot in anarchist theory is the failure to handle the question of leadership. A leader who directs the work of a group exercises power, but this may be done with the consent and approval of the group. As long as the leader is doing his or her job and not overstepping the bounds of his or her delegated powers, whoever challenges the leader challenges the group. It is not the use of power in social relations that is wrong, but the use of power in immoral ways or for immoral ends.

Another critic of nationalism ("nationality"), Lord Acton, produced his famous diatribe in 1862. Some of Acton's aphorisms are:

> The greatest adversary of the rights of nationalities is the modern theory of nationality.
> The theory of nationality is a retrograde step in history.
> Nationality does not aim either at liberty or prosperity, both of which it sacrifices to the imperative necessity of making the nation the mold and measure of the state. Its course will be marked with material as well as moral ruin. (Acton, 1907:297, 298, 299)

Acton is arguing against the fragmentation of empires (such as the the British and Austro-Hungarian Empires) into smaller states which he believed would be not only nonviable but lacking in the facilities to develop a higher civilization. In defending existing empires, he specifies that they should not be oppressive, but does not give any indication how such oppression can be avoided, nor what the nationality that feels itself oppressed should do. He feels frustrated, because the Roman Catholic Church, which had as its mission the overcoming of national differences, has been rudely thrust aside (ibid.:291). Acton is, in a word, a reactionary imperialist, with no feeling at all for the rights of oppressed peoples. When he says that nationality does not aim at either liberty or prosperity, he is ignoring history—since, as Marx and Engels pointed out in a letter to Kautsky at the time with reference to Poland, a people desiring development must first secure independence, and it is not the job of others to tell them that their national independence is a secondary matter (cited in Davis, 1967:17-18). But E. H. Carr, who at the end of World War II apparently still thought that it might be possible to preserve the British Empire, in his booklet *Nationalism and After* quoted Acton with approval (Carr, 1945:vi).

The material and moral ruin wrought by the Fascists and Nazis in the 1930s and 1940s was attributed by some to their nationalism. Both Mussolini and Hitler were of course chauvinistic nationalists, though Hitler's type of nationalism was different from Mussolini's and was sometimes camouflaged as racism.[16] It is true that nationalism may lead into chauvinism (Ginsburg, 1961:31). But must all nationalism be condemned on that account? As for nationalism leading to moral ruin, that comes poorly from Acton, who is able not only to wink at the monstrous immorality of imperialism but to defend it.

Of later students who were averse to nationalism, the name of Carlton Hayes of Columbia University comes to mind. His work was mainly historical, dealing with the nineteenth century. Hayes condemns nationalism for the most part by implication and innuendo rather than directly. His ostensibly neutral treatment slides from objectivity to judgments against nationalism "without pausing to warn the reader" (Silvert, 1963:9-12).

Another historian who is very much against nationalism is Arnold Toynbee, who called it "this disastrous corruption poisoning the political life of our modern Western society," a "false and maleficent religion." If we refuse to be overwhelmed by the authority of the distinguished author and read further, we find that (1) he refers to particular phenomena attributed to nationalism without showing that they follow from that cause alone; and (2) he is also, almost equally, against industrialism (Toynbee, 1939:163; Schuman, 1976:2).

Certain extreme manifestations of nationalism, such as chauvinism and jingoism, and even nationalism itself, have been cited as leading to war; and so nationalism has been condemned as a menace to peace. A moment's thought will show that this analysis is false. The system of competing states leads periodically to wars, and the causes of these wars may be studied; but it will be found that nationalism as such is an accompaniment to, rather than a cause of, wars.

Nationalism is indeed a menace if we define it to be so. Mazzini, who was the first to distinguish between "good" and "bad" nationalism, said that the former was marked by equality, peace, and cooperation among all nations; whereas the second was "savage, hostile, and quarrelsome." The first type was called by Mazzini "nationality"; the second type he called "nationalism," though some would be more inclined to use such a term as "chauvinism" or "jingoism." Yet Mazzini's terminology has come into general usage on the continent of Europe, and is used, in effect, by the United Nations. Thus we found in 1974 that UNESCO at one session (1) condemned colonialism *and nationalism,* and (2) asked the Director General to cooperate with the Palestine Liberation Organization to allow the Palestinians to "preserve their national identity" (*New York Times,* Nov. 24, 1974). But in the United States "nationalism" does not necessarily have an evil connotation. English usage is midway between the U.S. usage and that of continental Europe (Hertz, 1944:387).

What Mazzini called "good" nationalism is usually called "patriotism" in continental Europe. The term, "patriotism," also has positive moral connotations in the Anglo-Saxon countries. But this usage is extremely dangerous because it slips so easily into automatic endorsement of whatever policy the nation-state has a mind to follow. It also opens the way for demagogues to smear their opponents.[17]

Liberal opinion in Europe associates nationalism with reaction. The "nationalists" have been, in France, the reactionaries Maurras and Barrès (Robert, 1958:737); in Germany, Hitler; in Italy, Mussolini; and in the Soviet Union, anyone whom the government desires to condemn.

Edward Shils would have us believe that reactionaries ("traditionalists") are "almost always" nationalists (Johnson, 1962:47). This proposition cannot be accepted. The Fascists outside Germany and Italy in the 1930s and early 1940s were traditionalists but assuredly they were not nationalists. Quisling in Norway, Mussert in the Netherlands, Pétain and Laval in France, were following policies set out by a foreign power, in its own interests; they were antinationalist by any reasonable definition. Everything depends on the political conjuncture.

Robert Briffault points out correctly that a people with a distinctive language would not object to being part of a larger political unit with

a different language if it were not for the fact that they were oppressed. But he adds: "The evil arises from nationalism." No so, Mr.
Briffault! The evil arises from, indeed is, the oppression.

Elie Kedourie loosed yet another blast against nationalism. According to Kedourie, when the French introduced the principle of nationalism into European politics at the end of the eighteeenth century, they
began fighting for a principle, and as a result, compromise became
impossible (Kedourie, 1960:18).

His charges are documented and his treatment is erudite, but his
audacious generalization is simply not true. In the first place, while the
wars of Napoleon were ostensibly fought for a principle, they were
obviously not the first wars to claim high moral, even divine, backing.
In the second place, why should we take the battle cries of those wars
as statements of truth? Did not all countries claim to be fighting for
liberty in World War I? We cannot repeat too often that there has been
no morality in international politics—either before or following Machiavelli.

Wars are not fought for a principle, just because the publicists claim
such a justification. England did not go to war with Germany in 1914
to maintain the rights of small nationalities (say, Belgium). We may
recall that Napoleon's Marshal Ney said to a Swiss general: "You fight
for money; we fight for honor." And the Swiss replied: "Yes, we both
fight for what we have not got."

Kedourie does not agree at all with Kohn's argument that nationalism tends to be associated with democracy and liberalism; on the
contrary, he says, nationalism and liberalism are antagonistic principles
(ibid.:109). The essence of nationalism, says Kedourie, is that the will
of the individual should merge in the will of the nation, which makes it
logically a philosophy of despotism.

The arguments of Kedourie against nationalism seem to depend on
either (1) a misinterpretation of the term, making it much narrower in
scope than it actually is or has to be; or (2) an attribution to nationalism of vices that properly belong to international politics as such,
meaning violence, extremism, and so on.

Like Acton, Kedourie looks on nationalism as a force for disintegration of the old society. But actually nationalism is in the typical case an
important factor of reintegration of a society torn apart by the forces
of technical change. Indeed, where bourgeois social scientists have been

able to overcome their profound prejudice against colonial anti-imperialist movements, they have been obliged to recognize this constructive aspect of nationalism (A. D. Smith, 1971:49-50). Eric Wolf notes that in South Vietnam after World War II it was the National Liberation Front (NLF) alone that "offered a viable organizational framework and ideology for an atomized society striving to attain greater social cohesion" (Wolf, 1969:207). This cohesion no doubt meant much to the people involved; it had a moral dimension because the movement, the NLF, was engaged in advancing values that we have included as moral.

Leopold von Ranke (1795–1886) found many years ago that the state "pressed forward, with elemental might, toward ever greater self-assertion, toward ever fuller self-realisation" (Meinecke, 1957:xvii-xviii). This description, stripped of any psychological backing, was essentially the same as a proposition put forward by Thucydides. It was used by J. G. Fichte, one of the early prophets of German nationalism, in an article written in 1807, where we find the following:

> Your neighbor, even though he may look upon you as his natural ally against another power which is feared by you both, is always ready, at the first opportunity, as soon as it can be done safely, to better himself at your expense. He is forced to do it, if he is wise; and could not hold back, even if he were your brother.
>
> It is altogether insufficient for you to defend your own territory; on the contrary, you must keep your gaze fixed dispassionately on everything which could influence your situation, and you must in no way tolerate that anything inside those boundaries of your influence should be altered to your detriment, and never hesitate a moment, if you can alter something there to your advantage. For you can rest assured that the other will do the same, whenever he can; and if you delay in doing it now on your side, then you will get behind him. Whoever fails to increase his power, must decrease it, if others increase theirs. (Fichte, 1918: III:401f.)

Political scientists are not quite as grim about the inevitability of global conflict as this passage would suggest. Even Ranke fully appreciated that contrary forces are operating continuously to restrain the "drive for self-realization" of the several sovereign nation-states. The dynamic equilibrium of states has been compared to that of juxtaposed balloons, each ready to expand to fill any space that may be left by the deflation of some other balloon. That some will expand and others will become deflated with the passage of time has been recognized by writers before and after Lenin whose "law of uneven development" is indeed a commonplace of observation. But the question of whether the equilibrium will be upset drastically and war will result is another matter.

We also do not wish to imply that socialist states should imitate the international immorality of the capitalist states, just because they all must look out for their own interests as a condition of survival. Even Trotsky believed in defending the Soviet Union in the 1920s and the 1930s, while that country was building its industry and becoming able to defend itself.

But perversions of Marxist ideals such as took place under Stalin have to be condemned if Marxism is to retain its claim to be considered an ethical system. Indeed any socialist state has to be continuously evaluated and its mistakes criticized, by Marxists no less than by the enemies of socialism.

Marxists who wish to remain worthy of the name cannot, we insist, commit themselves to the continuing support of any one nation in the international power struggle; they will judge any particular policy on the basis of whether it brings closer the advent of socialism and welfare in general or in any particular country. The Soviet policy of coexistence was condemned for years by the Chinese as a piece of rank revisionism. Now, China finds it possible not only to coexist with imperialists but even to defend them on occasion. So, Russian "revisionism" turns out to have been merely a way of advancing the national interests of the Soviet Union, which in this respect is no different from China.

Maxime Rodinson, a French Marxist, believes that all nations, including socialist ones, tend to maximize their respective advantages; he contends that this idea derives from Marxian sociology. The similarity with Ranke's approach is apparent. But like Ranke, Rodinson recognizes that there are counterforces; otherwise how could Marxism have ever been considered part of the humanist movement (Rodinson, 1968: 148-49; 1973:190f.)?

It may be true that all nations, including the socialist ones, are still bound to follow a Machiavellian policy (*Realpolitik, raison d'état*) in their international relations. But the future of humanity does not, we repeat, stand or fall with the fortunes of any particular state or nation.

## NATIONALISM AS BOTH GOOD AND BAD

Nationalism may be considered on balance good; or on balance bad; or neither good nor bad; or both good and bad at the same time.

The last of these options was adopted by the late Harold Laski, an intellectual in the British Labor Party for a number of years and a respected liberal political scientist. Let us examine the argument that he made in 1932, when Fascism was threatening to plunge the world into a holocaust (as it ultimately did) and rational people were wondering whether civilization would survive at all.

Laski states: "In so far as we can give to each nation the power to express itself as a state . . . we liberate a spiritual energy which, beyond discussion, adds to the happiness of mankind." For one nation to refuse this power of expression to another is to "impoverish the spiritual well-being of the world." So far, clearly, nationalism is good, according to Laski (Laski, 1939:140).

It is no doubt true, as Laski says, that nationalism liberates spiritual energy. That is the big reason why nationalism is such a formidable implement for good or evil. Like Laski, Minogue attempts to give this spiritual lift a moral content. He says: "The nationalist struggle is a noble one, which dignifies a man's sufferings, and gives him a hopeful direction in which to work" (Minogue, 1967:32). Nationalism then takes people out of themselves, and induces a spirit of achievement and self-sacrifice. Is it not then ethical?

By no means. We fail to note any ethical content in the feeling of elation that accompanies a manifestation of national power. All we need to do to convince ourselves to the contrary is to ask (1) whether such manifestations of power are for a moral aim; and (2) whether the feeling of elation is followed by a feeling of depression. Even as careful a student as Rupert Emerson fails to ask these questions adequately, and falls into the same trap as Laski and Minogue. Emerson counts it a positive feature of nationalism that it "can give a lift to the spirits of even the oldest of nations"—referring to Britain during the Suez crisis of October 1956 (Emerson, 1960:384). But Britain's decision to attack Egypt was not a moral decision. Emerson refutes himself when he adds that this feeling of elation may leave some bad effects on the "morning after." Will Irwin as long ago as 1921 had compared war fever to a drunken spree (Irwin, 1921). Indeed, Emerson has pointed out elsewhere that the elation of nationalism, which is a potent factor in the colonial nations' struggle for independence, may fade out after independence, with dismaying consequences (Whitaker, 1961:36). Thus the good that Laski sees in nationalism turns out on examination to be a mirage.

Laski considers it an evil when nationalism (of the imperialist nations, that is) refuses subjected peoples the joys of nationalist elation. The evil is there, indeed, but a just appreciation would find it in the more fundamental fact of subjugation and exploitation.

Laski does find fundamental evils to be present in nationalism, but he mistakes their nature. He finds that nationalism threatens the continuance of civilization. The "profound and irrational" impulses of nationalism supply the state with an emotional force largely blind to the ideals of right and wrong, says Laski. Further, nationalism "throws a dangerous glamor around imperialist and mercantilist adventures." So, nationalism is not only wrong; it is irrational as well (Laski, 1939:191, 194-95).

Nationalism harnesses the "instinct of pugnacity," says Laski, in the service of private profit; it forwards the aims of a particular class in society. This result has been possible, he says, only because of the ignorance of the common people. The "only way out," in his view, is a public educational system that will educate the masses in the dark ways of imperialism.

Psychologists had rejected the concept of an instinct of pugnacity years before Laski wrote. But is it so irrational for the ruling class to harness the reactions of the unthinking masses to make profit for themselves? And has the ruling class ever allowed the public educational system to expose its own devious ways?

The masses who are supposedly misled into following nationalist policies are perhaps mistaken in their analysis, as Laski states. But is the imperialist power struggle a mistake? Is exploitation a mistake? Laski does not face up to this question. Like all liberals, he wants to eat his cake and have it too. He accepts the power struggle, and laments its inevitable consequences.

Ironically, it was in the year 1933, just after Laski wrote, that the British Labor Party at its annual conference endorsed the so-called Oxford Pledge, an absolute pacifist document. Needless to say, nothing further was heard of this extraordinary action. The Labor Party had long before accepted imperialism as a fact of life. Neither in 1933 nor later, when it assumed office in 1946, did the Labor Party live up to Laski's prescription and conduct a principled educational campaign against imperialism. Nationalism remained for it, as for him, an inscrutable, irrational force and at the same time quite reasonable from the point of view of those at the helm of the ship of state.

Laski failed to distinguish between "right" as a concept applied as between individuals and *raison d'état* which governs the relations of states. Like the General Council of the First International, he posited a moral standard for the country's government—a standard that could not possibly be lived up to, given the circumstances. He blamed nationalism and the instinct of pugnacity for the shortcomings of his own logic.

Nationalism is indeed a contradictory phenomenon, as Laski states, and it may be used for good or evil purposes, or for both at the same time. Where we part company with him is not on this general proposition but on his analysis of particular situations and his conceptions of what constitutes the good and evil respectively in class and national relations.

It is unfair to condemn nationalism for doing what it is supposed to do. It is equally unfair to condemn nationalism for not doing what it was never supposed to do.

Maurice Cranston writes that "because nationalism cannot be universalised, it lacks the moral dimension which all ideologies purport to possess" (Cranston, 1969:7). Another thinker who is apparently under the impression that nationalism is intended as a general organizing principle for society is Barbara Ward; in a thoughtful lecture delivered in 1966 she gave her reasons for thinking that nationalism had failed on this score (Ward, 1966:55-56). Listing the three areas of human need as kinship, cohesion, and economic function, she found that nationalism gave no adequate answer to the problems of human solidarity; "its essential nature is to leave other people out." Also, the nation-state was called economically anachronistic.

The burden that is here loaded onto the back of nationalism is imposing—and most unfair. Nationalism does *not* purport to be a general ideology. Ideologies need a moral dimension, but it has to be sought independently of the concept of nationalism, which is much more limited. Nationalism has not failed as an organizing principle on the cultural level. Nationalism has not emerged superior to the power struggle, nor can it be expected to do so. When and if this struggle is resolved, the nation may still serve as an organizing principle within specified limits, as Marx contemplated (see Davis, 1967:5-6).

The attacks on nationality and nationalism from the Left (Proudhon and the anarchist school) and from the Right (Acton, Kedourie) have left the nationalist movement substantially untouched; it has continued to grow and spread, so that Sun Yat-sen's classifying it as one of the three great movements of the nineteenth century can in no wise be challenged. It is all the more surprising—and alarming—that Marx and the Marxists should have made so little effort to understand nationalism and to integrate it into the general framework of Marxist philosophy and the Marxian moral code. For Marx, contrary to a widespread impression, had a moral code, the nature of which is all too little understood.

## NATIONALISM, MARXISM, AND MORALITY

Marx, as is well known, scoffed at bourgeois morality. Where he and Engels used the terms of conventional ethics, it will usually be found that the passages in question were forced on them. Thus Marx wrote the "Address to the First Meeting of the International Workingmen's Association," in which these words appear: "The simple laws of morals and justice, which ought to govern the relations of private individuals, should be the paramount rules of intercourse between nations." If Marx had been the author of these lines, we should have to put him down as not merely conventionally moralistic but incredibly naive in the bargain. However, as he explained in a letter to Engels, these phrases were put in by the committee that went over the manuscript. Marx hoped that they would not do too much harm (Marx, 1936:II:441-42, 432-33).

In practice, Marx and Engels wasted little time in moralizing about international relations. They analyzed each situation as it came up, and mapped a preferred course of action on the basis of what they thought would best advance the cause of socialism and human welfare. This was their frame of reference; this was, in effect, their moral code.

Marx and Engels had, and their followers have, the same goals as ethics in general; they seek freedom and welfare for mankind in the long run. It is in their conception of how best to arrive at this goal that Marxists differ from conventional moralists.

The society that Marx was interested in, and toward which he believed history was tending, was an egalitarian society, from which exploitation of all kinds—economic, political, racial, sexual, by age, and national—would be banished. He believed that private property was at the bottom of society's troubles, and that when the means of production were socialized not only economic exploitation but the other forms of exploitation as well would disappear, or at least become manageable. The way to arrive at socialism was, he thought, first to study the laws of motion of capitalism (and to this he devoted his life); when capitalism had, so to speak, dug its own grave and ceased to be a viable system, the proletariat would be prepared to take power, by a violent revolution if necessary, and introduce the new form of society.

Marx had a special commitment to freedom. He spent considerable time and effort in his early years, before he became a socialist, in fighting against the Prussian censorship (Marx, 1927: I:211-12).

Capitalism, according to Marx, tears a person away from all primary ties and primary group loyalties; he or she becomes alienated from the family, the nation, the community, the land, and craft. The struggle for the abolition of capitalism is thus at the same time part of the struggle for the ending of alienation in its several manifestations (see Meszaros, 1972).

Marx condemns group loyalties under capitalism, including loyalty to the nation; patriotism appears as a particular form of alienation (Marx, 1964:21; Marx, 1961:74-75; Berki, 1971:93-97). Under communism, human nature will be reintegrated; new bonds—national, natural, moral, and theoretical—will bind people to one another more firmly than ever.

One reason for thinking Marx envisaged the survival of the nation—aside from his explicit statement to that effect in the *Manifesto*—is his use of the vocabulary of the early German Romanticists, most of whom were at the same time nationalists. Marx was keenly aware of the constructive role of nationalism in Germany that was about to come into being (Meyer, 1954:57-58).

Marx never described the institutional framework of the future communist society that he envisaged. His belief that there must be some such framework is evident from his continued emphasis on the increasing scale of operations, which could only be kept going by an elaborate institutional network. Marx was no utopian socialist. His description of the person of the future as "self-determined" is not to be taken to mean that the individual will operate in isolation. He or she may not be—will not be—specialized in one exclusive occupation; but the "administration of things," as Engels called it, will remain after the coercive framework of the state has withered away: "In place of the old bourgeois society," wrote Marx and Engels in *The Communist Manifesto,* "we shall have an association in which the free development of each is the condition for the free development of all" (Marx and Engels, 1968:53).

Nationalism is thus part of Marx's vision of the future—not nationalism in the sense of chauvinism, seeking to advance the interests of one's own nation at the expense of others, but nationalism in Rousseau's original sense of patriotism, seeking the welfare of the collectivity.

But what of nationalism today, and in the period immediately ahead? It might seem that Marxists, as bearers of the tradition of humanism, would take the lead in organizing a world that would make an effective end to all major wars. A nuclear war among the major powers could mean the end of civilization; brinksmanship is about as safe as Russian roulette.

We do not believe that socialist nations will give such a lead, if that means being the first to lay down their arms. On the contrary—the nations professing Marxism are likely to overdo the tough talk if only to persuade their rivals (including one another) that they are not going to be victimized in any such way. We recall the Cuban missile crisis of

1962, in which the Russians acted so tough that their attitude was condemned as adventurism by the Chinese.

It is not unusual for self-styled Marxists today to condemn "all" nationalism. Sometimes this is done through the thoughtless taking of a statement of Lenin out of context. Tito condemns "all" nationalism in Yugoslavia—he has special reference to the "narrow" nationalism of the several republics (e.g., Croatia). Loyalty to Yugoslavia as a whole is by contrast lauded as patriotism. Again, some Marxists condemn "all" nationalism on the ground that the working class, in which they put their trust, is international. This way of thinking was widespread before World War I; those who still maintain it some sixty years later are guilty of wishful thinking. The working class is not any more international than any other class. When the Chinese workers consider that the Russian workers are their principal enemies, it is surely time to re-appraise the early blind faith in proletarian internationalism. To condemn all nationalism is unacceptable because it means condemning the national liberation movements of the colonies and semicolonial countries.

Communist theoreticians have seldom faced up squarely to the problems posed by continuing nationalism in a deeply divided world. Some blindly advocate world unification; but this surely is premature; it would involve not only the acceptance of imperialism, but at best the absorption of small nations by larger ones. Others put forward the nonantagonistic diversity of nations as a workable goal, but this too involves skipping over unsolved problems. R. N. Berki says that Marxists vacillate between these two positions (see Berki, 1971:85, 86). E. Kardelj of Yugoslavia takes a more realistic approach than most self-styled Marxists, but offers in the end nothing better than the traditional Machiavellianism (Kardelj, 1960:189).

For many years Marxists comforted themselves with the thought that the worldwide advent of socialism would bring an end to national-ism and international wars. Marxists should no longer make any such assumption. Milovan Djilas recounts a conversation with an otherwise unidentified Red army commander who supported the idea that when Communism had triumphed in the whole world, wars would then acquire their final bitter character. Djilas on reflection accepted this proposition (Djilas, 1962:50).

Even if the tendency to exploit is not instinctive, it clearly does exist, and we are not justified in assuming that the worldwide victory of socialism would lay it permanently to rest.[18] But we hope we have shown that the tendency to contain exploitation is at least as persistent. The ambition of any one nation (state) or any group of nations *can* be contained by the timely action of the others.

It would be somewhat ridiculous to assume that even a socialist future will be devoid of struggles. Evil will not be banished from the world in the next generation, or the next century, or at all. The future of humankind depends on its ability to recognize and control exploitation and domination, by the judicious and timely application of sanctions if necessary. But only a body of genuinely socialist nations would possess the moral authority to carry out such a move, and to make it stick.

# 3

## The Theory of Nationalism: Luxemburg, Stalin, Lenin, and Trotsky

### A. LUXEMBURG VS. LENIN

It is perhaps little known that despite Lenin's attacks on her, the philosophical position so ably expounded by Rosa Luxemburg in her articles of 1908–1909 was never refuted; that it was, on the contrary, adopted by a substantial section of the Bolshevik Party, which fought Lenin on the issue, using Rosa Luxemburg's arguments—and eventually, in 1919, defeated him, so that the slogan of the right of self-determination was removed from the platform of the Communist Party of the Soviet Union (CPSU). Later, when the issue was no longer so acute, the slogan was revived and today represents part of the CPSU's stock in trade. But the basic arguments in its favor are precisely those which were successfully opposed by Rosa Luxemburg and her partisans. The Soviet leadership is working with a blunted tool.

Julius K. Nyerere, president of Tanzania and one of the more subtle theorists of the new nationalism in Africa, has suggested that over-emphasis on the slogan of "self-determination" in the campaign for decolonization may make the eventual attainment of socialism more difficult. He says:

> Everyone wants to be free, and the task of the nationalist is simply to rouse the people to a confidence in their own power of protest. But to build the real freedom which socialism represents

is a very different thing. It demands a positive understanding and positive actions, not simply a rejection of colonialism and a willingness to cooperate in noncooperation. (Nyerere, 1968: 26-32)[1]

It might come as a surprise to Nyerere to learn that just this difficulty with the slogan was pointed out by Rosa Luxemburg sixty years earlier. Surely Marxism has been remiss in neglecting the theory of nationalism for so long.

Western scholars who are unaware of this situation have been hampered in their efforts to evaluate the "Great Debate" by the fact that only one side—Lenin's—has been available to them.[2]

The differences between Rosa Luxemburg and Lenin may be summarized under several headings as follows:

1. Lenin strongly emphasized the right of self-determination of nations. Rosa Luxemburg said that there was no such right, and putting forward this slogan when the terms were not defined carefully could mean not a contribution to solving the problem but a means of avoiding it.

Luxemburg's point was sound then and it is sound today, but she overstated it. There is a *moral* right of self-determination, when the terms are defined; and she should have so indicated. Her opposition to national oppression shows that she recognized the principle.

2. Lenin emphasized the role of the bourgeoisie in building modern nations. Luxemburg said that there were circumstances when the role of the bourgeoisie in nation-building was minimal, and she was correct, not only with regard to Poland but in relation to precapitalist economic formations, colonies, and so on.

3. Luxemburg allowed a place for federation and autonomy. Lenin's position on federalism was ambiguous. He at first opposed it, then later adopted it for the Soviet Union, at least nominally. Luxemburg's thinking was more flexible on this point, and her criticism of Lenin is receiving renewed attention today. But autonomy may mean little in an undemocratic state.

4. Rosa Luxemburg and her followers interpreted self-determination as meaning the self-determination of the working class. Lenin correctly opposed this formulation, but his statement of the case against it failed to carry conviction and he was overridden by the 1919 CPSU Congress, as we shall see.

5. Rosa Luxemburg opposed nationalism as leading to fragmentation. Lenin stressed the advantages of large national units, but at the same time appreciated the strength of the tendency to fragmentation, to which he was not entirely unsympathetic. Lenin was correct, as anyone today would have to concede.

Our main concern is with the first point above, the question of whether there is a *right* to self-determination of nations.

## THE HISTORICAL SETTING

Rosa Luxemburg was born and went to school in what was then Russian Poland. She came of middle-class Jewish parents. She early showed an interest in the revolutionary movement and attracted so much attention from the authorities that she found it advisable to leave Russia. She went first to Switzerland and then to Germany, where she completed her studies while continuing active in the social-democratic movement. She studied Polish history, and was later able to correct Lenin in his exclusive emphasis on the bourgeoisie as the creator of nationalism; for in Poland the nationalist movement was led for many years by the landed nobility (*shlachta*).[3] She always retained her interest in Poland; she worked among the Poles in East Prussia and was the German Social Democratic Party's expert on Poland. At the same time she participated—at a distance most of the time—in the social-democratic movement in Russia, where she usually sympathized with the Bolshevik position. Lenin, although he disagreed with her on a number of points, always had the highest opinion of her ability and sincerity.

The whole 1893–1914 period was characterized by a debate between two parties in Poland on the subject of national self-determination. The Polish Socialist Party (Polska Partia Socialistyczma—PPS) favored the reconstitution of Poland, and its branch parties in each of the partition states (Germany, Austria, and Russia) campaigned among the workers, the peasants, and the middle class on this strictly nationalist basis, hardly mentioning socialism. The Social Democratic Party of Poland— later, after the inclusion of Lithuania in 1899 known as the SDKPiL—

was founded by Rosa Luxemburg and others in 1893, and continued an earlier Marxist tradition in opposing self-determination for Poland.

First one and then the other of the parties seemed to have the ear of the workers. The International Socialist Congress at London (1896) heard both sides present their cases and decided, in effect, not to interfere. The SDKPiL seemed to have only a small following in 1903, but when the first Russian Revolution broke out in 1905 the workers in Russian Poland flocked into the SDKPiL and made common cause with the Russian workers. Barricades were erected and there was street fighting in several Polish cities. The PPS split: one faction gravitated toward the position of the SDKPiL and eventually (in December 1918) merged with it; a smaller group, led by Pilsudski, survived and eventually, after the war, took over the leadership in the newly reconstituted country of Poland.

Rosa Luxemburg's position on nationalism was that it was a movement in which the working class had only an indirect interest. She always maintained that the best and quickest way for workers to get rid of the bane of national domination was to bring about the international socialist revolution. In 1903, partisans of Rosa Luxemburg's point of view appeared at the Congress of the Russian Social Democratic Labor Party (RSDLP) and urged that the congress make no endorsement of self-determination. The RSDLP did come out for self-determination of nations, whereupon the Polish delegates left. Both Bolsheviks and Mensheviks favored self-determination.

The Poles again appeared at the 1906 Congress of the Russian Party, and this time did not press their opposition to self-determination, though they still held the same position as in 1903. They cooperated with Lenin at this congress, thus indicating the extent of the similarity between their views and his. But the basic philosophical question remained unresolved.

Rosa Luxemburg set forth her position in detail in a series of articles, "The National Question and Autonomy," which were published in 1908–1909 in her Cracow magazine, *Przeglad Sozialdemokratyczny*. Other Marxists also contributed to the discussion, and Lenin commissioned Stalin to write a pamphlet on the subject of nationalism.

However, no one had really answered Rosa Luxemburg, and Lenin himself undertook this task. "On the Right of Nations to Self Determination," written at the beginning of 1914, was directed specifically against her.

## THE "RIGHT" OF SELF-DETERMINATION

It is non-Marxist, said Rosa Luxemburg, to talk in terms of absolute rights, or indeed of rights at all, since the dialectic does not recognize the existence of rights in general; the "rights" and "wrongs" of a given situation must be arrived at by an analysis of the given historical circumstances.

Lenin as a Marxist had absolutely no answer to this contention, since he had often expounded this very point. He said both before and after 1908 that the interests of the proletarian revolution were paramount, and he was prepared to sacrifice the right of self-determination to the cause of the revolution at any time. He was also not in favor of self-determination in the abstract, for this might lead to unacceptable conclusions.

Luxemburg denied that there was any "right" to freedom from oppression. Such questions, she maintained, are questions of power and are settled as such. She said that telling the workers that they had the "right" to self-determination was like telling them that they had the right to eat off gold plates.

In a class society, to speak of self-determination for the "people" would ordinarily mean the self-determination of the ruling class; the workers would be left in a subordinate position as before. This was why in her discussions, with Poland very much in mind, she gravitated toward the position that self-determination was the self-determination of the *working* class. This, as we shall see, was a slogan that was used in the Russian Revolution.

Since Luxemburg was specifically opposed to the right of self-determination, it might be supposed that she would also have objected to any special consideration being shown to the minor nationalities as such. But that would not be correct at all. She had a strong feeling for the autonomy of Poland, the smaller nationality in which she was most interested. It is only necessary to read the sixth and last article of the

1908–1909 series in order fully to appreciate how hard she was prepared to work to come up with a plan which, while not based on any
general principle of self-determination, still would guarantee the requisite degree of self-government and cultural autonomy to her people.
Lenin complained that she limited her demands for autonomy to
Poland alone, but that did not necessarily follow. In the dialectical
method Lenin himself advocated, each case has to be considered on its
merits, and it is necessary to start somewhere.

Luxemburg took occasion to state why she thought Lithuania and
Georgia would *not* be suitable territories in which to apply the principle
of autonomy. The reason was quite simply that they were too small—
even Georgia with its 1.2 million people was not in her estimation a
viable unit. Lenin, by contrast, mentioned a figure as small as 50,000,
and indeed some of the nationalities in the Soviet Union are not much
larger than that.[4] Since Lenin was prepared to go in for mini-nations, he
was also prepared to carve up the administrative units of the old
Russian Empire where these included more than one nationality.

But did Lenin not realize that a nation with only 50,000 people
would not be capable of defending itself, or of developing an internal
market large enough to bring the advantages of large-scale production?
How could such microscopic nations survive at all? Luxemburg, following in the footsteps of Marx and Engels, emphasized the tendency to
form larger and larger national units. Her solution to the problem of
popular control was in the Marxist tradition: to have the proletariat of
the advanced nations, making common cause with the minor nationalities, overthrow capitalism and bring freedom to the smaller nationalities
and to the colonies from the center, under a socialist government.
Pending such a solution, it was Luxemburg's view that the smaller
nationalities would do better within the larger (imperialist) country.
She even criticized Marx for having advocated the independence of
Poland. She contended that such a move would have the effect of
solidifying the control of the gentry (and, later, the bourgeoisie), and
would be of little value to the peasants and workers, who should make
common cause with the workers and peasants of the larger country in
which they found themselves.

This was indeed a major difference between Lenin and Luxemburg,
but it was a difference more of judgment on the practical application of
the theory than of theory or method as such. Lenin's attempts to label

Luxemburg's theory "abstract" and "metaphysical" come down largely to matters of definition. Lenin asked Luxemburg, rhetorically, why she did not define the nation in accordance with Kautsky's historical-economic analysis and take specific exception to Otto Bauer's psychological definition. Here Lenin was on dangerous ground. In the first place, Stalin, with Lenin's apparent blessing, had just published an article containing a definition of the nation which was based partly on Bauer's "psychological" one. And in the second place, Kautsky, writing incessantly on the nation, had come to define nationality in terms of language, a definition so defective that Lenin himself was presently obliged to attack it. Lenin saved himself the trouble of defining a nation, but that did not give him the license to impose definitions arbitrarily on others.

In calling for the "right of self-determination of nations" Lenin was endorsing the idea that nations have rights. Luxemburg denied this absolutely; if she was prepared to talk about rights at all, it would be exclusively in terms of the rights of the working class. Since Lenin was fully aware of the economic advantages of large states—he intended to make a single economic unit of the socialist society of the future, which would be not only as large as the empire of the tsar, but much larger—and since he looked on the "right of self-determination of nations" as a qualified right, subordinate to the aims of the socialist revolution, was he then not seeking to deceive the smaller nationalities about the nature of this "self-determination"? Luxemburg maintained, in effect, that he was, and she proceeded to argue that in a contest involving nationality, the ruling class held all the trump cards. At any given time—short of socialism—any "democratic" determination of the wishes of the "people," even of the proletariat, might be expected to show a majority for the bourgeoisie.

This was a fundamental criticism of Lenin's position. Since Lenin advocated self-determination only up to a point, those who wished for self-determination beyond that point—those who were not interested in social revolution (except to combat it)—would of course charge Lenin with hypocrisy; and this was done, both at the time and later. Luxemburg's position was not any more palatable to the conservatives, but she did escape from the charge of hypocrisy.

By way of defining his position on the separation of small nations from larger, Lenin wrote (CW, XXI:410):

Never in favor of petty states, or the splitting up of states in general, or the principle of federation, Marx considered the separation of an oppressed nation to be a step towards federation, and consequently, not towards a split, but towards concentration, both political and economic, but concentration on the basis of democracy.

Lenin was prepared to have a small nation secede from Russia (the Soviet Union) because he fully expected that the economic advantages of belonging to a larger economic unit, plus, for the workers, the advantage of belonging to a workers' state, would bring any such seceding nation back again.

Luxemburg was opposed on principle to the creation of new, small, and as she saw it, nonviable states, even when it could be shown that all classes, including the workers, were in favor. Lenin saw as clearly as she the economic forces that were driving toward creation of larger and larger states. But he saw what she did not see (or chose to overlook), that the contrary forces, making for smaller states, were powerful too and in the short run perhaps determining. Further—and this was the crucial point—Lenin opposed *overruling* the nationalists even when he did not agree with them. They should be brought to see the error of their ways, while at the same time being allowed full *cultural* freedom for their respective nationalities.

Luxemburg was confronted with a particular situation in Poland (which was not necessarily typical, as Lenin pointed out). The Poles in Austria already enjoyed de facto autonomy and considerable democratic rights, and the Polish workers there had little to gain and possibly much to lose from being put into a reconstituted Poland dominated by bourgeoisie and landowners. Much the same could be said of the Poles in East Prussia with whom Rosa Luxemburg worked, and in Russia it was plain that the days of tsarist absolutism were numbered, so that the Poles in "Kingdom Poland" could reasonably hope for autonomy and/or democracy within the foreseeable future.

It was the analysis of the concrete situation that divided Luxemburg and Lenin, not the method of analysis or the starting point, both of which were nearly identical. Lenin, as a Russian internationalist, was fighting against Great Russian chauvinism. Luxemburg, as a Polish (German) internationalist, was fighting against Polish social patriotism (chauvinism). Paradoxically, they arrived at exactly contrary positions on self-determination. But Lowy finds that Lenin's position was superior in that it applied elsewhere too; it recognized the constructive aspects of nationalist movements in a way that Luxemburg's did not (Lowy, 1971:66-67).[5]

Is "freedom from national oppression" (a freedom which Luxemburg favored) the same as "self-determination of nations"? Her strong and continuing objections to the latter phrase make it seem as if she thought there was a difference. But if so, what? Or was she merely opposed to the idea that self-determination was a *right?*

Phrases like "national liberation" and "freedom from national oppression" are, to be sure, vague and general, but less so than "national self-determination." In either case, we have to define what the nation is supposed to include—that is, its territorial boundaries. There is also the question of who is to do the determining, or, alternatively, just what the nation is supposed to be liberated from. But the phrase self-determination is hopelessly vague on the question of whether what is meant is independence or some status short of independence. The anticolonial movements of recent years have been in favor of independence, and when they called themselves "national liberation" movements no one has doubted what was meant.

## FREEDOM FROM OPPRESSION
## AS A MORAL RIGHT

Perhaps Social Democrats do not have the duty to protest against national oppression. Rosa Luxemburg said that on the contrary, Social Democrats have the duty to raise such a protest, not because it is *national* oppression but simply because it is oppression. Luxemburg insisted that to be a socialist one had to protest against *all* kinds of oppression, and to this point Lenin had no real answer either.

When Luxemburg spoke of the *duty* of Marxists to protest against oppression, was she reintroducing, by the back door, the concept of morality and ethics which she had just thrown out the front door? It is not a contradiction to speak in terms of socialist morality, and that is the concept that Luxemburg had in mind.

Lenin said he was against "all exploitation." Against exploitation of women? Clearly. Against national oppression? Obviously. Lenin showed by his actions all through his life that he was prepared to fight against exploitation wherever it was found. What is the difference between him and Luxemburg? None at all on this point, unless it might be in the manner of phrasing and the priority given to economic (class) exploitation in Lenin's writings. Lenin thought that the class question was of overshadowing importance. But he was broadminded enough to admit that under certain circumstances the national question might assume prior emphasis. Thus, the national question takes its proper place in the hierarchy of social values, and a rounded socialist ethic becomes possible (CW, VI:434-63).

We find then that for Marxists to use phrases like the "right of self-determination" invites misunderstanding. Luxemburg's "freedom from national oppression" is superior on all counts.

In her basic theoretical articles, Luxemburg especially stressed the economic aspects of nationalism and understated the importance of the political aspects (Lowy, 1971:65-66). Her theory of nationalism thus lacks generality, and Lenin was right in criticizing her on this ground; further, the political aspects are of the greatest importance in the wars for national liberation which have dominated the scene since World War II. She also underestimated the importance, for the revolutionary struggle, of the allies of the proletariat, including both the minor nationalities and the peasants. However, we cannot accept a point that is sometimes made, namely that she overlooked the effect of national oppression on the working class. We interpret her eloquent denunciation of national oppression as such, and her insistence that resistance to such oppression has more emotional content than mere economic exploitation could evoke, as indicating a realization on her part that national movements affect the working classes profoundly. We cite here in proof a passage from a work heretofore not translated from the Polish, a preface to a compendium on the national question which she edited in 1905:

> To the credit of mankind, history has universally established that even the most inhumane *material* oppression is not able to provoke such wrathful, fanatical rebellion and rage as the suppression of intellectual life in general, or as religious or national oppression (Hentze, 1971:217).

The debate on self-determination continued up to and during World War I. When Luxemburg was in and out of prison in Germany, her point of view was argued in Bolshevik circles by Piatakov ("Kievsky") and Bukharin.

## THE FIRST WORLD WAR

In the "Junius" pamphlet, written anonymously from her prison cell in 1916, Rosa Luxemburg again discussed the question of self-determination. The phrasing is more moderate, but the point of view has not changed. "Socialism," she then said, "recognizes for every people the right of independence and the freedom of independent control of its own destinies." But at the same time she argued that self-determination was impossible to attain under capitalism, and added: "Today the nation is but a cloak that covers imperialistic desires, a battle cry for imperialistic rivalries" (Luxemburg, 1969:94-95, 98). National wars, said "Junius," are no longer possible. Lenin pointed out in the friendliest spirit (he did not at first know who had written the pamphlet) that, on the contrary, national wars *of liberation* were quite possible in the imperialist epoch and indeed were the order of the day (Lenin, CW, XXII:305-91). He also did not altogether accept Luxemburg's contention that self-determination was impossible under capitalism (ibid., 144-45).

Poles holding Luxemburg's point of view submitted theses on the national question to the Zimmerwald Conference; these were published in 1916. They opposed the independence of Poland. Lenin drafted theses in opposition, and wrote a special article to answer the Polish theses ("The Discussion on Self-Determination Summed Up").

## LENIN'S CONTRADICTORY POSITION

In this "answer," Lenin conceded Luxemburg's main point, namely that Poland would not be a viable state under existing conditions. He therefore advised the Polish Social Democrats not to press for Polish independence. At the same time, he tried to stick to his former advice to the Social Democrats of Germany, Austria, and Russia that they should recognize the *right* of Poland to secede. The result was a hybrid policy which cleared up nothing. According to Lenin:

> People who have not thought out the question find it "contradictory" that Social Democrats of oppressing nations should insist on "freedom to *secede*" and Social Democrats of oppressed nations on "freedom to *unite.*" But a little reflection shows that there is not and cannot be any *other* road to internationalization and to the fusion of nations, any other road from *the present position* to that goal. (CW, XIX:297; emphasis in original)

Professor Carr calls this a "somewhat nebulous" foundation for Bolshevik nationality policy, a restrained judgment indeed. Lenin's position had become very difficult to grasp (Carr, 1950b).

However, Lenin's platform on the national question had other planks, and it was for these quite as much as for the rather meaningless demand for "self-determination" that Lenin was fighting in his battles on the nationality question. The principles which he succeeded in impressing on his followers were primarily two: (1) equality of nations; and (2) the right of nationalities to a cultural existence of their own. There were also other aspects. It was Lenin who led the fight for the legal protection of national minorities against discrimination, for the right to schools and court proceedings in the vernacular, for writing down languages that had never been written down before, and for directing new investment precisely into backward areas with the avowed aim of bringing their standards up to those of the most advanced areas.

Lenin did not invent these principles, which were in general circulation at the time. They had been developed in struggle, on the initiative of the minority peoples themselves. It was to Lenin's lasting credit that he perceived that a general principle was involved, the right—which Marxists could not deny—for the working class to be free of *national as well as class* oppression. Lenin believed in this principle and acted on it; Luxemburg made it the cornerstone of her position.

## SELF-DETERMINATION IN THE RUSSIAN REVOLUTION

In 1919, at the Eighth Party Congress of the Bolsheviks, Bukharin took the point of view that the interests of the international revolution were paramount, and in this matter he was strongly seconded by Piatakov, then in actual charge of the Ukraine, who urged centralized control of all proletarian movements by the newly established Communist International. Piatakov condemned the slogan of the right of nations to self-determination as reactionary. The slogan of the hour was self-determination for the *working class* of each nationality, but this did not satisfy Piatakov, who said that Soviet Russia must keep control of the Ukraine, even against the wishes of the Ukrainian proletariat (Daniels, 1960:97). He thus pushed Luxemburg's point of view to its logical conclusion (Lenin called Piatakov a Great Russian chauvinist).

The slogan of "self-determination for the working class" seems at first blush to incorporate the bourgeois ideal of self-determination for a nation into the revolutionary theory of the Bolsheviks, which is based on the working class. Lenin had used the slogan himself in 1903. The Armenian Social Democrats had taken a position in favor of self-determination for Armenia. Lenin wrote then: "We on our part concern ourselves with the self-determination of the *proletariat* in each nationality rather than with the self-determination of peoples or nations." He was to repeat the same idea in "The National Question in Our Program" (July 1903). He objected to the emphasis on the right of self-determination because it obscured the class point of view (Lenin, CW, VI:329, 454, 460).

By 1919 Lenin had come to realize that "self-determination of the working class" was an unacceptable formulation. A close analysis will show that the slogan is not realistic. The working class that won independence for a national unit and set up a state would thereby have constituted a nation, actual or potential. If that state was free of class oppression, there would still remain the question of abolishing or guarding against other kinds of oppression. A social class may control a state, or (in Marxist theory at least) it may constitute a state, but it cannot exist independent of and outside of a state. The classless state, which has existed so far only as a theoretical concept, does not by its existence solve all problems of nationality. The Bolsheviks conducted a victorious revolution under the slogans of internationalism and the ending of class domination; but if they had not been guided, to the extent they were, by Lenin's principles of the freedom of nationalities, the "classless" state would hardly have survived. And Russian nationalism was not held in abeyance for long. "Self-determination for the working class," taken in context, meant "all power to the working class," to the Bolsheviks, and down with the bourgeois nationalists, the bourgeoisie. The utilization of a slogan from the field of nationalism in what was essentially a class struggle may have been legitimate as a revolutionary tactic, but it made no sense as a logical proposition; it was no contribution to the argument on self-determination.

The Congress actually did remove the phrase "self-determination" from the Bolshevik program. However, it left in the right of secession, so that Stalin was later able to describe the change as having made no difference (Stalin, 1942:140).

Those who took Lenin's theory of self-determination seriously and attempted to apply it to concrete situations were faced with insuperable difficulties. In the Ukraine, for example, people were unable to find out just how self-determination was supposed to be applied. This problem was discussed at the time (1919) by two writers who professed to be loyal Communists but who were also interested in the freedom of the Ukraine. They said: Show us how self-determination should be applied, and we will "openly and publicly renounce the independence of the Ukraine and become the sincerest supporters of unification" (1970:173). We do not have any means of checking up on these authors, but the point is that the dilemma they cite could have occurred. So Lenin laid himself open to an attack that was not long in coming. His "self-determination" was later called a "tactical propaganda trick to deceive [the non-Russians] and to bring about the 'speedy extinction of their national feelings'" (Smal-Stocki, 1960:43).

The situation in the Ukraine was not as bad for the Bolsheviks as Piatakov made it sound. The masses of the workers and peasants were, by and large, *for* the Bolsheviks, even if there was no possibility of testing the point by a plebiscite. The witness whose testimony has usually been accepted on this point is V. Vinnichenko, who headed the (bourgeois) Central Rada General Secretariat and the Directorate, and who was among those forced out of power when the Rada collapsed. He freely admitted that by the time of the Brest negotiations the Rada, whose representatives were admitted to the conference, had ceased to command the support of the people. By that time, he said, the "vast majority of the Ukrainian population was against us" (Carr, 1950b:298). And again: "If our own peasants and working class had not risen, the Russian Soviet government would have been unable to do anything against us. . . . We were driven out of the Ukraine not by the Russian government but by our own people" (Salov, 1972:90).

## LENIN'S TWO-PRONGED POLICY

The "official" Bolshevik version of this phase of Russian history is that Lenin's policy of self-determination for the border republics was a major reason for the success of the revolution. This contention calls for some discussion.

Lenin's policy toward the border peoples was two-pronged. On the one hand, the central Bolshevik government went to great lengths to recognize the desire of these peoples for freedom if they desired it. One of the first acts of the new government was to grant independence to Finland, and this was confirmed in an elaborate ceremony in which Stalin represented the Bolshevik government. The Baltic republics were also recognized.

The Georgian Mensheviks called themselves Georgian nationalists. They had never demanded secession from the tsar's empire, and did not seek to secede from the Kerensky government. When the Bolsheviks seized power, the Menshevik leaders proclaimed the independence of Georgia and organized a federation of Transcaucasian governments. Within a month, the Georgian authorities had invited the Germans to come in, and 3,000 German troops landed (Fischer, 1930:85).

With the defeat of the Germans in 1918, the Transcaucasian federation broke down. The British replaced the Germans in Georgia, at the invitation of the Menshevik government. In Azerbaijan, however, a Soviet republic was set up. On May 7, 1920, the Bolshevik government signed a treaty with the Georgian Menshevik government. According to this treaty, Georgia was required to break all contacts with the Russian counter-revolution, to have all foreign military forces withdrawn from

Georgia, to grant legality to Bolshevik organizations, and to recognize the Soviet Republic of Arzebaijan (Carr, 1950b:350).

Nationalist Armenia was given a kind of de facto recognition. Turkey was fighting the Greeks in Asia Minor, and the Bolsheviks wished to assist the Turks: "The Armenian delegates in Moscow in May 1920 were offered assistance if Armenia allowed transport of Russian troops over the Kars Railway to go to the rescue of the Turks" (*Encyclopaedia Britannica,* 1955, II:380). The Armenian government rejected the Russian offer.

Later Armenia, Azerbaijan, and Georgia were all brought into the USSR on a basis of formal equality with the Russian Socialist Federated Soviet Republic (RSFSR).

The Far Eastern Republic, which had been set up in eastern Siberia, faded out after the Bolsheviks established military control over the area. As a French newspaper headline put it at the time, the Far Eastern Republic "committed suicide for the beautiful eyes of Moscow."

The other prong of Lenin's policy toward the border peoples was to mobilize in each territory the friends of the revolution, to have them set up a revolutionary government, and to insure the accession of this government to power, with the aid of Red army troops if necessary (as it was). This policy is defended as not inconsistent with self-determination, since any other policy would have endangered the revolution without benefiting the masses (Rodinson, 1966:13).

Eventually most of the former colonies were reincorporated into the USSR. But where the Western powers had established their military occupation, as in Finland and the Baltic republics, or where the Red army was defeated, as in Poland, it was the self-determination of the bourgeoisie that won out.

The case of Finland is instructive in this connection. The newly recognized government of Finland asked to have the Red army units then stationed in Finland withdrawn. Lenin did not do this. The intention had been to stage an uprising of the Finnish Communists, who would be aided by the Red army in setting up a new government sympathetic to reunion with the Russians. But an expeditionary force of Germans under von der Goltz arrived in Finland in time to upset this plan.

In Poland it was the Luxemburgists, known as the "internationalists," who would have set up a government if the Red army had won the war with the Polish army. The failure of the Polish workers and peasants to support the Russians was of course a major disappointment to Lenin. With regard to the peasants, the nationality question furnished part of the explanation. In the Ukraine the peasants supported the Bolsheviks, but in Poland they did not. Carr points out that the landlords in the western Ukraine were mostly of Polish extraction, so that there was an element of national antagonism between them and the Ukrainian peasants: "The national problem became acute when it acquired a social and economic content" (Carr, 1950b:307). But in Poland, both peasants and landlords were by and large Poles. Also, the Polish Communist Party's land policy did not have sufficient appeal to attract many peasants.

The issue was settled finally, in the way that Rosa Luxemburg had predicted, by force of arms, although the outcome was as unpalatable to her as to Lenin.[6] The idea that the theory of self-determination was responsible for the breakup of the Russian Empire was just as badly overdrawn as the opposite proposition, that the adherence of the border republics to the Bolsheviks was due to the same theory. Concrete evidence is lacking that the theory of self-determination had much to do with the outcome one way or the other.

## B. STALIN AND TROTSKY ON THE NATION

Stalin's 1913 essay on *Marxism and the National Question* (Stalin, 1942:7f.) is not a first-rate handling of this thorny subject. But since the essay has passed for many years as the official Marxist treatise on nationalism, we must point out in some detail just why it is inadequate.

There is, in the first place, a lack of precision in the use of terms. Stalin uses "nation" and "nationality" interchangeably; "nationalism" refers to a variety of phenomena. He makes no distinction between the nationalism of the oppressing imperialist nation and the nationalism of the oppressed smaller peoples seeking their freedom.[7] In one sentence are grouped as examples of "nationalism" the spread of Zionism among the Jews (although he did not recognize the Jews as a nation); "the increase of chauvinism in Poland" (a deprecatory use of the term "nationalism," but the term is not consistently deprecated in the essay); "pan-Islamism among the Tatars" (surely an unusual kind of "nationalism"); "the spread of nationalism among the Armenians, Georgians, and Ukrainians" (these of course were then nationalities but not nations); and "the general tendency of the ordinary man to anti-Semitism" (perhaps the only time in Marxist literature that anti-Semitism has been called "nationalism"!) (ibid.:8).[8]

In contrast with current usage, Stalin did not include the national movements as movements for human freedom; when he speaks of "emancipation movements" he has in mind exclusively the social revolution, specifically, the one that had failed in Russia in 1905. Nationalism, whether of the tsar or of the several oppressed nationalities, is usually deplored.

Stalin's definition of a nation is noteworthy for its restrictiveness. A nation, he says, is an historically evolved, stable community arising on the basis of a common language, territory, economic life, and psychological make-up manifested in a community of culture.[9] If it lacks one of these characteristics, it is not a nation. Multilingual nations are ruled out; Switzerland, with three nationalities, is a state but not a nation; there is no national problem because the regime is democratic, said Stalin.

But long as is Stalin's list of indispensable characteristics, we note with amazement that one is lacking—and, according to Renan and others, it is the most important one, or even the sufficient one—that is, that the members of the community in question believe themselves to be a nation.[10]

It might be thought that Stalin's failure to emphasize the subjective factor of national consciousness was part of an attempt to define the nation in purely objective terms. But a purely objective definition would not be possible unless nationality were to be made dependent on racial and geographical factors alone; even the Nazis, who were strong on "race" and geopolitics, did not make this attempt. Culture is a matter of the psychology of individuals, and any definition of the nation that includes cultural and institutional factors at all must be classed as a subjective definition.[11] Stalin correctly included culture in his definition. This fact does not make his definition non-Marxist; the emphasis on culture is not inconsistent with a materialist conception of history. Stalin's definition is simply defective as a definition and as a tool of analysis. His error lay not in the fact that he included subjective factors in his definition, but in his whole approach, which was non-dialectical and non-Marxist and emphasized the wrong things.

It is not clear why Stalin insisted that a nation must be "historically evolved" or "stable." Pakistan was neither; it was created suddenly, on the spur of the moment, for reasons that were indeed "historical" in the sense that the thing happened, but that in retrospect seem quite inadequate. There was nothing stable about this nation either before or after its creation. Thus, it did not last. But the fact that it could be created at all throws doubt on the validity of this part of Stalin's definition. Most of the new African nations are not "historically evolved" or "stable" in Stalin's sense, but they still make great efforts to become consolidated as nations.

When we start to apply Stalin's definition in this way, we find repeatedly that it does not correspond to reality. One or the other of Stalin's points is missing in case after case. Take pre–World War I Poland, divided up among three other states. Did it have "unity of economic life"? But Stalin considered Poland a nation, as did Marx.

Stalin did not tackle the problem of what to do when language and territory do not coincide. It was to resolve this problem that Bauer and Renner suggested national-cultural autonomy. Stalin rejected the notion of national-cultural autonomy but did not explain how nations could be formed at all within his definition when the nationalities were all mixed in together.

The fact was that the celebrated definition was of limited usefulness from the beginning and could never be applied in any general way, not even at the time it was written. But worse, the whole approach was undialectical and scholastic to a degree. It was un-Marxist in concept. The listing of "factors" involved in nation-building is reminiscent of bourgeois social science at its worst (Davis, 1954).

The closest Lenin came to a definition of the nation was in his criticism of Rosa Luxemburg. He chided her for bypassing Kautsky's economic-historical definition and preferring the "basically psychological" definition of Bauer (Lenin, CW, XX:398). Stalin used Kautsky's definition (without credit) for three of the four points of his own, but the fourth part is based on Bauer. Thus, Lenin's criticism of Rosa Luxemburg is in part an implied criticism of Stalin.

Later students have complimented Lenin for the admirable way in which he struck a balance between an exclusively economic emphasis and a heavily psychological emphasis such as we find in Bauer (Nair and Scalabrino, 1971:33). Lenin laid the economic groundwork for his (Marxist) theory, but he always emphasized that the social revolution, and the theory of the state and the nation, are *political* matters. As Michael Lowy says:

> From the methodological point of view, the chief superiority of Lenin over most of his contemporaries lies in his capacity for "putting politics at the post of command," that is to say, his tendency, at the same time obstinate, inflexible, constant and tenacious, to catch and underline in each problem, in each contradiction, its *political* aspect. (Haupt et al., 1974:388-89)

We should indeed bear Lowy's remark constantly in mind when estimating Lenin's theory of nationalism, which was nowhere set forth in any systematic way. Some writers today attribute to Lenin the view that nationalism arose "naturally" from the economic aspects of capitalism, first in the eighteenth century, and later, responding to a different set of stimuli, in the time of imperialism. Actually, to Lenin, the *political* factors were determining in the short run, especially the circumstance that the nation-state was the most appropriate vehicle for implementing the aims of any particular group seeking to wield power in the modern period. (On this point see below, "Kardelj's Criticism of Stalin's Essay.")

To understand the national question in any particular country, we need, not a schematic definition, but a discussion of the interpenetration of various factors—an in-depth historical treatment which is indeed suggested but not at all adequately developed by Stalin.[12]

## STALIN AND THE JEWISH BUND

Stalin distorts history when he says that the Jewish Bund formerly laid stress on aims that were common to Jews and the other workers, but they gave prominence to "its own specific, purely nationalist purposes." Actually, the Bund had a checkered history. Though always devoted primarily if not exclusively to the interests of the Jews, it did seek to unite all workers when it participated in the call for the formation of a revolutionary social democratic party of Russia in 1898. This congress failed, however. By the so-called Second Congress, in 1903, Jewish sectarianism was at its height; indeed the Bund representatives withdrew from the congress because the others would not recognize the Jews as a nation. Later this demand was toned down; the Bund cooperated loyally with other nationalities in 1905 and participated in the St. Petersburg Soviet at a time when the Bolsheviks held back. The Bund's readmission to the Party in 1906 was largely at the insistence of the Bolsheviks, with whom the Bund cooperated at that time. After 1906 the Bund declined. By 1913, the time of the Stalin article, it had degenerated into an unimportant nonrevolutionary sect, interested mainly in national-cultural autonomy. It was when it was in this last phase that Stalin and Lenin attacked the Bund so violently. Stalin loses sight completely of the sectarian phase in 1903, interlarded as it was between two cooperationist phases. (On the Bund, see esp. Hessel, 1964; and Tobias, 1972: Chs. 10, 13.)

Stalin's anti-Semitism, which became so noticeable later, may well have had its roots in the operations of the Bund in the Caucasus, where he was active.[13]

The Armenians in Georgia and the Caucasus generally performed functions similar to those traditionally associated with the Jews in the Pale (money lending, for instance) and were scapegoats because of this. The Bund organized a special protective organization for Armenians, the Armenian Social-Democratic Labor Organization. Stalin, meanwhile, had been working to build up an organization of workers that would include all nationalities—no mean feat in Baku, that "kaleidoscope of national groups" (Stalin, 1942:66). So, this move of the Bund infuriated him (Hessel, 1964:47). Beginning before 1905, Stalin, then a virtually unknown agitator, had waged a terrific battle against the Mensheviks, who were strong in Georgia. In fact, it was his consistent carrying through of Lenin's policies that brought him to Lenin's attention.

The Bund had by 1913 gravitated to the Mensheviks. Stalin was willing to believe the worst of them and must have welcomed the chance to attack their pet policy (as it had become) of national-cultural autonomy.

The issue was of course not a new one. Much of the effort of the Social-Democratic periodical *Iskra* in 1901–1903 had been consumed in a debate with the Bund on the question of nationalism, in which the question of intra-Party federalism was also involved.

The Bolsheviks and Mensheviks did not convince the Bund, but they convinced themselves. The federative principle was decisively defeated and nationalism became a dirty word.

This result is ironic in a sense because Lenin considered nationalism to have been a progressive force in the period of the rise of the bourgeoisie to power in Western Europe, roughly from 1789 to 1871. In the countries that had not yet had their bourgeois-democratic revolutions, such as Russia, China, and India, it should logically have followed that nationalism would be a progressive force, and indeed Lenin welcomed the rise of what he thought was a progressive bourgeoisie in China.

It was not possible for the Russian Social Democratic Party to disregard altogether the social-democratic parties that were being set up on a national basis in certain divisions of the Russian Empire; and the Lettish and Polish Social-Democratic parties were given recognition in the Congress of 1906, but on a strictly limited basis. Later all semblance of national autonomy in the Party was to be done away with, and the Communist Party of the Soviet Union (CPSU) emerged, over the protests of certain constituent representatives, as a completely unified organization—one in which the Russians were to have an unchallengeable predominance.

## THE CLASS BASIS OF NATIONALISM

Just as Stalin's definition is narrowly limited, so also is his discussion of the circumstances that give rise to nations. The bourgeoisie occupies the center of the stage; the historically predisposing factors are economic. The analysis is reductionist to a degree. "In its essence," says Stalin, "the national struggle is always a bourgeois struggle, one that is chiefly favorable to and suitable for the bourgeoisie." Stalin sees the restrictions on suppressed nationalities as being imposed by the bourgeoisie of the dominant nation as part of its struggle with the bourgeoisie of the oppressed nation (Stalin, 1942:21). However, these limitations affect the workers quite as much as the bourgeoisie. And so, said Stalin in 1913, the workers should struggle against national oppression, but should not allow themselves to be incited against their fellow workers; such a struggle among workers would benefit only the bourgeoisie.

This treatment of the causes of national oppression represents a significant difference from Stalin's 1904 treatment of the same subject (Stalin, 1953:I:31). Citing the prevailing opinion that the rise of nationalism was the work of the bourgeoisie, Stalin then gave as an exception to this rule the national movement of the Georgian nobles soon after the tsar had taken over Georgia, in the early nineteenth century. To be sure, he also stated that a national movement properly so called did not develop in Georgia until the late nineteenth century. But he continued to think that the social basis of nationalism was the landed aristocracy, and specifically so stated in an article in 1917 (ibid.: III:17).

Stalin was on solid ground in 1904, and again in 1917, when he averred that nationalist movements might be led by some class other than the bourgeoisie. Yet we find him reverting to Lenin's rather dubious analysis in 1925 and again in 1929, when he said that prior to World War I the bourgeoisie had been exclusively responsible for nation-building (ibid.: VII:226f.; and XI:353f.).

Further, to complicate the problem, we find that for the period *after* World War I, Stalin was insisting:

> It is beyond doubt that . . . the peasant question is the basis, the quintessence, of the national question. That explains the fact that the peasantry constitutes the main army of the national movement, that there is no powerful national movement without the peasant army, nor can there be. That is what is meant when it is said that, *in essence,* the national question is a peasant question. I think that Semich's reluctance to accept this formula is due to an under-estimation of the inherent strength of the national movement and a failure to understand the profoundly popular and profoundly revolutionary character of the national movement. (Ibid.: VII:71-72)

This insistence on the peasants as the "main army of the national movement" and on the national movement as "profoundly revolutionary" may surprise those who are accustomed to associate such ideas with the name of Mao Tse-tung. In fact they were the common property of the Marxist theory of nationalism in the 1920s.

After World War I, and especially after World War II, Communists attempting to work out a policy to be followed in colonial and semicolonial countries repeatedly tried to follow the supposedly progressive "national bourgeoisie" and uniformly met disaster. Meanwhile authentic Marxists, such as Cabral, operating in countries where the class categories developed in Europe did not apply, made their own analysis on the basis of local conditions, and combined nationalism with Marxism in new and often highly successful ways.

Even in the industrial countries, which did have a bourgeoisie, it was not always this bourgeoisie that took the lead in creating the nation. David Horowitz remarks that Germany and Japan were created as states (and nations) primarily by the "fundamentally non-bourgeois" political and social superstructure (Horowitz, 1969:49).

It is now clear that no dogmatic statement can be made about which social class is the "natural" leader of a nationalist movement. Stalin's statement, referring to the period before World War I, that "the national question is in its essence a bourgeois one," has been attacked even in the Soviet Union, where K. Ivanov has denied that this part of Stalin's essay was inspired by Lenin (Ivanov, 1964:39).

## LENIN'S AND STALIN'S
## ATTITUDES TOWARD THE NATION

Richard Pipes, of Harvard University, in his zeal to destroy the authority of Stalin's essay, sometimes overstates his case. One such instance is the passage in which he charges that Stalin takes a "positive attitude" toward the nation, in contrast to Lenin's comparatively "negative" attitude (Pipes, 1954:40). We do not understand the basis for this remark. If it is a question of the respective attitudes of the two men toward national*ism*, then it is difficult to think of anyone in the party who was more hostile than Stalin. In an article that appeared just before *Marxism and the National Question*, Stalin strongly attacked the "national-cultural autonomy" ideas of the Mensheviks ("Liquidators") in the Caucasus (Stalin, 1953: II:295-96). Stalin had campaigned against nationalism in the Caucasus for years; it was probably because of his well-known opposition to national-cultural autonomy that Lenin asked him to write down his ideas on nationalism.

In Stalin's basic essay nationalism indeed comes off badly. Social-Democrats are warned against "nationalist vacillations" and "nationalist obfuscations" (Stalin, 1942:9). Nationality is a "bourgeois principle," which Stalin contrasts—unfavorably of course—with the "socialist principle of class struggle" (ibid.:38). National-cultural autonomy is condemned among other reasons because it "stimulates nationalism," which is "entirely incompatible with Social-Democracy" (ibid.:63).[14] "The national type of organization is a school of national narrow-mindedness and prejudice" (ibid.:67).

Did Lenin have a rather negative attitude toward the nation? He was against national secession from tsarist Russia, in practice, but he fought violently for the right of secession, in theory. He was also the principal fighter for the cultural rights of the small nationalities, including their rights to their own literature, to their own language in schools and courts—only not to "cultural-national autonomy" in the form proposed by Renner and Bauer.[15] What Lenin had in mind when he expressed opposition to "national culture," as the expression was then used, was the *bourgeois* culture of the minor nationalities, as is made perfectly clear in the passages from Lenin's article which Pipes cites (Pipes, 1954:43). Neither Lenin nor Stalin expressed opposition to culture that was national in form as long as it was socialist in content.

In his 1913 "Critical Remarks on the National Question," Lenin's position on assimilation is summed up in this sentence:

> The proletariat . . . favors the greatest freedom of economic exchange and welcomes every assimilation of nations except that which is carried through by main force or grounded in privilege. (Lenin, CW, XX:35; Smal-Stocki, 1960:40, distorts Lenin's position by leaving out the qualifying clause.)

Just what did this imply with regard to the survival of distinct national cultures?

In a review of Eduard David's book *Die Sozialdemokratie im Weltkrieg* (1915), Lenin described the world as being dominated by the big powers. The war (World War I) was being conducted precisely for the purpose of oppressing new nations. The Bolshevik slogan "for the defeat of the fatherland" was not an antinationalist slogan; rather it was based on a desire to secure the freedom of the smaller nationalities. It was thus a pronational slogan, said Lenin. The true socialists are those who recognize the right of the oppressed nations to liberation. But this can be secured only by overthrowing the international bourgeoisie.

When this occurs, when the world proletarian revolution has liberated the oppressed smaller nationalities, will these disappear? Will they become absorbed into the single proletarian state? By no means, says Lenin. National partitions will indeed disappear; but the differentiation of humanity, in the sense of "the wealth and variety in spiritual life, ideological trends, tendencies and shades," will increase "a million-fold." It is clear from the context that what is meant is that nationalism considered as a cultural phenomenon will survive and increase (Lenin, CW, XXI:273-74).

The survival of differentiation, the protection of the culture of the smaller nationalities, was also contemplated by Lenin for the Soviet Union when it had become clear that this might be the only socialist state to come out of World War I. Lenin's passionate defense of the Georgians, when he had become convinced that they were being browbeaten by the Great-Russian *dzerzhimorda,* has become a classic of Marxist literature. It does not seem possible to ascribe Lenin's position to a mere desire to meet "the exigencies of the moment," as suggested by Carrère d'Encausse (1971:224). Lenin had vowed that if he recovered his health he would devote himself to two campaigns, which were related: one, to curb the Great-Russian tendencies of the bureaucracy; and two, to reform the bureaucracy as such, to infuse it with new life and initiative. If it is true that from 1913 to 1922 Lenin's main concern with the forces of nationalism was to harness them to the revolutionary movement (Carrère d'Encausse, 1971:224), does it not make sense to imagine him continuing to seek inspiration and initiative from these same forces in the battle against the ossification of the bureaucracy?

Lenin's insistence on the virtue of differentiation makes mincemeat of the position of those who would ascribe to him a belief in an undifferentiated world working-class culture. The "international culture of the world working-class movement" to which he made reference in an often quoted passage is to be thought of as one comprising many different nationalities and a great deal of variety, including (how could it be otherwise?) national variety. "Spiritual life, ideological trends, tendencies and shades" are not matters of the individual; such an interpretation would make no sense. These are social phenomena to which Lenin referred; and the vehicle of "spiritual life" and "ideological trends" which is the most important in this day and age is the nation, or rather the nationality, since culture is associated more especially with language groups.[16]

We have thus to make a distinction between the national cultures under capitalism, which Lenin repudiated as bourgeois, and the national cultures of the future, under socialism, which will not necessarily be associated with distinct nation-states but which could vary from one another culturally as nationalities always have. Lenin thought that ultimately language differences (and cultural differences?) would disappear; but the intervening period might be quite long.

Lenin saw nothing wrong with voluntary assimilation; in fact he considered it progressive, and applauded the Jews who had taken the way of assimilation. In 1903, when the Bund was claiming for itself the right to speak for all of the Jews in Russia, Lenin took the position that the Jews were not a nationality. In an article on "The Position of the Bund in the Party" (October 1903), he wrote: "The idea of a Jewish 'nationality' is definitely reactionary." But a little later, in May 1905, when a period of collaboration with the Bund was beginning, he wrote a pamphlet issued in Yiddish, *To the Jewish Workers,* in which the Jewish workers are said to be a disenfranchised nationality, and this presently became the official position of the Bolsheviks. After the October Revolution Jews were recognized as a nation and are to this day so designated officially in the Soviet Union.

Lenin's strong opposition to forced assimilation, of the Jews or any other nationality, was continued by his disciples after his death. Thus we find Stalin, as late as 1929, in a polemic against Meshkov, Kovalchuk, and others, writing the following:

> You know, of course, that the policy of assimilation is absolutely excluded from the arsenal of Marxism-Leninism, as being an anti-popular and counter-revolutionary policy, a fatal policy. (Stalin, 1953: XI:362)

Later, with the vast intensification of repression, such remarks on

Stalin's part would have to be put down as window dressing; Stalin was in no position to clamp down on lesser bureaucrats who engaged in forcible suppression of manifestations of national sentiment, once free discussion was effectively terminated. And indeed the persecution of such sentiment has continued not only throughout the period of Stalinism proper but right down to the present time. But this is an anti-Leninist policy.

## LENIN'S RESPONSIBILITY
## FOR STALIN'S ESSAY

Current opinion tends to minimize Lenin's responsibility for Stalin's essay, which is usually presented as the work of Stalin primarily (on this point see Carr, 1950b:203; Shaheen, 1956:68-69 passim; McNeal, 1967:90; Pipes, 1954:40-41; Tucker, 1973:155; Ulam, 1973:119-20). Maxime Rodinson, a loyal Marxist, feels sure that Lenin would not have approved a work so defective in logic and scholarship (Rodinson, 1968:137).

Trotsky and his followers, by contrast, have always contended that Stalin was trying to be Leninist; that the essay was "the work of a diligent pupil" (Souvarine, 1939:134; see also Trotsky, 1947:156-58; Wolfe, 1964:578; Deutscher, 1949:119, 122). Stalin himself indeed looked on the essay as embodying Lenin's ideas (Djilas, 1962:157; Tucker, 1973).

Lenin at the time professed to be much pleased with the essay, which he described as *"a very good one"* (Lenin, CW, XXXV:90). At the end of 1913 he wrote that Stalin's article "stands out in first place," in the recent theoretical Marxist literature on the national question (Lenin, CW, XXIV:223). Lenin continued to work closely with Stalin on matters involving nationality. Stalin was accepted as the expert on the national question in the Bolshevik Party; he was made Commissar of Nationalities in the first Bolshevik cabinet.

Lenin did *not* think that Stalin's essay was the last word on the subject. He himself continued to write on nationalism for years, discovering more and more angles that needed development.

From what has been said, it is evident that there were no major theoretical differences between Lenin and Stalin before World War I. Stalin was quite ready to take over Lenin's distinction between the nationalism of the imperialist country and that of the colonial country. Lenin was to take exception to Stalin's treatment of Bauer; but this was plainly because on Bauer Stalin had not done his homework. In two instances where Lenin had made an incomplete or unhappy formulation of certain ideas, Stalin took them over, thus weakening his own essay.[17]

But it would be a most serious error to speak, as Stalin did, of the "Lenin-Stalin theory of nationalism." Neither the one nor the other had a rounded theory of nationalism. But further, before Lenin's death Stalin had several times diverged from both the letter and the spirit of Lenin's nationality policies. Stalin in the first year of the Revolution spoke of the "self-determination of the working class" when Lenin had abandoned that formulation. More serious, Stalin's original draft of the Constitution of the Soviet Union proposed "autonomy" instead of "national equality" for the lesser republics. And on the question of using force against the minor nationalities—of coercing them—the difference between the two men turned out to be so profound that Lenin was on the point of demanding that Stalin be removed as secretary of the Party. Lenin's last letters on the national question, which were forgotten for so many years, were directed principally against Stalin (see Lewin, 1968).

Stalin survived not because he really caught the essence of Leninist national policy but because with his strong sense of what was politically expedient he always avoided an open confrontation with Lenin. Thus in the end he was the only top leader among the Bolsheviks who could say that he had never opposed Lenin on any major point of policy. This was true—as far as public confrontations were concerned, there were none, on this or other subjects.

Stalin was later to pervert Leninist nationality policy so grossly as to deprive himself of any claim to be an authentic Leninist. But Stalin's 1913 essay was still considered authoritative in the Soviet Union, until the assimilationists set out after World War II to bypass Lenin and destroy Stalin in their drive for a new ideological conformity.

Lenin, who in 1903–1904 had considered the national question as completely subordinate, had elevated it to a position of major importance by 1913. The collapse of proletarian internationalism in World War I caused him to modify his views still further. National liberation, if combined with the struggle for socialism, could be a force for the world socialist revolution no less important than the class struggle of the wage workers in the imperialist countries (Lenin, CW, XXXIII: 500).

The national liberation struggle, then, deserved the attention of Marxists no less than the class struggle. Nationalism, instead of being a problem of a different nature, as Stalin had implied in his 1913 essay, was part and parcel of Marxist theory.

National exploitation is now recognized among Marxists as a category that must be mentioned in the appropriate place; those who persist in expressing all exploitation in terms of class run the risk of being called non-Marxist. (See, for example, Davidson, 1975:19.)


## TROTSKY AND THE NATIONAL QUESTION

Since the attempt is still made today to build Trotsky up as a prophet, or at the least a leading Marxist theorist, it is necessary to point out that on the national question his insights were not followed up, or were irrelevant, or were arrived at after the event. We cite a few leading instances.

First, Trotsky is cited as an early partisan of colonial liberation because he said that the social revolution might come first in underdeveloped countries (Krasso, 1967:67). Trotsky, in expressing this opinion in 1905, was speaking solely of Europe, however (Deutscher, 1954:154f.). Trotsky did say—following a remark by Marx—that the European revolution might start in Russia. He had no thought of applying this philosophy to other areas such as Asia. Trotsky believed even in the late 1930s that the Chinese Revolution would have to wait on the revolution in Western Europe (Deutscher, 1963:427-28). He was Eurocentric quite as much as the other leading Marxists of the early period.

Second, Trotsky did not believe before 1917 that national antagonisms would disappear with the coming of the proletarian revolution. He thought that on the contrary they would increase, and that the minor nationalities should be warned (Trotsky, 1970:25).

His point was well taken, but Trotsky did not expend much effort warning minor nationalities. Later, he was war commissar when the border nationalities were being brought back into the Russian orbit.

Third, Trotsky objected to the policies followed by the Communist International in the aborted Chinese Revolution of 1927. Indeed he did—after the event. Konrad Brandt, a student of Chinese history, satisfied himself that some of the decisions which the Executive Committee of the Communist International made on China, and which Trotsky later attacked, were made when Trotsky was present—one while he was actually in the chair![18] Trotsky does not seem to have offered any objection to these decisions at the time.

Fourth, Jairus Banaji notes that there is something wrong (to make an understatement) with the theory of proletarian internationalism as put forward today by the leading socialist states, and suggests that the man who had the correct approach to internationalism was Trotsky (Banaji, 1974:1540). To understand this contention, we have to recall how Trotsky's particular brand of "internationalism" arose and how it fared.

Trotsky belonged to the school of dogmatic internationalists who before and during World War I emphasized very strongly the economic tendencies making for the breaking down of national barriers and the fusion of existing nations into some kind of superstate. Marx and Engels in the *Manifesto* had given eloquent expression to this idea. But the "internationalists" often carried it too far. Parvus (cited by Banaji) forecast the disintegration of the nation-state as a viable economic form. Trotsky wrote in October 1914:

> The war of 1914 represents first of all the collapse of the *nation-state* as a self-sufficient economic area. Nationalism can continue as a cultural, ideological, psychological factor—the economic basis has been cut from under its feet. . . . The war heralds the breakup of the nation-state. (Deutscher, 1964:72)

The conclusion does not follow. The fact that the nation-state is not economically self-sufficient does not mean at all that it is through as a political entity (Haupt et al., 1974:380).

Banaji gives Trotsky credit, quite properly, for distinguishing between the nationalism of the colonial bourgeoisie, which can derail the movement for socialism, and the nationalism of the colonial workers and peasants. Trotsky wrote in 1930 (and Lenin had made the same point several times):

The nationalism of the most backward Indochinese peasant, directed against French imperialism, is a revolutionary element as opposed to the abstract and false cosmopolitanism of the Freemasons and other democratic bourgeois types, or the "internationalism" of the social democrats, who rob or help to rob the Indochinese peasant. (Trotsky, 1973:31)

But Trotsky's brand of internationalism was just as phony as the "proletarian internationalism" of the Soviet Union and, now, of China, though for rather different reasons. The latter type does not contemplate the only kind of internationalism that could be real or could last, the kind that Marx and Engels must have had in mind (though they did not spell it out): a free federation of legally equal socialist nations, without the de facto predominance of any one. Trotsky may or may not have contemplated such a federation, but since, like most of those who use the term "internationalism," he did not define his terms, he could not, and his followers cannot, be taken seriously on this point.

Trotsky's partisans can offer no explanation as to why, in early 1924, Trotsky failed to condemn in the Central Committee Stalin's highhanded coercion of the Georgians—when Lenin had specifically asked Trotsky to take this action. Lenin was too ill to be present at the meeting of the Central Committee where the matter was to come up.

If Trotsky had felt as strongly on the nationalities question as Lenin, he would not have needed to be asked twice. Even if he was indifferent to the national question, his duty as a Bolshevik might have led him to accede to Lenin's wish. In view of his known dislike for Stalin, he might have been expected to jump at the chance. Instead, he did exactly what Lenin had warned him not to do, that is, accepted a "rotten compromise" offered by Stalin and kept silent during the whole meeting of the Central Committee (Lewin, 1968; Deutscher, 1959:90).

When Lenin died shortly afterward, he left a "testament" in which he urged specifically that Stalin be removed as secretary of the Party, largely because Stalin had handled the nationality question so crudely. When the Central Committee heard this testament a little later, Trotsky not only did not press for Stalin's removal but remained silent again. The testament was suppressed, with Trotsky's acquiescence, and only given to the public many years later.

Altogether, as a champion of the rights of nationalities, Trotsky did not measure up. He had no special feelings on the subject and certainly no distinctive theory. It could even be argued that Trotsky's failure to react to the question of nationalities caused him to lose his best chance to emerge as Lenin's successor and leading Bolshevik—an effort which he made later in vain.

Trotsky belonged to the group of urban intellectuals, who were "rootless" and cosmopolitan to a degree. They were the "international-ists," especially Trotsky with his insistence that the revolution must be continuous and must spread. Stalin by contrast emerged as the Russian nationalist. In the running feud between Trotsky and himself in the late 1920s and early 1930s, Stalin began attacking Trotsky for his rootless-ness and lack of Russian patriotism—an ironic fate for the man who had directed the armed resistance to the invaders who aimed to upset the Revolution (Carr, 1950b:220).

Trotsky indeed remained to the end a Russian patriot. Even Stalinist Russia was a workers' state, in his view, and as such unconditionally worthy of being defended by the world proletariat (Deutscher, 1963:459).[19]

Trotsky was a prolific writer and his command of the world's problems was amazing. After his break with Stalin, his advice on any particular problem was sure to be different from, and opposed to, that of Stalin. Since Stalin was sometimes right, Trotsky was bound to be sometimes wrong. We are concerned not with particular policy judg-ments but rather with the underlying theory, plus such flashes of insight as Trotsky continued to contribute from time to time.

One such insight came early, in 1926; if it had been acted on, a number of Communist parties could have been saved embarrassment and discomfort. In the course of a debate aroused by his book *Where Is Britain Going?*, written in 1925, Trotsky wrote that in no country should the workers undertake any steps in the interests of the Soviet Union that did not follow from their own interests (Deutscher, 1959:222).

A Marxist treatment of nationalism must be a dialectic treatment showing how nationalism arises in history, under what conditions, how it is related to other great movements such as democracy and socialism, and specifically, what is the relation of nationalism to the class struggle. By the time of Lenin's death (1924), the theory of nationalism had taken a certain shape. Since this shape still persists, in the minds of many would-be Marxists, we have to pause a moment to recapitulate where the Marxist theory of nationalism then stood and what problems still remained to be solved.

Lenin's brief sketch of the origins of nationalism overemphasized the role of the bourgeoisie and gave no guidelines as to the place of nationalism in the socialist society of the future. It is true that Lenin, like Marx, wrote broadly of "proletarian internationalism," but this term has to be defined if it is to be more than shibboleth. We cannot accept the idea that "proletarian internationalism" means whatever fits in with the foreign policy of the Soviet Union—or People's China.

There were not in 1924 sufficient data to warrant generalizations about the relation of the socialist revolution to nationalism, and specifically what role particular social classes could be expected to play. On the problem of building a multinational state Lenin had made an admirable beginning, but differences between him and Stalin on the application of Lenin's theory had thrown the basic principles into doubt. Especially in doubt was the definition of the nation. Stalin's effort in this direction was demonstrably imperfect.

The theory of Lenin was developed to solve the national problem in the collapsing Tsarist Empire, and in East Europe generally. Our first task will be to show how far this task has succeeded in the Soviet Union. We shall then examine the experience of another multinational state, in Eastern Europe, namely Yugoslavia. Still another attempt to apply Marxist nationality theory has more recently been made in China. Contributions to the general theory have been made in both countries, and these can be appraised in the proper place.

New ground had to be broken before a Marxist theory of nationalism could be applied to Africa, and the needed students were not lacking. To round out the picture, our study touches on the special problem of Latin America. We shall then be in a position to see whether a rounded Marxist theory of nationalism applicable to the whole world is a practicable project.

# 4

## The National Question
## in the Soviet Union

### THE RUSSIAN REVOLUTION

It was fortunate for the Bolsheviks that their top leaders, especially Lenin and Stalin, had given some attention to the national question prior to World War I. The outcome of the Revolution depended largely on what attitude toward it the minor nationalities would take.

In this chapter we shall examine the Bolshevik policy toward these nationalities, both during the revolution and thereafter, down to the time of writing. We shall further face the problem of whether a correct Leninist nationality policy is consonant with the survival of the Soviet Union (or any socialist country) in a world of competing national states.

Both the Bolsheviks and the Mensheviks professed internationalism before the war, but when the war actually began, the Menshevik leaders supported the government. The Bolshevik leaders in Russia hesitated; but Lenin, who was in Austria when the war broke out, presently launched from Switzerland the slogan of "Defeat of the Fatherland," as in 1903–1905, and the other leaders fell in line. In 1915 and 1916 they sought to rally the Left social-democrats of all countries behind the slogan "No forcible annexations, no punitive indemnities," linking these ideas always with that of social revolution.

Once in charge of the government, the Bolsheviks became the de facto bearers of national policy. "Proletarian internationalism," as initially understood by the Bolsheviks, implied trying to extend the revolution to the West European countries. After October 1917 the Bolshevik government directed a major propaganda effort at the German army then invading Russia. John Reed thought that this effort was a significant factor in the ultimate collapse of the German armies. But for a time the armies continued to advance into Russia. Lenin signed the Peace Treaty of Brest-Litovsk, and entered into diplomatic relations with the Kaiser's government.

The shift to a policy of building socialism in one country was not adopted deliberately; it was forced on the Soviet Union. (This point is developed at length in Carr, 1970.) Trotsky and Zinoviev objected when the self-interest of the Soviet Union was officially made the cornerstone of policy, at the time of the Fourteenth Party Congress in 1925 (Lerner, 1970:139). But even at the very beginning, the interests of the Soviet Union were never sacrificed on the altar of internationalism. Leonard Schapiro is misleading on this point (see Schapiro, 1970:225). Schapiro also states erroneously that the Eighth Congress of the Communist Party of the Soviet Union (CPSU), March 1919, reaffirmed the right of self-determination (ibid.:226).

The importance of the Bolshevik nationality policy to the survival of the Soviet Union would be difficult to overestimate. The non-Russian peoples on the periphery of the old Tsarist Empire took a generally sympathetic view toward the Bolshevik government. Stalin always insisted that it was the sympathy shown to the Bolsheviks in the border republics in the critical days of foreign invasion that made the success of the Revolution possible. He wrote in 1923:

> The October Revolution at one blow smashed the fetters of national oppression . . . removed the grounds of the old national enmity, cleared the way for the collaboration of peoples, and won for the Russian proletariat the confidence of its brothers of other nationalities, not only in Russia, but also in Europe and Asia. . . . Had it not enjoyed this confidence the Russian proletariat could not have defeated Kolchak and Denikin, Yudenich, and Wrangel. . . . (Stalin, 1942:124)
> 
> If in the rear of Kolchak, Denikin, Wrangel, and Yudenich we had not had the so-called "aliens," the oppressed peoples, who disorganized the rear of these generals by their tacit sympathy for

the Russian proletarians . . . we would not have nailed a single one of these generals. (Ibid.:143)

The favorable attitude of the minority peoples toward the Bolshevik government has been attributed to Lenin's policy of self-determination for all peoples (Pipes, 1954:49, Ch. 2 passim). This interpretation is open to question, for three reasons.

In the first place, while nationalist agitation was of long standing in certain of the border areas (e.g., Finland, Georgia, Armenia), there were some other areas where nationalist sentiment had hardly developed. With regard to the Central Asian peoples, Philip Mosely's description would seem to apply:

> The leaders of the non-Russian groups thought generally in terms of satisfying the demands of their nationalities through the establishment of cultural and administrative autonomy within the framework of a federal state. (Mosely, 1948: VII:207)

The second reason for doubting that the policy of self-determination influenced the attitude of the peoples on the periphery was that this plank in the Bolshevik platform was removed in the 1919 Congress.

Third, the counter-revolutionary forces that overran outlying areas of the old Russian Empire were led by and largely composed of the tsarist oppressors. Denikin particularly was known as an instrument of tsarist domination, although Wrangel was much more lenient in his attitude. The peoples of these areas did not need nationalist sentiment to justify their support for those who had destroyed the old regime.

The Bolsheviks, although they were no lovers of religion, were willing to work with the Musulman nationalist movement in getting rid of the tsarists once and for all; they also had a following among the poor and oppressed in all the territory of the old empire.[1]

In many of the former colonial areas it was the Russians who assumed the leadership. But this leadership would hardly have been accepted if self-determination had been uppermost in people's minds.

In the key area of the Ukraine, it was not the "self-determined" (bourgeois) Rada, which the Bolsheviks actually recognized for a while, but the Russian-sponsored rival government that won popular support.[2] The class struggle, not the nationality policy, was decisive.

But if the slogan of self-determination was not the means of winning the allegiance of the outlying areas, it was certainly not, as Rosa

Luxemburg maintained, the means of losing them either. Lenin, the chief sponsor of self-determination on paper, never applied the doctrine in such a way as to injure the state interests of the Soviet Union. The issue of the affiliation of each of the colonial areas was settled by a combination of force and diplomacy, but chiefly, as Rosa Luxemburg had predicted, by armed force.

The ideas of Lenin and Stalin on nationality were by no means universally held in the Communist (Bolshevik) Party in the early days. Some Bolsheviks were in favor of downgrading the minor nationality cultures from the start, and driving for a single proletarian culture under the leadership of the Russians.[3] An attempt was even made to apply this theory in the Ukraine in 1920–1922. The spokesman for this point of view was Lebed.

This idea was not exactly popular in the Ukraine. General Makhno, for instance, strongly opposed the tsarists and the landlords, and his troops were part of the Revolution, up to a point; but Makhno was also an anarchist, opposed to centralized authority, and his troops at times fought against the Bolsheviks.

There was also a group known as the Borotbists, who stood for Ukrainian independence and cooperation with the Soviet Union. Even after the incorporation of the Ukraine into the Soviet Union, there were different theories of nationalism in high places. Skrypnyk, who was commissar of education in the Ukrainian Soviet Republic, was a follower of Otto Bauer. Around 1923 speech was quite free and several schools of thought contended, not only in the Ukraine (see Smal-Stocki, 1960:50-55).

As finally organized under Stalin's direction, the USSR is made up of fifteen Union Republics; these are nominally equal in respect of basic rights, but the Constitution gives so much power to the central (federal) government that the USSR cannot be considered other than a highly centralized state. The 177 nationalities in the USSR are all accorded a type of recognition, even though most of them lie wholly within the territory of some one of the Union Republics. There are some sixteen "autonomous republics," nine "autonomous regions," and ten national areas that are supposed to form "autonomous units" within the Russian regions or territories. But some nationalities, such as the Jews, the Tatars, and the Kazakhs, do not form a majority even in their area of greatest concentration.

The Great Russians, who under the tsar were a minority, have since come to comprise 55 percent of the population; with the Ukrainians (18 percent) and the Belorussians, the eastern Slavs make up 77 percent of the Soviet population (Kulski, 1954:191, 194; Raymond, 1968:245-46).

Article 17 of the Soviet Constitution states: "The right to secede from the USSR is freely reserved for every Union Republic." But the official *History of the Communist Party of the Soviet Union,* prepared under Stalin's direction, specifies that the decision on secession is in the hands of "the party of the proletariat" (*History,* 1939:190-91). This party, the CPSU, is "monolithic"; in it there is no national autonomy.

Stalin was Commissar of Nationalities, responsible for implementation of the nationalities policy. He wrote in 1920:

> It is necessary that all Soviet organs in the border regions—the courts, the administration, the economic bodies, the direct organs of government—as also the organs of the party—should as far as possible be recruited from among the local people acquainted with the customs, life habits, and language of the native population; . . . that the local toiling masses should be drawn into every sphere of administration of the country, including military formations, in order that the masses may see that the Soviet government and its organs are the product of their own efforts, the embodiment of their aspirations. (Stalin, 1942:80-82)

These words were not merely for foreign consumption; a serious attempt was made, under Stalin's direction, to implement them. Local people were pushed forward for administrative positions, although the supply of trained persons was obviously inadequate for a time. The policy was to give to each nationality administrative posts in proportion to its weight in the population of the territory; this policy was called *korenizatsiya,* or "striking roots."

Enemies of the Soviet regime have tended to scorn the policy of staffing government offices, economic bodies, and so on, with local people, as long as the real power rested with the CPSU, that is, with the Russians. Actually the Lenin-Stalin policy was of great importance to the local people, and had everything to do with their acceptance of Russian hegemony. A whole stratum was built up of minor officials who had a stake in the regime and were not likely to join in local nationalist agitation. Also of course, the people were able to get their grievances aired if not always corrected, in the knowledge that at least the officials knew what they were talking about. The contrast with the tsarist regime was apparent to all.

Great Russian chauvinism was for a time preached as the main danger, in the spirit of Lenin (Kolarz, 1956:16). This emphasis was to shift radically. Skrypnyk could say at the Twelfth Congress of the CPSU (1923) that the Party was

> . . . making a balancing act of the nationalities question. . . . Every reference to Great-Power chauvinism must always be compensated by a counter-reference to the chauvinism of state-less peoples, and thus we always get double bookkeeping. . . .[4] Thus in point of fact we have waged no struggle against Great-Power chauvinism (cited by Dzyuba, 1968:37).

Skrypnyk was arrested in 1931 and committed suicide in jail in 1933. He was later rehabilitated.


## NATIONALISM, THE PEASANTS, AND REVOLUTION

The Bolshevik Revolution, based as it was on the city workers, could not have succeeded without the assent of the peasantry, who at that time made up the overwhelming majority of the population. But the Bolsheviks had paid relatively little attention to the peasants. The party with a mass following in the countryside was that of the Social Revolutionaries.

After the February 1917 Revolution, the Social Revolutionaries emerged as a violently chauvinistic party; they favored "War Till Final Victory," and supported the offensive launched by Kerensky in the summer of 1917. The failure of this offensive, and the war-weariness of the people, were capitalized on by the Bolsheviks, who sought to end the war as soon as possible. They also took over a large part of the Social Revolutionaries' land program.

When the Bolsheviks, with whom were associated the Left Social Revolutionaries, signed the Treaty of Brest-Litovsk and entered into diplomatic relations with the Kaiser's government, the leaders of the

Social Revolutionaries were furious. They assassinated Count Mirbach, the new German ambassador, and tried to kill Lenin and Trotsky as well, on the grounds of offended nationalism (Deutscher, 1949:191). But the peasants were more interested in other things.

Much Marxist writing emphasizes Lenin's original attempt to base the revolution on the poor peasants, while conciliating the middle peasants and attacking the rich peasants (kulaks). In the emergency of 1918, when the cities had to have food, the requisitions in the countryside were indeed carried out by the poor peasants, organized in "poverty committees." But the class struggle which resulted turned many middle peasants against the revolution. When Lenin saw what was happening, he called for a shift in policy. The poverty committees were abolished on November 8, 1918, and for some years there was a deliberate attempt to cultivate the strategically situated middle peasants. These for their part were amenable to Bolshevik leadership since they had gained from the land distributions and were freed from the burden of the village usurer, usually a kulak.

The success of the revolution in the cities was crucial to the success of the revolution in the countryside because there had to be an outside force to swing the power to the middle and poor peasants. The soldiers who arrived back from the front when the tsarist army disintegrated changed the power relations in the villages; the victory of the Bolsheviks made the land expropriations stick.

In the villages, social relations had been shifted but not revolutionized. Power had passed into the hands of the soviets, but these were at first sadly lacking in vitality; they were consciously patterned after the old village councils, with the difference that the kulaks were excluded from participation (Anweiler, 1958:298). It was to require another major upheaval and many years of unsettlement before the collective farm system was established and social relations were stabilized on a new basis.

Throughout the turbulent period of the 1930s, the patriotic motive continued to be stressed, addressed to the peasantry no less than to the city workers. The socialist fatherland was accomplishing wonders; the socialist fatherland was in danger. Even peasants who had had no special interest in socialism could understand these slogans. So, nationalism came to the aid of socialism, and the new system was consolidated. It is only regrettable that the new system turned out to be Stalinism, which is so different from the original idea of socialism as almost to deserve a separate name.

In the collectivization drive, it was the poor peasants against the new class of kulaks, many of whom were of course former middle or even poor peasants. City workers, always the mainstay of the Bolshevik regime, were sent into the villages to act as agents of the government and see that the policy was carried through. The middle peasants had been revolutionary, but only up to a point.

## BOLSHEVIK NATIONALITY POLICY
## AND THE CENTRAL ASIAN REPUBLICS

The Bolsheviks would hardly have been able to consolidate their hold on the Central Asian Republics in the interwar period if they had not been able to win the minds of the people. The people of this area had staged a full-scale revolt against the tsar's government in 1916. The smoldering resentment at the long-time oppressive policies of the tsar had burst into flame when the tsar's minions, not daring to put guns into the hands of the Central Asians, but still needing their manpower, had tried to conscript them into labor battalions. It has been estimated that the 1916 revolt enlisted the participation of eight million out of the eleven million population of the area; these were thus predisposed to accept the leadership of the Bolsheviks, who were continuing the revolt which the Asians had in effect started. The major leader of the movement, Amangeldi Iman-uli, joined the Bolsheviks soon after Lenin had taken power (Mandel, 1974:7-8). Meanwhile, however, the blood-letting had been great. Nearly a third of the Kirghiz population had fled to China.

Central Asian (Moslem) nationalism and Bolshevism soon came into conflict. The principal theorist of Central Asian nationalism, Mir Sayid Sultan Alioglu, known as Sultan-Galiev, was a Tatar Musulman from Kazan. He was born about 1880, the son of a Tatar schoolteacher. The three and a half million Tatars were scattered in small groups through-out the territory of the Tsarist Empire, with the largest concentration on the Volga; but even there the Tatars were only a little more than half the population of the district, and cities, including Kazan, were 80 percent Russian.

Sultan-Galiev joined the Bolsheviks in November 1917. A talented orator and organizer, he rose rapidly in the ranks. He organized a Musulman Communist Party and participated actively in the fight against Kolchak. He was the president of the "Central Musulman Commissariat"; he obtained from the central government, over the opposition of the local Russians, the promise of the creation of a great Musulman state which would have had six million inhabitants; it was to include the domain of the Tatars and the Bashkirs on the Volga. This state was to become the nucleus of a much larger unit, including all the Musulman peoples of Russia. Musulman bureaus were actually set up in all the Musulman cities, to propagate Communism in the Musulman world (Bennigsen, 1957:649).

Stalin, in charge of nationality problems for the Communist Party of Russia, demanded that the Musulman Communist Party fuse with the Russian Communist Party. Sultan-Galiev refused, and proposed a federative Communist party. Instead of this, a Musulman section was set up in the CPSU. The Musulman committees got progressively less power and eventually the idea of a separate Musulman state was dropped. Stalin led a fight—the first of many—against "indigenous nationalism." Sultan-Galiev condemned the Russian tactics in Islamic territory and called instead for humane and supple methods that would preserve the progressive features of Islam (ibid.:650-52).

In order to understand the running battle between Sultan-Galiev and Stalin, which ended in the complete defeat of the former, we have to study the relation of forces in the Tatar and Bashkir areas and in the Central Asian districts generally, in the period of the Revolution and immediately thereafter. Under the tsar, Russians had come into the Tatar and Bashkir districts and into the Central Asian colonies as well, in the capacity of teachers, government officials, skilled workers (especially railroad workers), the army garrisons, and some peasants. After the Revolution, these groups continued to exercise power to the virtual exclusion of the local ethnic elements. In the Crimea, for example, the big estates of the Russian nobles were confiscated, but instead of being given to the Tatar peasants, they were turned into state farms. In other former colonies the estates were distributed, according to one authority, to Russian colonists (Pipes, 1954:163, 190).

The uprisings against the Russians which took place after the Bolshevik assumption of power were looked on in the former colonial areas as a continuation of the struggle for national liberation from the colonial oppressors (the Russians).

Sultan-Galiev, generalizing on his own observations, denied that the proletariat of the advanced countries came to the colonial areas in the role of liberators. He said that the industrial proletariat—not only that of the traditional imperialist powers such as England and France, but even that of the socialist country, the Soviet Union—were interested not in liberating the peoples of the East but in exploiting them. The proletariat's seizure of power meant for the colonial peoples merely a change of masters (ibid.:261; quoting a Tatar document of 1924 setting forth Sultan-Galiev's views).

The real conflict, in Sultan-Galiev's view, was between the industrial metropolis and the colony. The "proletarians" in the colony were not the industrial wage earners—of whom there were very few, and these mostly of the imperialist country—but the indigenous people as a whole; the colonial nation was a "proletarian nation," and all classes of natives were "proletarian."[5] Sultan-Galiev thus favored basing the liberation movement in the colonies on the peasants, on the small bourgeoisie, and even on the progressive elements of the big bourgeoisie. The class struggle was of secondary importance; it would be limited to suppressing a few "inconvertibles" (Bennigsen, 1957:645-46).

Sultan-Galiev soft-pedaled the idea of class altogether, stressing instead the antagonisms between native and imperialist, between the rural colonized peoples and the industrial metropolis. The former, he said, should band together and form a colonial international alongside the Communist International and independent of it. The Russian socialist system, he thought, would turn into state capitalism. On the other hand, the colonial international would be genuinely socialist, under native Communist parties. The liberation of the Asian colonies would deal a death blow to European capitalism. The colonial international would win the political hegemony over the industrial metropolises (ibid.: 646-48).

Our knowledge of Sultan-Galiev's ideas is fragmentary. He left no systematic statement of his philosophy. We have only short articles and speeches, some excerpts from long documents (such as that cited by Pipes), and the works of Sultan-Galiev's disciple and compatriot, Hanafi Muzaffar.

It is not clear whether Sultan-Galiev had developed his whole philosophy by the time Stalin moved against him in 1923. In any case, in that year Sultan-Galiev was put on trial and summarily removed from his Party offices. He was the earliest of a long line of Stalin's enemies who were given legal lynchings, although the penalty was not death in this case, and he remained active for a number of years thereafter.[6] Other leading Bolsheviks, who were to be attacked in their turn by Stalin, regretted afterward that they had not protested this first arrest of a prominent Party member made on Stalin's initiative (see Trotsky, 1947:417). Perhaps they were willing to condone behavior toward a representative of a minor nationality which they would have opposed if it had been exercised toward a Great-Russian. Their blindness was to cost them dearly.

The Russians in Central Asia were early deprived of the special privileges that they had enjoyed under the tsar. Stalin insisted strongly on this point (see Stalin, 1942:80-82). But as the only elements in the area with command of the Russian language, the Russians alone could act as agents of the central government and Party, and this they tended to do, even though their knowledge of and devotion to Marxism were often very sketchy. There is a great deal of evidence that many Musulmans looked on them as merely continuing the Russian domination of the area (Carr, 1954:286-87).

The influence of Islam was pared down by gradual changes in the law, and in 1928 a general assault on Islam was begun. It was conducted by the Party, the schools, the Komsomol, and especially the League of the Militant Godless (disbanded in 1937), and continued until 1941 (Bennigsen and Lemercier-Quelquejay, 1968:150f).[7]

Sultan-Galiev's lack of emphasis on class seems non-Marxist on the face of it. But the Russian Communists also preached class peace in Central Asia (Bennigsen, 1957:647). Sultan-Galiev was criticized because he favored collaboration of the peasants with the bourgeoisie, including elements of the upper bourgeoisie. But collaboration between workers, peasants, and bourgeoisie in the national liberation struggle was recommended by Lenin and practiced by Mao Tse-tung, as we shall see. The idea that the revolution of the colonial peoples was to be identified not with the class struggle but with the common struggle of all the oppressed peoples for a transformation of their destiny was common currency in the area, according to the early Bolshevik historian G. Safarov (cited in Carrère d'Encausse, 1966:242-43). The Turks evidently thought that they and not the Russians should be considered the authentic spokespersons for the revolutionists of the area.

Lenin was alive up to the time of Sultan-Galiev's trial and exclusion from the Party in 1923. Lenin shared the responsibility for the forcible reconquest of the Central Asian Republics, which had enjoyed a de facto independence in 1919 and 1920. But the policy toward the indigenous populations which he favored and would have liked to apply was indicated in one of his last papers, which was not published until 1956. In it he refers to the awakening of the East:

> It would be an inexcusable opportunism that the day before this movement of the East, at the dawn of its awakening, we should ruin our prestige in their eyes by the least brutality, the least violence against our indigenous populations. (Lenin, CW, XXXVI:610-11)

Sultan-Galiev with his call for a "humane and supple" nationalist policy was clearly in the spirit of Lenin.

Marxist nationality theory did not rise to the challenge cast down by Sultan-Galiev. Later, when some of the same points were raised by Frantz Fanon, Marxists were thrown into confusion.


## GREAT-RUSSIAN NATIONALISM IN THE 1930'S

Stalin deliberately emphasized Great-Russian nationalism in the 1930s. This emphasis appears most obviously in the reversal of the official attitude toward M. N. Pokrovsky's interpretation of Russian history (see Pokrovsky, 1968). Pokrovsky, who had described the Russian tsars as imperialists and the resistance movements against them as anticolonial movements, had been much admired by Lenin. After Pokrovsky's death in 1932, his interpretation fell into disrepute. The expansion of the Russian state came to be seen as a progressive phenomenon. Sympathetic movies were produced glorifying Ivan the Terrible and Alexander Nevsky. (Earlier the former had been depicted as a madman.)[8] The tsarist generals Suvorov and Kutusov were rehabilitated and military decorations were named after them.

Stalin's revision of the attitude toward Russian history extended even to events within his own—and Lenin's—lifetime, and put him in sharp opposition to his own early pronouncements. The Social-Democratic Party had taken a position for the "defeat of the fatherland" in the Russo-Japanese War. Stalin in 1945, in his broadcast on V-J Day, said:

> The defeat of Russian troops in 1904 left a grave imprint on the minds of our people. It was a black stain in the history of our country. Our people were confident and awaited the day when Japan would be routed and this dark blot be wiped out. We men of the older generation have awaited this day for forty years, and now it has come. (Hunt, 1963:214)

It is necessary to understand the rationale of Stalin's move. Although the glorification of the tsarist conquest of the outlying areas was resented in those areas, to the majority Kutusov symbolized the Russian resistance to Napoleon. No doubt Stalin wanted to build up a sense of national pride and adequacy. In a speech delivered in 1931, he recalled that Russia

> . . . was beaten by the Turkish beys. She was beaten by the Polish and Lithuanian gentry. She was beaten by the British and French capitalists. She was beaten by the Japanese barons. All beat her—for her backwardness. . . . We are 50 or 100 years behind the advanced countries. We must make good this distance in 10 years. Either we do this, or they crush us.

There was something to be said for getting rid of the devastating Russian inferiority complex.

Stalin, who by this time had outmaneuvered his political enemies and was the unquestioned master of the Soviet Union, based his policies of industrialization and rapid and complete collectivization on frankly nationalist grounds. The collectivization was carried through clumsily and brutally, and provoked widespread opposition among the peasantry. At the beginning of the drive for collectivization, the Central

Committee of the CPSU had decided to proceed with caution in the outlying areas, such as Central Asia. At Stalin's instance the Sixteenth Party Congress reversed the Central Committee and fell in line with Stalin's policy of rapid and complete collectivization in all areas. The result was a revival of nationalist sentiment and agitation. Stalin was led to remark that "traces of capitalism in the minds of men are more tenacious of life in the sphere of nationalism than in any other" (Avtorkhanov, 1959:ch. 23; Stalin quote is from Stalin, 1942:474).

Not only was collectivization pushed on an all-union scale, but a campaign for denomadization was launched in Kazakhstan and carried through against massive resistance. Hundreds of thousands of Kazakhs lost their lives or left the area altogether.[9]

In all the national republics, resistance against collectivization crystallized into antigovernmental movements. Some of these operated partly in the open, professing loyalty to the Revolution but demanding greater local autonomy; others were counter-revolutionary and operated illegally. Underground groups in the Ukraine included the Union for the Liberation of the Ukraine, created in 1930; the Ukrainian National Center (1931); and the Ukrainian Military Organization (1933). Other nationalist groupings in the early 1930s included followers of Sultan-Galiev in Tataro-Bashkiria, followers of Sadvokasov in Turkestan, former "national deviationists" in the Caucasus, and so on (Avtorkhanov, 1959:Ch. 23).

The Soviet Union did indeed become industrialized, and did become able to defend itself, as World War II showed. But the cost was very great. One of the casualties was the whole system of socialist legality. The secret police ran wild; purges decimated the intelligentsia, and a system of prison camps for political dissenters was established on a scale never dreamed of by the tsars. The whole socialist regime was brought into disrepute.

Another of the casualties of the 1930s was the Leninist nationality policy. Spokespeople for the rights of the smaller nationalities were mercilessly purged for the "crime" of nationalism. Among the many so liquidated were Aghassi Khandian in Armenia (1936), and Premier Faizala Khodzayev and Party Secretary Akmal Ikramov in Uzbekistan (1938).

The list of those executed for nationalist deviations which is presented by Roy A. Medvedyev is striking for the fact that so many have

Russian-appearing names (Medvedyev, 1971). Actually in this period many of the officials in the outlying republics still were of Russian origin, but this fact apparently did not prevent them from taking the point of view of the peoples in those republics as against the center. Party officials and non-Party leaders alike were purged. All but one of the Central Committee of the Ukrainian Communist Party were executed. The purge did not exclude executives of foreign parties who were living in the Soviet Union. The whole Central Committee of the Polish Communist Party was killed; of the Yugoslav Central Committee only Tito was spared. Since the purges affected equally the middle officialdom of the Russian Socialist Federated Soviet Republic (RSFSR), they cannot be connected with nationalism except where this charge was specifically alleged.

Although great numbers of people knew of cases where justice had miscarried and innocent persons had been executed, criticism of the government had been effectively silenced. Critics were accused of disloyalty and were in great personal danger. Thus there was no general appreciation of the extent of the violations of socialist legality. Even abroad, where the criticisms were fully aired, many people were inclined to attribute them to anti-Soviet bias on the part of the accusers. The anti-Communists had cried "Wolf!" too often in earlier years. In the Soviet Union itself, the general feeling of elation at the success of the five-year plans and the imminent threat of war and invasion sustained morale and, later, made possible the amazing showing of the war years.

## RUSSIAN NATIONALISM AND PATRIOTISM IN WORLD WAR II

When the fabulous German war machine invaded Russia on June 22, 1941, and drove to the outskirts of Moscow and Leningrad, taking 3,400,000 prisoners on the way, many predicted that the morale of the Soviet peoples would collapse.

The Western world had before it the example of a country such as Norway, where Quisling and his followers welcomed the invading Germans and where the Communists, confused and disoriented by the

Molotov-Ribbentrop Pact, at first offered no resistance. It also had in mind the showing of France, where national morale sank to very low levels after the military defeat; the majority of the people not only accepted the collaborationist government of Pétain and Laval, but would have voted for it, as we are reminded in *The Sorrow and the Pity,* the remarkable documentary film about that period. When it was started, the underground had to contend not only with the Nazis in command of the occupation but with its own neighbors who informed on it and denounced it to the occupying authorities. Some of the French youths were so much in sympathy with Hitler's anti-Communism that they formed a special group of French Fascists and went to fight in Hitler's armies.

It was known that there had been massive disaffection within the Soviet Union in advance of the war. It was known, too, that there were concentration camps in which opponents of the regime had been confined. The West had only vague ideas as to how many were in the camps, but Stalin's violations of socialist legality were recognized as being widespread. It was known that organizations of local nationalists were active in the Ukraine and in half a dozen other Soviet republics. How could national Soviet morale be sustained under such adverse conditions?

Somehow the national morale and the strength of Soviet resources were adequate to absorb the initial reverses and turn the enemy back (lend-lease aid did not begin to arrive in any quantity until after the Battle of Stalingrad). And as if to emphasize that the patriotism of the Soviet people had deep roots, partisans numbering some two hundred thousand formed detachments and operated behind the enemy lines, in occupied territory.

At the same time, however, a mass defection was taking place among the prisoners, hundreds of thousands of whom were inducted into the German armed forces and served for two or three years in that capacity. This phenomenon would seem to indicate a low level of patriotism in the Soviet army. This requires further examination.

In order to understand this mass defection, it is necessary to examine the circumstances. Most of the defections took place in the winter of 1942–1943 (Fischer, 1952:136). At this time the condition of the prisoners was difficult in the extreme. Hundreds of thousands had died of hunger and exposure. Fischer, who interviewed a considerable number of defectors, leaves no doubt that the desire to survive was the reason for most of the so-called voluntary enlistment (ibid.:44).

There was an additional motive for some of the defectors: the desire to get rid of Stalin.

In discussing the psychology of the former prisoners, Fischer emphasized their political "inertness." Their manner of survival in the Soviet Union was not to question Stalin's authority. However, when that particular inhibition was removed and Stalin was presented to them as their real enemy, many were ready to accept that idea. They were influenced, among other things, by the example of General Vlasov, a Russian who was taken prisoner and expressed willingness to lead an army of defectors against the Soviet Union. (It never materialized.)

But if it is conceded that the bulk of the prisoners who were inducted into the German army really had no choice in the matter, what about their later behavior? Might they not desert back again at the earliest opportunity?

We may assume that this idea occurred to the German generals on the eastern front, where the *Osttruppen,* as they were called, were first organized. These "voluntary" troops, or *Hiwis* (a German abbreviation for "volunteers"), were attached to the German regiments as "drivers, stable-boys, cooks, medical orderlies, and interpreters" (von Rauch, 1959:343) and were assigned to rear-area police duties. Beginning in the summer of 1943—that is, at the earliest practicable date—four-fifths of them were removed from the eastern front to other parts of Europe, doing antipartisan work under Himmler, in Poland, the Balkans, Slovakia, Italy, and France. Göring, for one, had a very low opinion of them, saying they were not good for anything but deserting (Steenberg, 1970:152). That at least some did exactly that is attested by a *New York Times* dispatch of October 14, 1944, which recounts that during the Allied invasion of Southern France, Russian, Caucasian, Georgian, and Ukrainian troops showed a propensity to shoot their German officers and to desert.

The picture of a mass defection on the part of the Soviet troops is affected by two other considerations. In the first place, although the defectors were very anti-Stalin, they were never anti-Soviet. Fischer is vehement on this point. He says they were intensely nationalist, even chauvinist (Fischer, 1952:152).

A second point has to do with the number who actually defected. If we take at face value the statement of General Koestring, the last general who had the *Osttruppen* in charge, that there were "well over a million" of them, then some one-third, or 1,100,000, of the prisoners defected. This figure is difficult to reconcile with another, the number of Soviet citizens from the prewar area who did not return to the Soviet Union. We may assume that an active defector would have realized what a chance he was taking in returning home; he knew the low esteem in which "Vlasov men" were held. Yet the number of "non-returners" for whatever reason was only about 250,000 by Fischer's estimate (ibid.:45,.112).

Smal-Stocki has tried to show that the defectors were mainly non-Russians who wanted to fight against the Russians (Smal-Stocki, 1960: 67-68). He even presented a table of the number of defectors from non-Russian areas, classified according to nationality, totaling 647,000.[10] Fischer denies that the movement was anti-Russian. The Vlasov element was predominantly Russian; the top men around Vlasov were nearly all Russian. The Ukrainian nationalist organizations that were approached to endorse the Vlasov movement refused; only with great difficulty did Vlasov eventually get some Ukrainian leaders to back his committee (see Armstrong, 1963; Fischer, 1952:137-38).

The episode of the Soviet defectors does not testify to any mass disaffection with the Soviet regime, among either the Russians or the minor nationalities. Soviet national morale remained strong in spite of occasional exceptions. Russian anti-Soviet forces included General Pannwitz's Cossack battalions, and the forty thousand troops assembled by the Organization of Ukrainian Nationalists, who fought against the Nazis, against the Red Partisans, and in 1944–1945, against the Red army as well.

When whole nationality groups in the Soviet Union were deported during the war, this move implied that they had collaborated with the enemy en masse. However, all but one of these groups, the Crimean Tatars, were eventually rehabilitated and returned home. There was no mass disaffection here either, only hysteria in the central government, similar to that which caused the removal of first- and second-generation Japanese from the Pacific Coast during World War II.

## NATIONALITY POLICY AFTER WORLD WAR II[11]

The anti-Islamic campaign was revived in 1947, after the war. The alphabet was made Cyrillic, the languages "cleansed," and history rewritten in a way favorable to the Russians; much of the traditional literature was condemned. By the time of Stalin's death in 1953, Central Asia was apparently "de-Islamized."

The question of more freedom of self-expression for the non-Russian nationalities was one of the issues among the candidates for the successor position after Stalin died. Beria led the movement for greater freedom; Khrushchev opposed it. Beria's policies seemed to be making progress up to 1956. For example, in Stalin's postwar drive to weed out remnants of anti-Russianism, the inhabitants of Daghestan had been deprived of their national hero, Imam Chamil (1829–1859), who had resisted the encroachments of the Russian tsar and had taken refuge in the hills from which he waged guerrilla warfare. Chamil had always been considered an early hero of resistance to imperialist aggression. From 1950 to 1956 he was attacked as an enemy of progress; but in 1956 he was rehabilitated, and Baghirov, who had been leading the campaign against Islam, was executed (Bennigsen, 1957:657-59).

A new period of toughening began with Khrushchev's accession to the leadership. Khrushchev considered that in the Soviet Union as a whole, a period of rapprochement of the cultures, called *sblizhenie,* was due to be followed by amalgamation of the cultures, or *sliyanie.* At the Twenty-second Party Congress (1961) Khrushchev launched an attack on all forms of localism (*mestnichenstvo*) but particularly on national localism. He hailed the Soviet Union as a new type of ethnic community, higher than the nation.

Khrushchev's resolution, according to which "the nations will draw still closer together until complete unity is achieved," was adopted and became national Soviet policy. The resolution, while making the usual bows in the direction of the sovereignty and "free development" of the several republics, said that "the Party will promote . . . consolidation [of the several national cultures], and thereby the formation of the future single worldwide culture of communist society" (*Moscow News,* Aug. 5, 1961:13).

There was no question that the regime contemplated the absorption of the several nationalities into a single integrated whole, the Soviet nation. As an article in a Soviet periodical put it at the end of 1961:

> Mutual assimilation is, in substance, denationalisation of the autonomous national territories, even of the Union Republics; the Soviet society is thus approaching the point where a complete national fusion can be seen as a matter of the near future. (Cited by Penner in Goldhagen, 1968:227)

In August 1958 Gafarov had written an article in *Kommunist* foretelling the development of a single language (Solchanyk, 1968:339). The August 1962 issue of *Voprosy Filosofii* contained an attack by A. N. Maslin on the notion that a culture could be national in form and socialist in content. Several other articles attacked Stalin's idea of a new international language that would develop out of the "best elements" of all the other languages. Russian, it was said, was the only international language for the Soviet Union.

In February 1963 the Supreme Soviet issued a resolution establishing the Central Asian Economic Region which would unite the Tadzhik, Kirghiz, Turcoman, and Uzbek Soviet Socialist Republics. All major policy matters concerning Central Asia were to be reviewed by the Central Asian Bureau of the Central Committee. This bureau was made up of eleven members, seven of whom (including the chairman and the deputy chairman) were Russians. The only Central Asians were the first secretaries of the four republic parties. These first secretaries had enjoyed little power in any case, since each had been assisted, in the usual Soviet fashion, by a powerful second secretary who was always a Russian.

In May 1964 it was reported that the Central Asian Economic Region was not functioning properly. Every request for funds crossing republic lines had to be approved by the separate republic finance ministries, who sabotaged the whole arrangement by retreating into a maze of bureaucratic red tape. Later that year the attempt to amalgamate the Central Asian Republics was officially abandoned.

Khrushchev fell from power the same year. The "line" regarding the minor nationalities changed noticeably. An editorial in *Kommunist* stated that the tsarist autocracy had slowed the development of the borderlands by "merciless exploitation" (*Kommunist*, no. 16,

1964:11). In 1965 and 1966 several articles in *Kommunist* reaffirmed the policy of bilingualism and hailed the fact that "the culture of the large nations does not crush and swallow the cultures of the smaller nations" (*Kommunist*, no. 5, 1966:69-70). The way seemed open for a rehabilitation of Pokrovsky. This did not occur; but Brezhnev, in his report to the Twenty-third Congress of the CPSU in March 1966, called for a slowing down of the movement toward assimilation. In the congress itself, both points of view, for and against rapid amalgamation, were expressed; the speakers favoring conservation of national traditions in the several republics were by no means overwhelmed or even outnumbered.

Through the 1960s and into the 1970s the debate continued. At stake was the whole conception of the USSR as a federation of equal nation(alitie)s, as laid down by Lenin. The alternative concept was that of the Soviet Union as a single integrated nation.

The assimilationists did not attack Lenin directly, but they had no such scruples about Stalin, whose 1913 essay was declared to be out of date. Stalin had mentioned four essential characteristics of a nation—community of economy, territory, language, and psychological make-up. The historian E. M. Zhukov in 1961 declared that only the community of language remained to distinguish one Soviet nationality from another. The unity of interest of all Soviet peoples and the mixing of the national groups through migration had made the other criteria meaningless (see *Voprosy Istorii*, no. 12, 1961).

This approach, and that of the writers who had been arguing that language differences were disappearing, were demonstrably defective. When the results of the 1959 Census became available, they showed that the tendency for Russian to be adopted as the native language in new areas was not nearly as marked as some had thought. In 1926 58.5 percent of the population of the Soviet Union had counted Russian as their first language; by 1959 the proportion had risen only to 59.3 percent. And in matters of nationality, as we have attempted to show, it is not the language alone that matters, but the will to be separate and distinct.

P. M. Rogachev and M. A. Sverdlin argued that since a common economic life is an important part of Stalin's definition of a nation, and since the several Russian republics are increasingly being integrated into a single unit, the "psychological" basis of separate nationhood is being undermined; the growth of national consciousness in the several republics (which they do not deny) is being deprived of its objective basis.[12] Rogachev and Sverdlin think that national differences tend to disappear under "classless" socialist conditions. They distinguish between "socially heterogeneous," "transitional," and "socially homogeneous" nations, with the obvious implication that the Soviet Union is approaching the last stage. But others (e.g., Tavakalian) deny that the Soviet Union has reached that point in its development.

Although it has evolved as a highly centralized state, the Soviet Union is legally and constitutionally a federation, in which all the states are equal. This is the legacy of Lenin. Thus for the USSR to absorb the constituent republics and leave them as only cultural reminders of the past would pose awkward problems at law. Part of the intellectual drive of the assimilationists was to undermine the conception of the constituent republics as self-determining states, and reduce them to non-self-governing, nonself-determining units of the whole.

Rogachev and Sverdlin thought with Lenin that nations tend to set up independent states, but Semenov suggested that that only applied to capitalist states; in a multinational socialist state, nations would survive but not as states. Mnatskanian by contrast sought to vindicate the separateness *at law* of the several republics in the Soviet federation; these were thought of as having come together voluntarily.

The British historian Peter Howard found that the 1966 articles in *Voprosy Istorii* were tortuous and lacking in forthrightness, but other critics have expressed admiration for the degree of freedom of expression evidenced.[13]

The fact that the debate was permitted at all, in a country where political dissidence is discouraged, is an indication of the importance the regime attaches to the subject. It is surely a sign of progress that a document that for so many years was considered authoritative (Stalin's 1913 article) should be subjected to searching criticism; and while the original purpose of the criticism—to further a government campaign for assimilation—cannot be judged consonant with Lenin's ideas, the discussion seemed to bring Soviet nationality theory back into the realm where it can be seriously debated.

A certain amount of assimilation of quite small tribal groups goes on without necessarily being forced in any way. This assimilation as a rule is to the large group with which the small group is most closely associated. Thus between 1960 and 1970 the small peoples of the Altai-Saian highlands merged with two larger peoples, the Altais and the Khakasy (Bruk, 1972:357-58).

The groups that are large enough to retain their tribal or national identity on the other hand not only do not show any tendency to merge but are increasing in size; this trend is observed of all the eighteen tiny peoples having between 400 and 9,000 members (Mandel, 1974:34; quoting *Izvestia*).

Evidence accumulates from various quarters in the USSR that interest in nationality surges among the young even more than among the old. This is admitted in the official press. Young poets sing the praises of Armenia, the Ukraine, Lithuania, and Turkmenistan, without mentioning Russia or the Soviet Union, and continue to do so even when penalized for it (Kulski, 1954:108-10; *Kommunist* [Yerevan], March 6, 1966). In Central Asia, a new generation of intelligentsia, loyal to Communism though not necessarily to Russian tutelage, has revived Sultan-Galiev's idea of an oriental Communism controlled by orientals (Bennigsen, 1957:656).

The idea that assimilation is just around the corner, so to speak, or that nationalities will disappear in the foreseeable future, is not held today by anybody (Mandel, 1974:44). This represents quite a change from the policy announced by the Party in 1961.

But the cult of the Soviet nation continues to be preached. The term was officially adopted at the Twenty-fourth Congress of the CPSU.

So, a collision course is indicated.

## SOVIET ATTITUDES ON NATIONALITY

The survival of national languages and national differences on a large scale has led to the demand for more information on the whole subject. In 1963 there was held in Frunze in Central Asia a nationwide conference which decided to launch a massive ethnosociological investigation of nationality attitudes in all major regions of the Soviet Union. The first publication of findings, with details on the Tatar Republic, appeared in 1967 (Drobizheva, 1967). Since the studies employed a small army of researchers using the most up-to-date Western techniques, it is evident that a new standard has been set for study of the nationality question in the Soviet Union.

While the study showed in general that there was a high degree of tolerance of other nationalities in all the areas studied, there was a residue of the "self-contained nationalist" point of view, especially among the older members of the population. "Nationalism" (in the sense of intolerance toward those of other nationality groups) was usually stronger in the country than in the towns, and was a little stronger among young people who had just entered the labor market and were competing for jobs for the first time than among those still in school or those who had settled into their jobs and "gotten over the cultural shock of adjusting to a life of work" (Mandel, 1974:27).

Those who objected to working with members of other nationalities, or had no friends outside their own group, or disliked having a chief from another nationality, or demanded ethnic schools, did not number more than 20 or 25 percent in any of the areas. This figure includes those who expressed "no opinion" or declined to give an answer.

Among the workers, the higher the education and the more urban the group, the less prejudiced were the attitudes. However among professional people and intellectuals, including the younger ones, the amount of national antagonism expressed was higher than among workers, though still not by any means overwhelming. This finding applied especially to work relationships. The explanation offered was that Soviet *workers* do not feel themselves in competition with one another for jobs, but professional people do (ibid.). In Kazan, highly educated Tatars showed significant job dissatisfaction, while among the highly educated Russians job satisfaction was almost complete (ibid.:28).

There are those who would discount heavily any Soviet sociological study of attitudes, on the ground that the respondents would not feel free to express their real opinions for fear of reprisals. This criticism, if applied to the study in question, must contend with the fact that respondents were always given an out: they could say that they had no opinion or simply that they did not care to answer. Even when those of indeterminate opinions are included with the outspoken nationalists, no mass dissatisfaction with Soviet nationality policy can be read into the findings.

But the fact that a "residue" of national feelings still exists gives point to the remark of one supporter of the regime—a remark made in another connection. S. Kaltakhchyan, a respected scholar, wrote in 1972:

> The statement that "the nationalities question has been solved" obviously does not mean . . . that there are no more problems. The solution of the nationalities question means the removal of political, economic and cultural inequality, and the rise of an atmosphere of friendship of nations. But so long as nations exist, there will also be the problems intrinsic in the relations between the nations and the state they constitute. Another ever-present task is the fostering of socialist internationalism. . . . We still have a good deal of work ahead of us. (Kaltakhchyan, 1972, I:2, 10)

The spirit of socialist internationalism obviously has not been built, and it is an open question whether this can be done as long as the Russians in the central government feel obliged to throttle critical discussion in the country as a whole. The heritage of Stalin casts a dark shadow over social relations in the Soviet Union. (Drobizheva, 1967, cit. by Mandel, 1974:44)

The Soviet studies find extreme national chauvinism among 5 to 10 percent of the Soviet population. It is probable that if the question were put, there would turn out to be an idealistic "internationalist" group at the other end of the spectrum, who would be determined to have done with the animosities and jealousies of the past. Whether this group would also be 5 to 10 percent of the total is impossible to say. But the "undistributed middle" is the determining factor in the situation. If things began going badly, in economics-plus-politics, this group in the non-Russian areas might still follow an anti-Russian lead. Nationalism could give real trouble, as in Hungary in 1956 and Croatia in 1971.

When nationalist agitation appears on a considerable scale, what attitude does the central government at Moscow now take? Armenia recently furnished a test case.

Armenia is a republic of three and a half million, in which the Russians constitute only 3 percent of the population. For many years Armenia was a showpiece; it received a good share of the investment funds available, and production and the scale of living increased rapidly. Some 220,000 Armenians who had emigrated abroad returned to help build up the Armenian Socialist Republic.

In 1965, anti-Russian sentiment was reported in Armenia. When 100,000 Armenians gathered in Lenin Square to commemorate the Turkish massacres of fifty years earlier, although the occasion was primarily one of protest against the Turks, the authorities thought they detected anti-Soviet overtones, and police were sent to disperse the crowd. In 1974, a portrait of Lenin was reportedly burned in Lenin Square.

Eventually it became evident that what at least some of the protestors had in mind was not merely resentment at Russian domination but opposition to socialism, and secession from the Soviet Union as a step to reintroduce capitalism. The physicist Andrei D. Sakharov reported the existence in Armenia of a National Unity Party which avowed such aims. Eleven young persons were sentenced to prison for terms of two to seven years for the crime of Armenian nationalism, according to Sakharov (*New York Times,* Nov. 17, 1974).

Karen S. Demorchyan was appointed (not elected) as secretary of the Communist Party of Armenia (CPA) in November 1974, and the following February he delivered a report on the situation he found. He attacked what he described as wholesale "embezzlement of socialist property, abuse of official position, bribe-taking, influence-peddling, speculation, avarice, hooliganism and other negative manifestations" (*New York Times,* Feb. 16, 1975). The Communist Party had virtually lost control of the economic and social life of the republic. The quality of the goods produced had deteriorated alarmingly, according to Demorchyan, and corruption had reached into the courts and prosecutors' offices, the medical profession, where drugs were diverted for speculation, and educational institutes, where grades and diplomas were falsified (ibid.).

Corruption is of course not peculiar to Armenia or to the Soviet Union. But Armenia is no advertisement for the policies followed there, of relaxed control from the center without (as is now admitted) an adequate education in the principles of socialism, or an adequate contact with the masses of the people, who have suffered more than anyone from the corruption at the state level.

The housecleaning foreshadowed by the Demorchyan report may be looked on as the third stage in the Russian reaction to Armenian nationalist agitation. The first stage was apparently to leave things alone—a risky policy (or lack of one), since as Bernard Shaw once remarked, when you leave things alone they go to the devil. The second stage was reached with the conviction of the antisocialist separatists. The third stage, presumably looking toward a remedying of the grievances, followed immediately after.

The question of what part was played in the antisocialist agitation by the 200,000 repatriates who had lived in capitalist countries, would be an interesting subject for investigation. But it is not necessary to resort to the scapegoat theory to explain the nationalist movement. The people obviously had grievances, which were not being corrected. The blame for this rise of Armenian nationalism, which was obviously a reactionary movement, must be placed on the authoritarian regime in the USSR, which brings the whole idea of socialism into disrepute. It is indeed ironic that socialism, which came to maturity as a democratic movement, should be discredited in such a way.

In spite of the fact that academic and scientific discussions of nationalism in the Soviet Union have reached a new high, criticism of the government's nationality policies is still severely limited. Objections to these policies on behalf of the minority nationalities are suppressed like much other political criticism; as fast as one dissident is let out of prison, another is put in. In the Ukraine, more than twenty intellectuals were arrested for "nationalism" in 1966 and tried and convicted in the deepest secrecy; Vyacheslav Chornovil, a journalist who called attention to what had happened, was convicted of "slandering the Soviet system" and spent eighteen months in a prison camp. In January 1972 he was arrested again, together with two other well-known critics of Russian operations in the cultural field, Ivan Svitlychny and Ivan Dzyuba (*New York Times,* Jan. 19, 1972). Dzyuba, after one and a half years in prison, acknowledged that he had been mistaken in some of his earlier ideas and was released (*New York Times,* Nov. 14, 1973).

The attitude of the central government in Moscow toward manifestations in the Ukraine was expressed in *Pravda* in July 1968 by Aleksandr P. Botvin, the Communist Party chief of Kiev. He said: "Some people are . . . ready to grasp at the putrid theories spread by hostile propaganda about the necessity of a 'democratisation' and a 'liberalisation' of socialism." Nothing of that nature would be tolerated, Botvin indicated (*New York Times,* July 14, 1968).

If discussion were free in the Soviet Union, defenders of the regime could point out that it is simply not possible to satisfy everybody. If the Russians fail to push industrialization in a non-Russian republic, they are accused of not seeking to bring the backward areas up to the level of the advanced. If they push development so fast that the local population cannot meet the increased demand for labor, and Russians flow in, as in the Baltic republics, the Russians are accused of seeking to "colonize" the area. On the other hand if the increased demand for labor is met by recruiting in other non-Russian areas, the Soviet leaders are accused of mingling and reshuffling the population to prevent the development of homogeneous nationalities (Dzyuba, 1968:20). If they do not give jobs to the local intelligentsia, they are accused of antilocal bias; if they do, they are accused of fostering nationalism (Pipes, 1967:128).

The movement of Russians and Ukrainians into the outlying republics which began under the tsar continued unabated under the Soviet regime. Sometimes the movement was deliberately fostered by the central government, which recruited tens of thousands of Russians to go to Siberia and Central Asia to plow up the steppe and plant grain, in Khrushchev's "virgin lands" program. The Russians in Kazakhstan actually came to outnumber the Kazakhs. The only republic in which the proportion of ethnic Russians failed to increase between 1959 and 1970 was Georgia (*New York Times,* July 31, 1972).

Recently, however, the scope of this migration has abated with regard to Central Asia, where the indigenous rural population is increasing very rapidly and some farmers are moving to the towns. The proportion of Russians in the population of most of the national republics is now diminishing. Only in the Baltic republics, such as Latvia and Estonia, is the natural increase of the population small, and Russians have been coming in to run the newly developing industries. They come as unskilled laborers, with the natives forming a kind of aristocracy, as in the United States in the period prior to World War I.

In Central Asia it is said that the collective farmers now have a scale of living higher than that of the city workers, who have always been largely Russians. The Russians form a minority in very many cities throughout the Soviet Union, and have begun to complain that they are an oppressed minority! In the Soviet Union, it is illegal to publish the complaints of the Russians, on the ground that this might tend to stir up national hatreds. Radio Liberty, always willing to fish in troubled waters, however, has picked up the theme: "The Russian nation is the most underprivileged national unit in the USSR," it announced in 1971 (Mandel, 1974:3). How this contention can be squared with the other line of the anti-Sovieteers, to the effect that the Russians are an imperial power dominating over the weaker nationalities, is Radio Liberty's problem.

Despite the moderating effect of the slowing of Russian migration, the grievances of the spokespeople for minor nationalities remain many and varied. In Georgia, the social-democratic tradition has not died out; a Georgian historian recently recalled affectionately the Menshevik regime of 1919 which invited in the British rather than join as part of the Bolshevik-led Soviet Union. He was deprived of his doctoral degree (see *New York Times*, May 14, 1972). In Latvia, as in other republics, the main complaint is about the underrepresentation of the indigenous population in the organs of power, both local and national. Latvians also complain that the Russians who administer the country are not taking adequate care to replenish natural resources; one such group asserts, for example, that depletion of forests has exceeded reforestation every year since World War II (*New York Times*, Feb. 27, 1972).

Dzyuba, a Ukrainian nationalist born in 1931, attaches great importance to the development of a *national* culture. He quotes: "A man deprived of the feeling of nationality is incapable of a wise spiritual life" (Dzyuba, 1968:20). He continues with a statement of his own: "Communism is impossible if we do not foster the enrichment and proliferation of national cultural attainments" (ibid.:23).

Dzyuba, who does not demand Ukrainian independence, says that what is needed is a wider circulation of Lenin's last letters, which were not given to the public until 1956 and have not been much circulated since (ibid.:39). With this opinion we are in hearty agreement. But Dzyuba overstates his case. The future of culture does not depend on any particular national culture, nor on the national cultures as a group.

The argument for the survival of those cultures rests on quite other grounds, mainly on the wishes of the people concerned, of which Lenin was always most solicitous.

The "most formidable" of the articulate Ukrainians is said to be Valentyn Moroz, an historian. Two volumes of his essays have recently been published in English (*Boomerang: The Work of Valentyn Moroz*, edited by Yaroslav Bihun, Baltimore, 1974, and *Report from the Beria Reserve: The Protest Writings of Valentyn Moroz*, edited and translated by John Kolasky, Toronto and Chicago, 1974). He was tried in 1970 and sentenced to fourteen years of imprisonment and exile. At his trial, which was held in secret, he hurled this defiance at his persecutors:

> The awakening of national consciousness is the deepest of all spiritual processes. . . . Your dams are strong, but now they stand on dry land, bypassed by the spring streams, which have found other channels. Your drawgates are closed, but they stop no one. . . . You stubbornly insist that all those you place behind bars are dangerous criminals. . . . You can pursue this absurd policy for, let us say, ten more years. But then what? These movements in the Ukraine and in the whole country *are only beginning.* (Reddaway, 1974:38)

We might expect the nationalism of the minor republics to be associated with the general movement for freer discussion, and there have been instances in which two lines of criticism coincided in a single individual. We are thinking of General Pyotr G. Grigorenko, a well-known liberal who in 1969 took up the cause of the Crimean Tatars. Members of this nationality, though exonerated of charges of collaboration with the enemy in World War II, have not been allowed to return to their home (see *New York Times,* May 8, 1969). Grigorenko was ruled insane and sent to a mental hospital, where he remained for five years; his rank was reduced to private, and he was expelled from the Party (*New York Times,* June 27, 1974).

Yet there is not necessarily anything liberal or democratic about the nationalist agitation in the Russian republics, as the Armenian episode illustrates. Similarly, the nationalist movement in Lithuania is led by the Roman Catholic Church.

Cynics may see in the attitude of the Soviet central government a revival of the psychology of certain German nationalists of the early nineteenth century. These nationalists feared that the growth of civic liberty and self-government in the separate German states would tend to consolidate and crystallize these states, and thereby hinder the development of a strong central German state. Fichte is quoted to the effect that people who have developed a communal consciousness, with free institutions, cannot fit themselves into a new nation, meaning a large, integrated nation (Namier, 1952:22; Fichte, 1918: VII:549).

This contention suggests the futility and narrow outlook of those who try to argue that democracy and nationalism are "naturally" associated with each other. One type of nationalism, intent on the development of state power, fears the growth of another kind of nationalism which is indeed associated with liberty and democracy.

## ON THE USE OF NATIVE LANGUAGES

In the early days of the revolution, the government went to great lengths to see that children were enabled to attend schools in their own language, whether they lived in the country or in the city. Then in 1937–1940 a change took place, and the rule became that in the city schools only two, or sometimes three, languages were taught: Russian, and the language or languages of the most numerous local nationality.

Although this change seemed rather abrupt at the time, it corresponded to what is now recognized as the general trend. Today the demand for Russian language schools actually exceeds the supply, even in the rural areas (Mandel, 1974:18). The decline in the language schools has accompanied increasing urbanization and industrialization.

Even the desire of the Jewish people for Yiddish-language schools is declining. When the Jews left the tiny ghetto towns of the Pale for new residences in the interior, they expressed their willingness to learn and use the language in the new environment, much like the Jews who migrated to another country such as the United States. A Jewish woman is quoted: "It may sound paradoxical, but it is a fact: Jewish mothers closed the Jewish schools" (ibid.:19).

There are still some spokespersons for the smaller nationalities who insist not only that members of a given nationality should have education available in their own language wherever they are, but that they should be forced to use it; Dzyuba has said that "all Ukrainians, no matter in which republic they live, [should] be obliged to study the Ukrainian language" (ibid.:20-21).

It is not only in connection with the schools that the question of native languages arises. Some of the languages of the border republics had never been written down; when they were, they were at first rendered into Latin script, then after 1939 this was changed to Cyrillic. Many Russian words were introduced into the native vocabularies. These moves have been attacked as an attempt to Russify the languages and so the peoples.

Actually some linguistic experts are still of the opinion that the Cyrillic alphabet is better adapted to reproduce the sounds in certain of the native languages. The introduction of some Russian words was surely inevitable, since the objects described by them were new to the people and so to the language. Should a native word be invented corresponding to, say, telephone? Or should the Russian word be used? Convenience would seem to dictate the latter.

On the broader question of the extent to which the native language should be used, opinions still differ widely. Russian is introduced into the school curriculum early, and is used increasingly for instruction at the higher levels, against the preference of some spokespeople for, say, Ukrainian. The argument for economy is frequently used to win this debate. How many college textbooks should be translated into Ukrainian, which is not too different from Russian, when the students are expected to know Russian anyway? It is not considered a hardship in the Netherlands when university students are assigned readings in an English or a German text.

The same kind of problem is encountered in relation to the other mass media. A correspondent for the *New York Times* visited Yakutsk, in Siberia, early in 1972. In Yakutia 44 percent of the people are Yakuts. He found that there were schools where the language of instruction was Yakut, but Russian was introduced as a subject of study in the first grade. Yakutsk has its own television station, on which programs are broadcast in the Yakut language. However most of the programming is in Russian: only 200 of 2,700 hours annually are in Yakut. Does this constitute discrimination against the Yakut language? (*New York Times*, May 4, 1972).

In general, the 1970 census confirmed that national languages are not dying out in the Soviet Union or even diminishing appreciably. The Tatars are an interesting illustration. Of the six million Tatars in the Soviet Union in 1970, 90 percent still declared Tatar to be their native language. This is true even though only one-fourth of the Tatars live in the Tatar autonomous republic; the rest are scattered in small groups in various parts of the Soviet Union. Two-thirds of them are fluent in Russian, but they still resist cultural assimilation (*New York Times*, Jan. 24, 1972).

The non-Russians have quite a good command of Russian; half of them speak it fluently. (Indeed thirteen million members of non-Russian nationalities list Russian as their native tongue.) But the widespread bilingualism does not necessarily imply that the minor nationalities are due to disappear. On the contrary, Professor Suren Kaltakhchyan argued in a 1972 article that knowledge of Russian,

> ... far from preventing the development of national cultures, helps to develop them. ... Bilingualism makes it possible to improve knowledge of both languages, broadens the mental outlook of those who speak them and provides wider scope for their intercourse. (Kaltakhchyan, 1972:10).

The spread of literacy and new techniques of communication in the whole of the USSR has resulted in the local intelligentsia's being able to appeal directly to the masses of workers and peasants through the mass media (or they would be able to do so if the restrictions on free expression of opinion were not so drastic). It is perhaps for this reason that the central government is allergic to expressions of national dissatisfaction, even when it realizes that the undoubted progress made by the national republics since 1917 predisposes the masses to support the regime.

The whole Leninist theory of equality fails to make sense except in a democratic milieu.[14] When agitation for separation is prosecuted as treason, what becomes of this "right"? "Strange freedom this," comments S. Shaheen. "One could not exercise it. This is high casuistry indeed" (Shaheen, 1956:128).


## DIMINISHING THE DIFFERENTIAL
## AMONG THE SOVIET REPUBLICS


One of the important canons of Leninist nationality policy is that the backward nations should be brought up to the level of the most advanced. Thus at the Tenth and Twelfth Party Congresses (in 1921 and 1923) it was declared to be the duty of the Russians to help the national borderlands catch up, and to abolish inequalities (Avtorkhanov, 1959:168-69).

V. Holubnychy, a recent student of the Russian scene, has asserted that contrary to this announced policy, the *Russian* Soviet Republic has been developing *faster* than the countrywide average, and that the non-Russian republics are industrially more backward in comparison to Russia than they were before the Bolshevik Revolution (see Goldhagen, 1968:72).

This conclusion does not correspond to the work of other American students of the contemporary scene.[15]

Statistical statements of long-term trends, especially in a field such as the level of living, are not usable as they stand because there is no such thing as a constant unit of measurement. Thus, even if the Russian

*Table 4.1*

*Relative Growth of Industry and Agriculture*
*in the Several Soviet Republics: 1913–1966*

|  | 1913 | | 1940 | | 1966 | |
|---|---|---|---|---|---|---|
|  | Ind.[1] | Agr.[2] | Ind.[1] | Agr.[2] | Ind.[1] | Agr.[2] |
| Russian SFSR | 1 | 1 | 8.7 | 1.3 | 67 | 2.5 |
| Ukrainian SSR | 1 | 1 | 7.3 | 1.6 | 44 | 2.7 |
| Belorussian SSR | 1 | 1 | 8.1 | 1.7 | 64 | 2.7 |
| Uzbek SSR | 1 | 1 | 4.7 | 1.8 | 32 | 4.5 |
| Kazakh SSR | 1 | 1 | 7.8 | 1.0 | 101 | 6.0 |
| Georgian SSR | 1 | 1 | 10.0 | 2.5 | 62 | 5.8 |
| Azerbaijan SSR | 1 | 1 | 5.9 | 1.6 | 25 | 3.2 |
| Lithuanian SSR | 1 | 1 | 2.6 | 1.4 | 52 | 2.2 |
| Moldavian SSR | 1 | 1 | 5.8 | 1.6 | 99 | 3.9 |
| Latvian SSR | 1 | 1 | 0.9 | 1.8 | 18 | 2.0 |
| Kirgizian SSR | 1 | 1 | 9.9 | 2.0 | 117 | 5.1 |
| Armenian SSR | 1 | 1 | 8.7 | 1.6 | 119 | 4.3 |
| Tadjik SSR | 1 | 1 | 8.8 | 2.5 | 64 | 5.9 |
| Turkmen SSR | 1 | 1 | 6.7 | 1.5 | 33 | 3.9 |
| Estonian SSR | 1 | 1 | 1.3 | 1.5 | 25 | 1.9 |

[1] Gross industrial output (1913 = 1)
[2] Gross agricultural output (1913 = 1)

*Source:* Compiled from *Soviet Union Fifty Years: Statistical Returns*, 1969: 310-38.

tsars had compiled figures on the level of living of populations, they would not be comparable to the modern figures. Russian figures on national income have actually been compiled only since 1957.

Figures on the growth of "industry" and "agriculture" are more helpful but they are not decisive. Thus industry has developed more rapidly between 1913 and 1966 in Armenia, Kirghizia, Moldavia, and Kazakhstan than in Russia. But all the other national republics showed *less* rapid industrial development than the Russian republic, according to the official figures.

*Table 4.2*
*Level of Education of the Population, by Union Republics*

| | Persons with Higher or Secondary Education, per 1,000 of Population Over Age 10 | | Percent Rise, 1939 to 1970 |
|---|---|---|---|
| | *1939* | *1970* | |
| USSR | 108 | 483 | 447 |
| Russian SFSR | 109 | 489 | 449 |
| Ukraine | 120 | 494 | 412 |
| Belorussia | 92 | 440 | 478 |
| Uzbekistan | 55 | 456 | 829 |
| Kazakhstan | 83 | 470 | 566 |
| Georgia | 165 | 554 | 336 |
| Azerbaijan | 113 | 471 | 417 |
| Lithuania | 81 | 382 | 472 |
| Moldavia | 57 | 397 | 696 |
| Latvia | 176 | 517 | 294 |
| Kirgizia | 46 | 452 | 983 |
| Tadjikistan | 40 | 420 | 1,050 |
| Armenia | 128 | 516 | 403 |
| Turkmenia | 65 | 475 | 731 |
| Estonia | 161 | 506 | 314 |

*Source:* Bruk, 1972:353; based on Soviet Census of 1970.

Russia in 1913 had the beginnings of industry, including heavy industry, but it was predominantly agricultural, and the standard of living was low.

Much lower was the standard of living in great areas that indeed were part of the Russian Empire but were not modern in any sense; there precapitalist and semifeudal relations prevailed. For example, in Central Asia not even a beginning had been made on education or public health work, and industry was mostly handicraft.

Russia is now a major industrial area; its techniques are comparable with, and in some areas quite the equal of those of the West, and its standard of living is approaching that of mass consumption.[16]

The outlying republics have been effectively modernized. Their conditions have improved with educational facilities that have set the stage for further advances.

*Table 4.3*
*Medical Services in Soviet Central Asia and Selected Other Countries*
*(per thousand population)*

| Country | Year | Physicians | Hospital Beds |
|---|---|---|---|
| Soviet Central Asia | 1913 | .03 | .24 |
| | 1940 | .44 | 3.59 |
| | 1961 | 1.39 | 8.18 |
| Soviet Union | 1913 | .17 | 1.26 |
| | 1940 | .74 | 4.15 |
| | 1961 | 1.97 | 8.54 |
| India | 1956 | .17 | .44 |
| Iran | 1959–1960 | .25 | 1.01 |
| Turkey | 1959–1960 | .34 | 1.71 |
| Japan | 1959–1960 | 1.09 | 9.01 |
| France | 1959 | 1.01 | 14.74 |
| United Kingdom | 1960 | .91 | 10.63 |
| United States | 1961 | 1.28 | 9.26 |

*Source:* Wilber, 1969:166.

Especially striking is the fact that the formerly illiterate Central Asian Republics now have nearly as many highly educated people in proportion to the population as the Western republics. Equalization in this field has been truly remarkable.

No less striking has been the reduction in the death rate, and the improvement in health facilities generally, with the percentage increase being the greatest in the most backward group.

Note that in Soviet Central Asia while the number of physicians per thousand population in 1961 was not as great as in the Soviet Union generally, it was greater than in leading West European countries—greater than in the United States!

But what of the welfare of the republics generally—in terms of what is measured in the West as "national income"?

Here the problem of measurement becomes more difficult, because Soviet statisticians do not like the concept of "national income." "Gross social output," which they have been calculating since 1957, does not mean the same thing, and cannot be used without discussion even to measure differences within the Soviet Union. (For instance, "gross social output" does not include services.) The concept of earned income per capita and per worker avoids most of the difficulties inherent in the other methods. Figures have recently become available that make possible a calculation of earned incomes in the several republics, so that a meaningful statement of the extent and trend of the differential has become possible for the first time.

The Soviet Union has always kept before it the goal of equalization of incomes among the several national republics. This goal has been sought in general by way of speeding up the development of the backward areas rather than subsidizing them out of the general funds, though this latter method is by no means scorned in principle. The recent emphasis on policies tending to integrate the whole economy has led to a wide extension of nationally equalized wage rates, to the great benefit of the areas of lower productivity. Thus in general the basic wage scales for each branch of the economy are uniform for that branch throughout the USSR, although sometimes the urban and rural scales differ. In 1970, this system of centrally fixed wages covered 76 percent of the total civilian labor force (Schroeder, 1973:2). As a result of these policies, differences in wage levels among the fifteen republics of the USSR are quite small. In 1970, average annual money earnings of the state labor force varied from 84 percent of the USSR average in Moldavia, the lowest, to 111 percent of the national average in Estonia, the highest. The ranking of the several republics had changed little from 1960.

*Table 4.4*

*Indexes of Average Annual Wages in the State Sector of the USSR, by Republic: 1960 and 1970*

| | Average Annual Money Wages | | | | Average Annual |
| | 1960 = 100 | | USSR = 100 | | Social Wage[1] |
| | 1960 | 1970 | 1960 | 1970 | 1970 |
|---|---|---|---|---|---|
| USSR | 100 | 151.4 | 100.0 | 100.0 | 100.0 |
| Russian SFSR | 100 | 151.7 | 103.1 | 103.4 | 104.0 |
| Ukraine | 100 | 147.1 | 97.1 | 94.4 | 96.0 |
| Belorussia | 100 | 128.0 | 78.4 | 87.2 | 87.9 |
| Uzbekistan | 100 | 163.6 | 87.0 | 94.0 | 96.6 |
| Kazakhstan | 100 | 156.5 | 100.2 | 102.7 | 102.7 |
| Georgia | 100 | 142.6 | 92.8 | 87.5 | 87.4 |
| Azerbaijan | 100 | 146.0 | 93.3 | 90.0 | 93.6 |
| Lithuania | 100 | 164.4 | 89.8 | 97.5 | 96.0 |
| Moldavia | 100 | 152.5 | 83.6 | 84.3 | 81.5 |
| Latvia | 100 | 160.0 | 97.4 | 103.0 | 105.5 |
| Kirgizia | 100 | 148.4 | 92.3 | 90.5 | 93.6 |
| Tadjikistan | 100 | 150.2 | 97.1 | 96.4 | 97.9 |
| Armenia | 100 | 161.8 | 93.5 | 100.0 | 110.0 |
| Turkmenia | 100 | 153.3 | 103.6 | 104.9 | 93.6 |
| Estonia | 100 | 165.2 | 101.6 | 110.9 | 111.9 |

[1] Also presented for 1970 are indexes of relative levels of average annual "social" wages, which consist of money wages plus a Soviet statistical category called "payments and benefits," covering mainly such items as transfer payments and state noninvestment expenditures for education, health, and housing maintenance.

*Source:* Schroeder, 1973:23; based on statistical handbooks of the republics.

Data that have recently become available make it possible to calculate for the several republics a much more comprehensive statement of the relative levels of income. This comprehensive figure includes not only wages and salaries in the state sector, to which reference has already been made, but the earned income of collective farmers from all sources, and the incomes of state farm workers from private plot activities. The only parts of income that are omitted are transfer payments and military pay; the latter, at least, would tend to increase the uniformity of incomes from the whole country since there is no distinction by republic in military pay.

Earned income per caput in the republics varies from two-thirds of the national average in Azerbaijan to more than 25 percent above the average in Estonia. Thus in Estonia, per caput income is nearly twice as high as in Azerbaidjan (ibid.:27). In the United States, by comparison, per caput disposable income for Connecticut, the highest income state, is 2.16 times that for Mississippi, the lowest.

A refinement in the statistical technique is to calculate earned income per worker instead of per caput. When earned incomes are expressed per worker, the differentials among the republics are considerably reduced, because the republics with the lowest incomes (in general, the Central Asian Republics) are also the ones with the largest families. Even if incomes per worker were equal throughout the USSR, the incomes per caput would be lower in these regions. Incomes per worker are quite close together for all of the regions. Estonia, the highest of the republics, is only 14.6 percent above the average for the country, while the lowest, Moldavia, is 21.2 percent below the average (ibid.:29).

An indication of the direction and intent of Soviet policy is that the government introduced in 1974 family income supplements providing a minimum of fifty rubles per month per family member. This establishment of a national minimum will have little impact in most of western Russia but a great deal in Central Asia.

As in the case of the figures on wages, the figures on earned income per worker show that differentials did not change substantially between 1960 and 1970. Average wage and salary income differentials decreased slightly during the period, while the differentials in collective farmer incomes increased moderately (ibid.:17). Other studies confirm that the rank ordering of the various republics is fairly stable over time. All

*Table 4.5*
*Relative Levels of Earned Income Per Worker, by Republics: 1970*

*Earned Income*
*per Worker*
*(USSR = 100)*

| | |
|---|---|
| USSR | 100.0 |
| Russian SFSR | 105.5 |
| Ukraine | 90.1 |
| Belorussia | 86.2 |
| Uzbekistan | 96.1 |
| Kazakhstan | 111.3 |
| Georgia | 86.4 |
| Azerbaijan | 93.8 |
| Lithuania | 94.2 |
| Moldavia | 78.8 |
| Latvia | 106.1 |
| Kirgizia | 92.6 |
| Tadjikistan | 93.9 |
| Armenia | 107.1 |
| Turkmenia | 109.0 |
| Estonia | 114.6 |

*Source:* Schroeder, 1973:29.

participate in the general advance without greatly changing their relative position. The policy of equal payments for the same work in all parts of the USSR, plus the supplemental benefits just mentioned, point to a policy of substantial equalization.

We are thus unable to take seriously Holubnychy's contention that the advanced parts of the Soviet Republic are farther ahead of the less advanced than before the Revolution. At the same time, the direct influence of the Leninist nationality policy as such is hard to trace. The substantial equalization that we have noticed may have been the result of features of national policy having little to do with Leninist policy. Schroeder, on whose results we have drawn extensively, mentions the policy of "drawing together," which involves breaking down republican boundaries with respect to income differences among other things.

The development of all areas and the general result of substantial equalization have been made possible because the USSR has been generally successful in carrying through its economic policies. It does not follow that other socialist states could duplicate its results by imitating its policies. The sheer size and strength of the country, as evidenced in the last war, enable it to concentrate attention on its problems of development without having to adapt itself to external pressures, at least in recent years. The contrast with a country like Yugoslavia is obvious.

Even in the areas where attempts at modernization were once met with fierce resistance, the inhabitants do not today express regret that the modernization took place. Kazakhstan, once pointed to as an example of modernization that had been forced too fast, has today a scale of living far higher than it had, or would have had if the localists had been allowed to set the pace. Kazakh industrialization is a favorite exhibit of proponents of Soviet nationalities policy. Proof that the Kazakhs themselves approve was furnished dramatically when sixty-thousand Kazakhs crossed the border from Sinkiang, China, in 1962.

## POSTWAR ANTI-SEMITISM IN
## THE SOVIET UNION AND EASTERN EUROPE

The Jews, who in spite of great efforts on the part of the Bund had not won official recognition as a nation by the time of the Russian Revolution, did win it soon after in the Soviet Union, where the Yiddish culture was treated like a national culture.[17] Jews were relieved of all discrimination and treated like ordinary Russian citizens, as in everyday life they still are. The plaint of the Jewish nationalists about the decline of interest in Judaism in the Soviet Union was a complaint not so much against the government as against their own young people, who increasingly thought of themselves as Russians; they were losing their Jewish consciousness.

In the 1930s, however, some disquieting rumors began to circulate. It was said that Jews were not able to rise to the highest levels in either diplomatic circles or the government (Kaganovich was the last Jew to be taken onto the Politburo, in 1926); and there was even said to be a quota on the number of Jews admitted to certain institutions of higher learning (Goldhagen, 1960:39). The setting up of Biro-Bidjan as an autonomous republic in the late 1930s was a recognition by the government that Jewish nationalism existed, but at the same time was an indication that the government was not in touch with the sentiment in the Jewish community, which had not demanded this "solution" of their problems and took little interest in it from the start. Also, Zionists were excluded from Biro-Bidjan from the beginning. Thus, when vast numbers of Polish Jews fled to the Soviet Union to escape the Nazi invasion of Poland, they could not go to Biro-Bidjan; Zionism had by then become an article of faith with them (Heimann, 1947:206).

In the Stalin terror which reached a peak about 1937, some Jewish intellectuals were executed. There was no indication at that time that Jews were especially singled out for persecution; not only the number of ethnic Russians killed but even the proportion was much greater.

In World War II (the "Great Patriotic War" in the Soviet Union) there was of course no question as to which side the Jews were on. If anything, they exceeded the Russians in their patriotism. In Belorussia there were scores if not hundreds of Jewish generals; some of the leading national heroes were Jews who looked on Belorussia as their homeland. Nor was the loyalty of the Jews in the Ukraine and elsewhere noticeably less. The Jews, perhaps the fifteenth largest nationality in the Soviet Union ranked fifth in the number of heroes of the Soviet Union (Medvedyev, 1971:200).

The establishment of Israel as a state after the war removed any lingering doubts that the Jews might be considered a nationality, especially as the Soviet Union was among the first to recognize the new state (in 1947). But a campaign was presently launched against "cosmopolitanism" which had anti-Semitic overtones; and when the new state of Israel established a de facto alliance with the United States, then the Soviet Union's principal diplomatic enemy, the Soviet government's campaign against Zionism reached hysterical proportions.

The Jews were made the scapegoats for the country's ills. Jews were forced out of their positions with all kinds of organizations. Many were arrested and some were shot. The "Doctors' Plot" touched off a wave of anti-Jewish actions; pogroms actually began in some localities (ibid.:186-87).

After Stalin's death in 1953, tens of thousands of Jews were restored to their former organizations but not to their former senior positions. The higher jobs in the military, the diplomatic service, the government, and the Party remained closed to Jews. Medvedyev charged that a quota was being enforced on the number of Jews admitted to many establishments of higher education. The quota was informal and oral; nothing was in writing (ibid.:188).

The anti-Semitism of certain top Soviet leaders was noticed by foreign visitors, and was a factor in causing the splits that took place in various national Communist parties, for example, in the Canadian Labor-Progressive (Communist) Party in 1956. J. B. Salsberg, a leader of that party, visited the Soviet Union. He was quoted in the press as saying that Khrushchev was possessed of "a backward prejudice against the Jewish group as a people."

The Yiddish schools, which had had one hundred thousand pupils, were not reopened after the war, and the Yiddish theater and the Yiddish press have been starved for funds (Ginsberg, 1961:19). For the Jews, over a million in number, who had arrived from prewar Poland, this was a matter of great importance. They began a campaign, which still continues, for recognition of the Yiddish culture (see various issues of *Jewish Currents*).

Israel, eager for immigrants from the Soviet Union, has conducted a major propaganda campaign of its own to convince the world that the Jews in the Soviet Union are the victims of persecution and discrimination. The campaign has had some effect in the United States. In 1971, when the United States sought to moderate its violently anti-Soviet stance, the U.S. State Department took the extraordinary step of informing the U.S. Congress that Jews in the Soviet Union were not living in a state of terror (*New York Times,* Nov. 10, 1971). However the Yiddish culture is still denied facilities, individual Jews have been persecuted for protesting against the restrictions that still exist, and many Jews who wish to emigrate are still not free to go. Also it is not denied that virulently anti-Semitic novels (e.g., by Shevtsov) have appeared in the Soviet Union, although it is maintained that the Party had immediately condemned and withdrawn them.

Medvedyev points out that even a little anti-Semitism is more noticed and more resented now than would have been the case formerly. "The very fact of the existence of an independent Jewish state completely alters the *sensitivity threshold* of the Jewish population in any country to anti-Semitism" (Medvedyev, 1971:194).

The rise of Jewish nationalism in the world as a whole, which resulted from Israel's military victories, did not leave the Soviet Union untouched. The younger generation, while not especially religious nor necessarily interested in preserving Yiddish culture, still danced in the streets to celebrate Israel's 1967 victory. (According to C. L. Sulzberger, ten thousand participated in the demonstration; *New York Times,* July 1, 1970.)

Since the official policy regarding Jews is one of assimilation, considerable interest attaches to the 1970 Census figures. These showed that the number of Jews declined from 2.27 million in 1959 to 2.15 million in 1970, which in an official analysis was held to show that assimilation was indeed progressing. The proportions of Jews who gave Yiddish as their "first" language declined from 21.5 percent in the 1959 Census to 17.7 percent in 1970. In the Ukraine in 1969 one-third of all marriages involving Jews were mixed marriages (*New York Times,* May 8, 1971).

Some students have professed to find something discriminatory in the fact that the Jews alone among the nationalities have been "condemned" to total assimilation (Goldhagen, 1960:43). However this unique treatment may arise from the uniqueness of the Jews' demographic dispersion.

Why does anti-Semitism persist in the Soviet Union and other Eastern European Communist countries? Paul Lendvai, a non-Marxist student with wide experience in Eastern Europe, believes that the latest exhibitions of Soviet government anti-Semitism are a case of scapegoating. He writes:

> The rekindling of latent anti-Semitism [in the Soviet Union] is a concomitant of the rise of social tensions in a conservative society which for a variety of reasons (loss of inner dynamism, evasion of major unsolved problems, a political vacuum at the top, the threat of China, and the growing strains in Eastern Europe) in periods of insecurity whips up party discipline and heroic traditions, nationalism and xenophobia, racialism and the hatred and fear of the alien. (Lendvai, 1971:11)

All of these reasons boil down to the attempt to pillory the Jews as the group responsible for the country's failure to solve its critical problems. The "essential breeding ground" of East European antiSemitism is seen by Lendvai to have been the economic and political crisis that gripped Poland and Czechoslovakia in 1967–1968. We will see that the resurgence of Croatian nationalism after 1967 was also associated with a deep-going economic crisis.

Specifically, beginning shortly before the Russian troops moved into Prague in 1968, a number of anti-Semitic resolutions were adopted and publicized by organizations in East Germany, the Ukraine, and Poland, and a major anti-Semitic campaign was presently launched in Czechoslovakia itself by the Soviet occupying authorities. The burden of their argument was that the alleged counter-revolutionary activities that had led to the occupation had been part of an "international Zionist conspiracy" in which leading parts had been taken by the "Jews" Hajek, Goldstuecker, and Sik. Others were also mentioned as having been part of the "plot."

Goldstuecker, as it happened, had been purged before; he was involved in the Slansky "plot," the victims of which have since been rehabilitated. In 1968 he was chairman of the Writers' Union; he had been Czech minister to Israel and Sweden; and he was indeed a Jew. Deputy Premier Ota Sik, however, had been treated as an Aryan even by the Nazis. And in Foreign Minister Jiri Hajek, who in *Izvestia's* tirades was said to be a "passed" Jew who was originally named Karpeles, the anti-Semites in Moscow caught the wrong man. *Volksstimme* (Vienna) explained:

> Dr. Jiri Hajek was never a Jew nor ever called Karpeles. . . . There is really a Hajek, not Jiri but Bedrich, who was once called Karpeles. He changed his name in 1945 to Hajek. . . . But apart from his having once been called Karpeles, *Izvestia's* allegations do not fit this Hajek either. (Lendvai, 1971; quoting *Volksstimme,* Sept. 5, 1968, and *Le Monde,* Sept. 6, 1968)

This anti-Semitic campaign, it must be repeated, was official; it was not only known to the Party chiefs in Moscow; it was obviously planned and directed under their supervision.

Besides the scapegoat theory of anti-Semitism, another theory has sometimes been advanced: that anti-Semitism stems from the economic rivalry between Jews and non-Jews. Poland,where a disgraceful anti-Semitic campaign sponsored by the government erupted in 1967, provides a test of this theory.

The Nazi holocaust had left only about twenty-five thousand Jews in all of Poland. A small group of these, some two thousand, were the public bearers of the Jewish religion and culture; they were not disturbed. Most of the remainder considered themselves Polish rather than Jewish, and worked in various capacities in trade, education, industry, and the government.

The minister of the interior, General Mieczyslav Moczar, who had been in charge of the secret police for almost twelve years, launched an old-fashioned anti-Semitic campaign in 1967, using some of the techniques made famous by the Nazis. The Gomulka government did nothing to check the campaign, which resulted in most of the Jews leaving the country.

Was this campaign the result of pressure by Poles eager to get the jobs or the apartments of the victimized Jews? (It was estimated that some fifty thousand persons so benefited.) Lendvai argues with a wealth of detail that, on the contrary, the campaign was the result of a factional battle for power. Moczar hoped to use the campaign to advance his own political fortunes.

He was disappointed; the campaign did not achieve this end, although Lendvai remarks cynically that it might have done so if it had been combined with an anti-Russian campaign—in the psychology of the Poles anti-Russianism was stronger than anti-Semitism (ibid.:231). Moczar had been part of a Communist-led government. The failure of Gomulka, then the Party chief and real master of Poland, to condemn the anti-Semitic campaign deprived the Party of any claim to moral leadership in the field of ethnic or nationality relations.

The rest of Lendvai's argument on the causes of anti-Semitism is quickly summarized. In Hungary, where Jews had occupied so many leading posts in the government, after World War II, and in Romania, where the number of Jews in the 1960s far exceeded the number in Poland, anti-Semitism barely appeared at all, even though Romania had once been the country of all others in East Europe with the worst record in this field.

Lendvai thus sees the phenomenon of anti-Semitism as a government creation, making the Jews the hapless victims of some power play that the government, or government officials, have in mind.

The cases cited do not furnish any support for the widely held idea that in Eastern Europe anti-Semitism persists below the surface in the popular consciousness. It was not the (supposed) latent anti-Semitism of the masses that caused the government campaigns, but the government campaigns that sought to build up such a consciousness where it did not exist. Given a strong Leninist leadership in the government, Eastern Europe would have nothing to fear from anti-Semitism.

It would be quite possible for the Yiddish culture to be granted at least as much consideration by the Soviet Union as is shown to the cultures of other minor nationalities. The refusal to allow freedom of emigration is not a specifically Jewish problem, although there are cases of obvious hardship affecting Jews, and these have been widely advertised abroad. As for the policy of assimilation, we need only recall that while Lenin welcomed the assimilation of Jews, he warned specifically against using any pressure to bring about such assimilation.

## CONCLUSION

The ideas of equality of nationalities, of freedom from individual discrimination based on nationality, of special attention to the development of backward nationalities, and of freedom for national cultures to develop have survived in the Soviet Union and set a new standard of morality for the world in this field—a standard that the Russians are still far from living up to, by their own admission, but which minority peoples outside the Soviet Union continue to regard with admiration.

At the same time, we have to remember that nationality consciousness in the several republics is at least as great today as before the Revolution, and that inattention to the needs of the people in any of the republics is likely to be followed by nationalist outbreaks in that republic. So, the "solution of the national question" is contingent. Assimilationist policies followed by the central government are counterproductive. They tend to keep alive the pride of nationality which in Leninist theory fulfills an honorable role.

Whatever may be said about the need for national unity in wartime, the indefinite continuance of a war psychology is not consonant with correct Marxist theory. The adoption of a "humane and supple" nationalist policy is an urgent need of the hour.

# 5

## "Solving the National Question" in Yugoslavia

If a nation is a way of organizing people for struggle, then Yugoslavia is a nation par excellence. This socialist nation in its tempestuous history has been read out of the Marxist comity of nations—first by the Russians, later by the Chinese, and at various times by most schools of Marxist thought. But it is still there, still impenitent, and still claiming to be Marxist, although the attacks on its probity continue unabated.[1]

Like China and the Soviet Union, Yugoslavia is a multinational state. But the several nationalities are more evenly balanced in Yugoslavia than in any other socialist country. Yugoslavia's several nationalities must learn to live together and to participate jointly in the leadership; otherwise the survival of their country as a unified one will be impossible. For this reason the nationality problem is more important for Yugoslavia than for any other socialist country—and we do consider Yugoslavia a socialist country.

With regard to Yugoslavia, we are concerned about how it has sought to weld together previously warring nationalities into a unified state; how it has handled the problem of national minorities; and what have been the apparent causes of the persistence of national antagonisms among its several constituent republics even under socialism. Of interest also are the relations between Yugoslavia and the original socialist state,

the Soviet Union, although we cannot attempt an in-depth study of this topic.

Southeastern Europe—the Balkans—were until the twentieth century still largely dominated by the Ottoman Empire. Marx and Engels had supported the Turks against the Russian tsar. But by the early years of this century, democratic and socialist opinion turned against the Sublime Porte, and hailed the wars of the Balkan states against Turkey in 1912–1913 as wars of national liberation. To Lenin, economic liberation was the really important question. In Macedonia, the main battlefield, the landlords were Turks and the peasants were Slavs. The expulsion of the Turks, Lenin argued, would mean the creation of a more or less free class of peasant landowners and the opening up of the social development of a whole area that had been retarded by absolutism and feudal relations (Lenin, SW, IV:424).

Southeastern Europe, at the time of World War I, was, like tsarist Russia, still predominantly agrarian but with cities and a working class somewhat acquainted with Marxism. The Lenin-Stalin theory of nationalism, which had little relevance to Western Europe generally and even less to the colonial areas (at least as regarded its class analysis), was developed with reference to just this type of social setting. So Yugoslavia is a good testing-ground for the theory.

Certain of the minor nationalities are distinguished from the rest by their language. But the major groupings in Yugoslavia all speak Serbo-Croatian, and are distinguished from each other by their religion. The Slovenes and Croats are Roman Catholics; the Serbs, Montenegrins, and Macedonians are Orthodox ("Greek") Catholics; and one and a half million Bosnians are Moslems, having adopted the religion of their conquerors during the Turkish occupation.

Yugoslavia was set up as a country with its present borders in 1919. It is organized into six republics; there are also two autonomous regions, the Vojvodina and Kosovo (or Kosmet, Kosovo-Metohija), both administered by Serbia. The standard of living in the western republics, Slovenia and Croatia, approximates that in the neighboring countries, Italy, Austria, and Switzerland; the standard declines toward the east and south and is at its lowest in Kosovo, which borders on Albania.

The Communist Party of Yugoslavia (CPY) was born in 1919 in a wave of enthusiasm for a unitary Yugoslavia. All the regional Com-

*Table 5.1*

*Population of Yugoslavia According to Nationality,
by Republics and Administrative Divisions: 1971*

| | Yugo-slavia | Bosnia & Herze-govina | Monte-negro | Croatia |
|---|---|---|---|---|
| *Population according to nationality* | | | | |
| Total | 20,522,972 | 3,746,111 | 529,604 | 4,426,221 |
| *Persons who declared nationality* | | | | |
| Macedonians | 1,194,784 | 1,773 | 723 | 5,625 |
| Moslems—nationality declared | 1,729,932 | 1,482,430 | 70,236 | 18,457 |
| Slovenes | 1,678,032 | 4,053 | 658 | 32,497 |
| Serbs | 8,143,246 | 1,393,148 | 39,512 | 626,789 |
| Croats | 4,526,782 | 772,491 | 9,192 | 3,513,647 |
| Montenegrins | 508,843 | 13,021 | 355,632 | 9,706 |
| Albanians | 1,309,523 | 3,764 | 35,671 | 4,175 |
| Bulgarians | 58,627 | 284 | 394 | 676 |
| Italians | 21,791 | 673 | 70 | 17,433 |
| Hungarians | 477,374 | 1,262 | 296 | 35,488 |
| Romanians | 58,570 | 189 | 22 | 792 |
| Ruthenians | 24,640 | 141 | 38 | 3,728 |
| Slovaks | 83,656 | 279 | 31 | 6,482 |
| Turks | 127,920 | 477 | 397 | 221 |
| Czechs | 24,620 | 871 | 74 | 19,001 |
| Austrians | 852 | 44 | 5 | 352 |
| Wallachians | 21,990 | 52 | 6 | 13 |
| Greeks | 1,564 | 48 | 23 | 93 |
| Jews | 4,811 | 708 | 26 | 2,845 |
| Germans | 12,785 | 300 | 109 | 2,791 |
| Polish | 3,033 | 757 | 18 | 819 |
| Romany-Gypsies | 78,485 | 1,456 | 396 | 1,257 |
| Russians | 7,427 | 507 | 116 | 1,240 |
| Ukrainians | 13,972 | 5,333 | 10 | 2,793 |
| Other | 21,722 | 174 | 96 | 759 |
| *Persons who did not declare nationality according to Article 41 of the Constitution* | 32,774 | 8,482 | 521 | 15,789 |
| "Yugoslavs" | 273,077 | 43,796 | 10,943 | 84,118 |
| Regional appartainance | 15,002 | ——— | 1,204 | ——— |
| *Unknown* | 67,138 | 9,598 | 3,185 | 18,626 |

*Source: Statistical Pocketbook of Yugoslavia, 1971:30-31;
based on Census of 1971.*

| Macedonia | Slovenia | Serbia | | | |
| | | All | Serbia Proper | Vojvodina | Kosovo |
|---|---|---|---|---|---|
| 1,647,308 | 1,727,137 | 8,446,591 | 5,250,365 | 1,932,533 | 1,243,693 |
| 1,142,375 | 1,613 | 42,675 | 25,100 | 16,527 | 1,048 |
| 1,248 | 3,231 | 154,330 | 124,482 | 3,491 | 26,357 |
| 838 | 1,624,029 | 15,957 | 10,926 | 4,630 | 392 |
| 46,465 | 20,521 | 6,015,811 | 4,699,415 | 1,089,132 | 228,264 |
| 3,882 | 42,657 | 184,913 | 38,088 | 138,561 | 8,264 |
| 2,346 | 1,978 | 125,260 | 57,289 | 36,416 | 31,555 |
| 279,871 | 1,281 | 984,761 | 65,507 | 3,085 | 916,168 |
| 3,334 | 139 | 53,800 | 49,791 | 3,745 | 264 |
| 48 | 3,001 | 566 | 330 | 211 | 25 |
| 229 | 9,785 | 430,314 | 6,279 | 423,866 | 169 |
| 105 | 43 | 57,419 | 4,412 | 52,987 | 20 |
| 59 | 66 | 20,608 | 452 | 20,109 | 47 |
| 46 | 85 | 76,733 | 3,912 | 72,795 | 26 |
| 108,552 | 53 | 18,220 | 5,735 | 241 | 12,244 |
| 80 | 445 | 4,149 | 1,341 | 2,771 | 37 |
| 9 | 278 | 164 | 118 | 38 | 8 |
| 7,190 | 5 | 14,724 | 14,653 | 66 | 5 |
| 536 | 24 | 840 | 529 | 296 | 15 |
| 32 | 72 | 1,128 | 603 | 513 | 12 |
| 77 | 422 | 9,086 | 1,825 | 7,243 | 18 |
| 72 | 194 | 1,173 | 453 | 704 | 16 |
| 24,505 | 977 | 49,894 | 27,541 | 7,760 | 14,593 |
| 516 | 302 | 4,746 | 2,490 | 2,082 | 174 |
| 50 | 143 | 5,643 | 633 | 5,006 | 4 |
| 16,702 | 307 | 3,684 | 1,968 | 699 | 1,017 |
| 414 | 3,073 | 4,486 | 3,284 | 1,025 | 177 |
| 3,652 | 6,744 | 123,824 | 75,976 | 46,928 | 920 |
| 684 | 2,705 | 10,409 | 4,895 | 5,255 | 259 |
| 2,491 | 2,964 | 30,274 | 22,333 | 6,341 | 1,595 |

munist parties were merged into a single Party. Later, when the Party
was declared illegal (in 1921), it developed two wings, but both wings
supported the idea—which was by no means generally accepted—that
Serbs, Croats, and other national groups formed a single national unit
that had to be supported. And indeed, from the traditional Marxist
viewpoint, the formation of Yugoslavia was a progressive step (Burks,
1961:113).

The Soviet Union, however, saw Yugoslavia as a tool of French
imperialism, an artificial construct forming part of the anti-Soviet bloc.
It sought to dismember Yugoslavia. The Communist International
strongly supported the Soviet view, and a faction of the CPY in Croatia,
led by Anton Ciliga, came to accept this orientation.

Although Stalin's arguments against a unitary Yugoslavia were
special pleading in the sense that they were intended to serve the
interests of the Soviet Union, and although the interventions of the
Communist International in Yugoslavia sowed disunity and delayed the
formation of a strong national party, the insistence, in words, on a
really international point of view did finally impress the Yugoslav
leaders. Thus, somewhat ironically, they give Stalin credit for having set
them on the right road in this respect. As explained much later by
Kardelj, the contribution of Stalin was to raise the whole debate to the
level of principle. He argued that certain Yugoslav peoples were exploited as such—in a fashion analogous to the exploitation of the
working class—and thus helped orient the Yugoslav workers' movement
in the direction of unity with the national liberation and anti-imperialist movements in the rest of the world (Kardelj, 1960:57-58; Shoup,
1968:37).

The key point in Stalin's new formulation was the introduction of
national oppression as a Marxist category, related to class oppression
but not identical with or subordinate to it. This has always been the
position of Tito and his group in the Communisty Party of Yugoslavia,
and since they continued to adhere to it after Stalin had in effect
abandoned it and become a Great Russian nationalist, the further
development of this idea may be considered a Yugoslav contribution to
Marxist theory.

In any event, a strong Communist party did not develop in Yugoslavia in the 1920s. When King Aleksander introduced a military dicta-

tørship in 1929, the Party leaders fled abroad, and Party membership was reduced to a few hundred in all of Yugoslavia (Shoup, 1968:36).

Dinko Tomasic distorts history when he maintains that the rather large vote cast for the newly formed CPY in 1920—13 percent of the total, in a relatively free election—was due to the Party's having opposed centralism and having thereby won the adhesion of non-Serbian national and regional groups (Tomasic, 1946:11). The positions he attributes to the Party are from 1925, not 1920, and refer to the Communist International and Stalin, not the CPY. Tomasic does not analyze the most likely reason for the electoral successes of the CPY, namely, its socioeconomic program.

A change in the intellectual climate during the 1930s made possible the Party's emergence as the leader of the resistance in World War II. The Communist International in the period of the United Front quietly dropped its opposition to a united Yugoslavia. The Yugoslav intelligentsia and the liberals, sickened by the long years of military dictatorship, came to accept the need to work with, even to follow the lead of, the Communists. But what really gained the CPY the leadership of the underground movement was its ability to weld together a nationalist resistance to the foreign invasion.


## THE PEASANTS AND NATIONALISM

Chalmers Johnson, basing himself on the traditional idea that peasants are "naturally" nationalist, implied in *Peasant Nationalism and Communist Power* (1962) that the Communist Party of Yugoslavia adopted nationalism as a tactic in order to appeal to the peasants, who were already, in his view, nationalist-minded. He writes:

> It was not until . . . the winter of 1941 that the Party began to act like a nationalist party and began to receive strong support from the peasant masses. (C. Johnson, 1962:167)

Shoup, however, has rejected this interpretation of the peasants' attitude; he found that they were, if anything, more inclined toward parochial (regional) loyalties during the war than before. According to

Shoup, it was the Communists who educated the peasants to take a broader, all-Yugoslav point of view; he points out, in specifically criticizing Johnson, that the CPY had had this point of view before the war (see Shoup, 1968:97-100).

It is of course true that the Yugoslav Party, like the Chinese Party, shifted its social base to the countryside in the course of its operations. In the interwar period—that is, before World War II began—Burks found that out of 511 members of the central committees of the Party, about half (51.5 percent) were from the middle class, two-fifths (39 percent) were workers, and less than one-twelfth (7.7 percent) were peasants (Burks, 1961:20-21). During the war, however, nearly all of the fighting men were peasants (see C. Johnson, 1962:169; Burks, 1961:46). The urban population was not in any sense passive or neutral; it was in constant touch with the partisans, whom it furnished with supplies, and whom it aided by creating diversions in the enemy's rear. But the city residents had to move with much caution. The occupying authorities were strict and occasionally ferocious; massacres, Lidice-style, in reprisal for actions of the guerrillas, were not unknown.

The bulk of the fighting fell to the peasants. If it had not been for the swing of the peasants to the Communist-led resistance, there could have been no resistance. This swing, which was to have such vital consequences for the Party and for Yugoslavia, requires some explanation. We will mention the most important factors.

First, the Yugoslav Party was in effect the only all-Yugoslav party in the field. Since an all-out collective effort was the only possible way of winning the war, those who sought to preserve the country's independence had little choice but to join the Partisans. There is no question that a great many peasants were conscious of the menace of foreign domination. Many had vivid recollections of the war to oust the Turkish overlords; and at least some had been engaged in the interwar struggles against the Austrians and the Hungarians. All could readily transfer their feelings of opposition to the invading Germans, Italians, Hungarians, and Bulgars.

Second, the Slavic peasants not only knew whom they were against— they also had a fairly good idea whom they were for. Already in the interwar period there was considerable interest in Russia, the traditional ally of the Slavs in the Balkans (Burks, 1961:85). This interest, of course, became much greater when the Soviet Union was invaded on June 22, 1941, and the Russian alliance became a reality (Shoup, 1968:51). Many Slavs looked on the CPY as the party most likely to be able to work with the USSR.

Third, self-preservation was a major motive for many peasants. The original nucleus of the Partisan army was made up largely of Serbs who were living in other parts of Yugoslavia and who existed under the constant menace of being exterminated by the Croatian Ustasha, who during the early part of the war killed altogether some seven hundred fifty thousand defenseless people, mainly Serbs (Shoup, 1968:67-68; Lendvai, 1969:75). Croatians living outside Croatia were menaced by Mihailovich's Chetniks (chauvinist Serbs). The Partisans fought both these Chetniks and the Ustasha most bitterly; Mikhailovich was completely defeated by the Partisans in armed struggle during the Nazi occupation.

Of course, self-preservation worked both ways. In the Italian-occupied territories and in Serbia proper there was some disposition to make a deal with the enemy and to live peacefully until the end of hostilities. The Partisans naturally sought to upset these understandings.

Fourth, ideology as such was a minor motive for the peasants, although some may have been attracted by the anti-Fascist program. But some adventurers may have foreseen that the victory of a peasant and mountaineer army would offer opportunities to a social stratum that did not stand to get rich in any other way; and this indeed turned out to be the case, although the spoils were more in the form of power than in the traditional form of loot (see Halperin, 1958:30; Lendvai, 1969:Ch.3, passim).

Fifth, the Yugoslav Party's nationality program was popular in Macedonia, which was offered equality with the other nationalities. So, some peasants came to the Partisans from Macedonia and similar areas (Shoup, 1968:90-91, 96; Burks, 1961:105). The importance of this element in the actual fighting should not be overstressed however. According to Tito the national composition of the Partisan army in 1944 was as follows: Serbs, 44 percent, Croats, 30 percent, Slovenes, 10 percent, Montenegrins, 4 percent, Moslems, 2½ percent, and others 6 percent (Shoup, 1968:95).

Sixth, the behavior of the Partisans toward the civilian population won them many friends, even in areas that were originally hostile to them. The policy was to use a minimum of coercion and always to treat the people fairly (Shoup, 1968:64-65).

We may thus question Shoup's statement that it is a mystery how the Communists managed to get *any* following among the peasants (Shoup, 1968:93). The Partisans' following was secured as the result of the policies developed under the leadership of the CPY. These policies were not those depicted by Johnson: the Communists did not appeal to the peasants' supposedly pre-existing loyalty to Yugoslavia as a whole. On the contrary—they convinced the peasants of their sincere respect for the peasants' *local* loyalties, and gradually educated the peasants to a national (or, as they are accustomed to phrase it, "international") point of view.

In Yugoslavia, as in China, the Communists took the lead in a war of national resistance to invasion, and in both countries they eventually won the peasants to their economic program as well as to their conception of nationalism. In both countries the attitude of the peasants was of crucial importance to the success of the revolution. But it does not follow, as Johnson contends, that the attitude of the Communists on the national question was, in effect, opportunist. The Communists in both Yugoslavia and China—and, we might add, elsewhere—had a program of opposing national oppression and to that extent their nationalism was an integral part of their program, not an opportunist dodge.[2]

In Yugoslavia the Party did not emphasize its own leadership. It put forward the Anti-Fascist Front. The full socialist program was held in abeyance. However Tito and his group never had any idea other than to carry through the socialist revolution, even when Stalin was specifically advising the opposite. During the war, Tito told his biographer Dedijer that the time "had come for the party to seize power and to seize it in such a way that the bourgeoisie would never regain it" (Lendvai, 1969:89; Dedijer, 1953:Ch.13).

## THE NATIONAL PROBLEM
## AFTER WORLD WAR II

Just after the war, when the new constitution had been drawn up and ratified, Tito announced that the national problem had been solved.[3] The first constitution created a state which was unitary in its basic structure; but in deference to the national feelings of the constituent republics it was officially described as a federal state (Vucinich, 1969:253).

In 1953, a new constitution was adopted, which deemphasized the autonomy of the republics and omitted altogether the right of self-determination. A long-run campaign for internal unification began the same year. Newspapers were criticized for not giving enough space to happenings in the other republics. School textbooks published separately in the several republics were found to be uneconomical and an effort was made to consolidate them. Nationalism (that is, loyalty to the individual constituent republics) was called a "bourgeois prejudice" (Vlahovic, 1964:175).

It was suggested that eventually there would be a merger of the national cultures into a single Yugoslav culture. Exchanges among republican cultural societies were promoted. A Serbo-Croatian dictionary was prepared. Minorities were pressured to merge with the dominant culture (Shoup, 1968:186-94).

The cultural exchanges were not very successful, and the merger of ethnically different schools was resisted. The peripheral republics did not entirely trust the center, which they suspected of harboring Greater-Serbian national pretensions. Coverage in the media of news and opinion from other republics remained sparse and inadequate.

The survival of (republic) nationalism was accompanied by a growth in what can only be called localism, or particularism: a disposition, especially pronounced in rural areas, to seek new industries and to protect them when they were obtained. This localism was not necessarily connected with nationalism (Shoup, 1968:242). It is quite comparable with similar efforts on the part of small towns in capitalist countries, all of which seem to fancy themselves as centers of industry. Tito thought that the uneconomic location of industry was due more to localism than to nationalism (speech at Second Plenum of Central Committee, November 1959; see Shoup, 1968:246). Djilas said that in some of the regional councils chauvinism was greater than in the national republican governments (Djilas, 1957:101).

Although he had built up the Partisan army on the basis of full recognition of the equal rights of the nationalities, and correctly adhered to this principle, Tito was still a centralist, in the sense that he believed that the country should be integrated and even that the nationalities should die out.

For Tito, as for the Russians, "nationalism" is a dirty word, reserved for the particularist psychology of the individual republics. Tito calls loyalty to Yugoslavia as a whole "social patriotism," which "is in its essence internationalism." "We are [republican] nationalists to the exact degree necessary to develop a healthy socialist [all-Yugoslav] patriotism among our people." Tito was prepared to admit that there were "positive national factors" which he said should be "a stimulus to, not a brake on, the development of socialism in our country" (Tito, 1963:98, 103, 105). Mostly, however, republican nationalism is described as "either a cloak concealing anti-socialist tendencies and selfish and particularistic interests," or a "product of uneven development" among different parts of the country (*Programme of the League of Communists of Yugoslavia,* Belgrade 1958; quoted by Vucinich, 1969:256f.). Tito complained that "various defects of a nationalist character still hamper our efforts to build socialism"; these should be eradicated.

It might have been thought that the Yugoslav leaders would have condemned the Soviet operations in Hungary in 1956, but they took a moderate position on that occasion.[4] They have continued to reserve the right to make independent judgments. They were practicing "polycentrism" long before Togliatti coined the term, though they reject the designation of "national socialism" or "national communism" (Neal, 1958:18).

In the early 1960s, with economic problems still far from solved, the country was shaken by an internal crisis involving the Party leadership, and turning partly on the national question. Alexander Rankovich, a Serb, had been in charge of the secret police ever since the formation of the Yugoslav government after World War II. He had engaged in gross violations of national (republican, district) sovereignty in the areas in which Serbs held key positions, most conspicuously in the Kosmet area, but also in Bosnia-Herzegovina, where the Serbs out-numbered the other nationalities but were still not a majority (see Table 5.1 above).[5] The facts about the personal machine, staffed mainly by Serbs, that he was building up did not become generally known at first, and when they did begin to leak out, Tito at first threw his influence on the side of Rankovich. Tito seems to have seen himself as supporting centralism and the authority of the Party in which Rankovich held an important position.

Only in 1965, after it had been disclosed that Rankovich had been bugging Tito's private office, was Rankovich exposed, and later (1966) removed and expelled from the Party. The secret police as an organization was broken up and many of its powers transferred to the republics (Lendvai, 1969:200). Tito admitted that he had been in error in not moving earlier against Rankovich (ibid.:185-86). At the same time, the campaign for amalgamation of the republics into a unified Yugoslavia was quietly dropped. As early as 1960, Tito had been quoted as saying: "It is impossible to create a single nation here" (King, 1973:250). Now, after the Rankovich affair, it became more acceptable to express republican-nationalist sentiments.

## DECENTRALIZATION AND
## THE NEW RISE OF NATIONALIST SENTIMENT

Beginning in 1965, the CPY decided to subject Yugoslavia's enterprises to some foreign competition, with the responsibility for meeting the competition resting on the individual enterprises. The tariff was reduced; the currency was made almost completely convertible; the profit motive was frankly introduced at the plant level; and Yugoslavia was launched on a program of long-term integration into the world (capitalist) economy (Vucinich, 1969:266-67).

The new policy did have a stimulating effect on some enterprises, and those that survived and prospered were in a position to accumulate considerable surpluses. But since the emphasis was on workers' control in the individual plants, there was little incentive for the plants in the advanced sectors to invest their surpluses in the backward areas. This remained the responsibility of the central government, and the criticism of its alleged uneconomic allocation of investment became increasingly strong. A few successful Yugoslav enterprises even obtained permission to invest their surpluses abroad; a plant was set up and run by Yugoslavs across the border in Italy.

Many more Yugoslav enterprises were unable to face the foreign competition and had to close down, so that unemployment in Croatia shot up. Yugoslavs received permission to emigrate, and did so en masse, to countries such as Germany, Switzerland, and France, and their remittances to their families assumed major proportions. But when Western Europe entered on a period of moderate recession, as it did in 1966-1967 (and again in 1970-1971), many of the emigrants had to return home, and no jobs were waiting for them. It was said that West Germany was exporting its unemployment to Yugoslavia.

The swing toward capitalism resulted in the partial reintroduction of private profit. A private employer may employ up to five workers. Since the number of enterprises that can be conducted by one man is not limited, the way is open for the appearance of "socialist millionaires" (and there have been some). Economic tensions and continued regional inequality soon produced signs of unrest in the cultural spheres. In March 1967, 130 prominent scholars, including 80 Communists, issued a declaration on the language question. The declaration asserted that the Croatian dialect was being discriminated against in everyday use, and proposed that Serbian and Croatian should be recognized as two separate languages. The Serbs counterattacked with a mass campaign of their own, and the Croatian Communists who had signed the declaration were expelled from the Party (Lendvai, 1969:204).

The wave of student unrest that swept Western Europe in 1968 spread also to Yugoslavia. As in France and Germany, the lead was taken by students having an anarchist and internationalist orientation. In Belgrade, where students occupied all university buildings for seven days in June, Tito praised the students and endorsed all their demands, which included abolition of bureaucratic privileges, further democratization, solution of the problem of mass unemployment, reduction of social differences, and university reform.

In Zagreb, however, the official reception was not nearly so friendly. The Croatian Party, in the hands of Croatian nationalists, undertook to crush the student movement. The attack was led by Marko Veselica, a Zagreb University professor and an official of the CPY (the League of Communists). Using Croatian nationalist slogans, Veselica falsely charged that Rankovich had started the student movement. The Roman Church and students from the poorer districts (for instance, Bosnia) joined the opposition to the students. The student movement was developing roots; the situation became dangerous. Yet the top leadership of the League of Communists failed at first to react strongly.

An important issue that came to a head in 1971 was that of where the central government should allocate its investment funds—in industrialized sectors like Croatia or in the underdeveloped areas. The demand for new capital to re-equip industry became insistent especially in Croatia where unemployment was the most serious. A vocal group in Croatia had long maintained that Croatia's interests had been sacrificed to those of the backward areas. They charged that big hydroelectric developments had been initiated and sometimes completed in hill areas having no industries to use the power, and that big harbor developments had been undertaken in Montenegro where a productive hinterland was lacking. They said that money had been thrown away on prestige projects that made good advertising for socialism but did not yield commensurate returns in terms of goods and services.

A favorite whipping boy in this connection was the Belgrade-Bar Railway. This project has long been a dream of Serb nationalists. It would connect Belgrade directly with the sea and attract shipments that now are sent via Rijeka, in Dalmatia (Croatia). However, the territory through which the line would pass is mountainous and little traffic would originate there. Croatians have always maintained that the line would be excessively expensive to build and operate.

Some funds were allocated for the project by the federal government, and by 1971 the sections from Belgrade to Valjevo and from Titograd (capital of Montenegro) to Bar, ninety miles in all, were in operation, and fifty miles more were due to be completed shortly. To finance $75 million in excess costs, over and above the original estimate of $240 million, a bond issue was put out and sold to Serbians to whom the railroad had become a symbol of national pride (*New York Times,* Apr. 26, 1971).

Statistics do not bear out the contention that Croatia's interests have been sacrificed to those of the other republics. For the period 1947 to 1966 (see Table 5.2) income per capita advanced in all the republics, but most rapidly in the more advanced areas, including especially Croatia and Vojvodina. The relatively backward republics have not benefited disproportionately; to the contrary, most of them have advanced on the whole less rapidly than the national average, so that Kosovo, Bosnia, and Montenegro are farther behind than ever.

*Table 5.2*
*Income per Caput as Percent of Yugoslav Average*
*by Regions: 1947 and 1966*

|  | 1947 | 1966 |
|---|---|---|
| Yugoslavia | 100 | 100 |
| Bosnia and Herzegovina | 83 | 66 |
| Montenegro | 71 | 64 |
| Croatia | 107 | 119 |
| Macedonia | 62 | 66 |
| Slovenia | 175 | 176 |
| Serbia | 95 | 99 |
|    Serbia proper | 96 | 104 |
|    Vojvodina | 108 | 120 |
|    Kosovo & Metohija | 52 | 38 |

*Source:* Rakic, 1968:29, 44.

The situation is not as bad as the Croatian nationalists have painted it. Thus the development of a textile industry around Belgrade and an aluminum plant at Titograd in Montenegro and the improvements to the port at Bar each seems uneconomic taken by itself, but taken together, and assuming the completion of the Belgrade-Bar railroad, they might not prove so uneconomic (Lendvai, 1969:177-78).

The whole idea according to which goods or services produced in a given area "belong" in some sense to that area rather than to the economy as a whole is un-Marxist and inconsistent with the socialist idea of economic life. But the agitation of the Croatians could not be disregarded.

The Croatian nationalists presented a series of demands to the (all-Yugoslav) League of Communists, on behalf of both Croatia and Slovenia. The demands were partly political and partly economic. In the latter field, they had to do especially with the allocation of the national surplus and of the foreign exchange. Such matters had theretofore been subject to discussion in the appropriate organs of the federal government, and the several republics were supposed to accept the collective decision (Vasilev, 1961). The Croatians, in effect, proposed dropping the presumption that there was no conflict between the interests of the several republics and the national interest; they put forward the Croatian interest as such, and demanded that concessions be made to this interest.

The Croatians maintained that their state brought into the country a very large share (43 percent) of the hard currency earned abroad; this was largely derived from tourists who visited the Dalmatian Coast resorts, but included also exports, and sizable remittances from hundreds of thousands of Croatian emigrants in Western Europe. But Croatia had been allowed to retain for investment only 8 percent of the country's hard currency (*New York Times,* Dec. 17, 1971). Under a new arrangement announced at the end of 1971, Croatia was allowed to keep 20 percent of its export earnings instead of 7 percent, and 45 percent of tourist earnings instead of 40 percent (*New York Times,* Jan. 25, 1972).

Another grievance of the other republics against Serbia arose from the fact that since Belgrade was the capital, Serbian "businessmen" were able to get their problems attended to more easily. The big financial organizations controlling international trade, Genex and Inex, were also located in Belgrade. After 1971, their operations were decentralized.

Croatia and Slovenia also pushed through a constitutional amendment according to which the investments in the backward areas (under control of the federal government) would be limited to 1.9 percent of the national income—surely not an excessive amount. At the same time, it was provided that where disputes on economic matters arose among the republics and the autonomous provinces, they should be settled by means of "parity committees," and where a decision had to be taken for the whole of Yugoslavia that might affect some one of the republics or provinces adversely, compensation was to be paid (Vratusa, 1971:161).

A political devolution of powers accompanied the economic reforms. In a series of amendments to the constitution in 1971, the central government was left with control of national defense, foreign affairs, the organization of internal commerce, and aid to underdeveloped areas; all other powers were transferred to the individual republics (Bourdet, 1971:237).

The trend toward decentralization even affected the League of Communists, which was broken up into eight regional parties (for the six republics and two autonomous districts); these were free to develop different ideas on day-to-day policies, though not on program, which was centrally determined as before.

Despite the reforms, the situation continued to deteriorate, politically and socially. The central government tried to avoid intervention, as much as possible, quite in the spirit of the free enterprise system. Since authority had to be exercised somewhere, there was a tendency for the republics to step in and fill the void; but economic problems continued to accumulate. To rationalize the frustration they felt, the republic governments blamed the federal government, and clubbed together to further limit its powers. The periphery took the point of view that the center was perversely accentuating its problems.

The agitation in Croatia had reached proportions where it attracted international attention. Mass meetings were held at which only Croatian flags were shown, Croatian nationalist songs were sung, and anti-Titoist slogans and signs were carried. Croatian party leaders Mika Tripalo and Savka Dabcevic, attempting to persuade Tito that nothing was wrong, were themselves accused of sponsoring the demonstrations, and Tito forced their resignations. Thereupon the students at Zagreb University went on a strike that lasted eleven days; among the demands were the reinstatement of Tripalo and Dabcevic, remedying of economic grievances, and a seat for Croatia at the United Nations!

Croatian émigrés, especially in West Germany, Sweden, and Australia, became active. They murdered the Yugoslav ambassador to Sweden; and when the Swedish government arrested six Croatians in connection with the murder, three Croatians hijacked a plane and flew it to Spain; they forced the Swedish government to release the six. In July 1972 it was reported that a band of nineteen émigrés had entered Yugoslavia and made their way to the mountains of Bosnia with terrorist intent. They were rounded up and killed.

The central government and the League of Communists decided that the time had come to crack down—hard. Over one thousand people were arrested, including hundreds of students; many minor officials of the Party in Croatia were expelled: one account put the number at 740. Veselica was put on trial and sentenced to three years in prison; other Croatian nationalist leaders received sentences of up to four years.

Among those expelled from the Croatian Party were two professors of economics who had, in their public utterances, been very critical of the Serbian minority living in Croatia (*New York Times,* July 25, 1972). This incident recalled the time during the last war when the Ustasha murdered hundreds of thousands of Serbs in cold blood. We are reminded of Renan's remark that in order to build a nation it is necessary to forget a good many things. The government, by way of justifying its crackdown on the professors, permitted publication of a theretofore suppressed book, detailing the wartime atrocities of the Ustasha. In the end the Party leadership was purged not only in Croatia but in the other republics as well.

The crisis of 1972 showed that the League of Communists still retained enough authority to reorganize the several republican parties and to curb the swing toward capitalism. But it also showed that much remains to be done before Yugoslavia can be considered a unified nation. Tito himself commented that the explosion in Croatia might have resulted in civil war if it had not been checked.

The revival of strong central control of course disappointed those who had been hoping for a continuation and extension of methods close to democratic liberalism in the Western sense. But it was precisely the liberalism of the system, with production and employment determined by the market, that had failed.

The economic problems of Yugoslavia were not solved automatically by the checking of decentralization. In fact there is no easy solution for them. But the spirited reassertion of the authority of the central government and the central Party served notice that the Yugoslav economy was going to remain socialist, at least for the time being. The revival of planning and the downgrading of the market as the prime economic regulator were necessary corollaries.

An important question that remains unanswered is whether the idea of equalization among the several republics will be revived. Until recently, the trend was in the other direction. The effect of using the market as a regulator was to cause the advanced sectors to develop more rapidly than the backward ones (Rakic, 1968:47), and of course the Croatian demands for a larger share of investment funds was frankly aimed at speeding up Croatian development even if that meant that the less developed republics had to wait. The defense of the Croatian position was in terms of the need to bring the whole country, led by Croatia and Slovenia, closer to the West European level. As one Croatian writer put it:

> We are the locomotive that is pulling the Serbs, the Bosnians, the Montenegrins and the Macedonians into Europe. (*New York Times,* Feb. 3, 1972)

## NATIONAL AND RELIGIOUS MINORITIES

Quite aside from the national republics and nationality districts that have autonomy with regard to nationality questions, there are large numbers of people in Yugoslavia who live in areas where they do not constitute a majority and who are thus classified as national minorities. According to the Census of 1961 there were then 1,906,576 such people, or one-tenth of the population.

Tomasic has argued that Communist policy in all countries tends to use nationalist feelings as a morale builder and psychological energizer, and that therefore the minor nationalities, whose members feel no stimulation from being of "Soviet," or "Yugoslav," or "Czechoslovak" nationality, tend toward apathy and indifference, while the top positions in Party and state are filled by members of the dominant nationality (Tomasic, 1960:72).

This argument runs afoul of the well-known fact that in all the countries that have carried out a social revolution and attempted to apply Lenin's theories on the national question, very strong attempts have been made to build up feelings of self-esteem among the minor nationalities—the very ones which Tomasic claims "tend towards apathy and indifference." In fact, both the Soviet Union and Yugoslavia have been criticized for precisely the opposite reason: that they have paid *too much* attention to writing down languages for small tribes that had not asked to have them written down, and perpetuating the existence of ethnic groups that were quite prepared to terminate their separate existence.[6] It is true that the policy of the Party and of the several states has not been altogether consistent and continuous on this point. But Yugoslavia has been among the countries in the socialist bloc that have shown the greatest evidence of seriousness in the application of a Leninist nationality policy. Tomasic is apparently not aware of the Yugoslav policy (and the analagous policies in China and the Soviet Union) according to which all organs in a nationally mixed area are to be constituted in proportion to the national composition of the region.

Among the rights of minorities specified in the Constitution of 1946 and accompanying directives are the right to use one's own language before the courts, and the right to have a school in one's own language wherever twenty or more students request it (Shoup, 1968:103). How much of a change was involved may be appreciated when it is recalled that in the interwar period the Shqipetars (Albanians) in the Kosmet area had no rights as such, and there was not a single school where Albanian was taught (Jončič, 1969:186).

The rights of minorities were further spelled out in general terms in the Program of the League of Communists (CPY) in 1958 and more specifically in a minute adopted by the Central Committee of the League in March 1959. According to the latter document:

1. National minorities are a continuing fact of life and cannot be solved by redrawing frontiers or exchanging populations but must be accorded full rights;

2. The problem of alien minorities in Yugoslavia and Yugoslav minorities in other countries are one and the same problem;

3. The minorities from other countries retain their culture and their adherence to the countries of their origin while enjoying full rights in Yugoslavia. Under socialism, the national minorities have a social function of drawing together different nations and states (ibid.: 211-12).

One of the rights of nationality is the right to keep one's nationality secret, which is done by registering simply as "Yugoslav" (ibid.:207-08). However one cannot be compelled to register that way. Before Rankovich was exposed and dismissed, a campaign sponsored by Tito and Kardelj to have everyone register as a Yugoslav had to be dropped because people feared that the group around Rankovich was trying to use this means to impose Serbian nationalism on the whole of Yugoslavia (Shoup, 1968:223-26).

According to Antun Vratusa, formerly Yugoslav representative to the United Nations, "In a nationally mixed area all organs from bottom to top, from workers' council in a factory to the organ of government of the region, are constituted in proportion to the national composition of the region." But, Vratusa adds, this system has not worked as well in practice as in theory because there is frequently a shortage of trained personnel in the minority group (Vratusa, 1971:33).

Also, as long as power in all important questions continues to be exercised by the League of Communists, and as long as its bodies are themselves not constituted proportionally to nationalities in the several regions, the minorities are dependent on the goodwill of the Communist establishment. However, the minorities do receive some protection from the central government. If there were a devolution of power to the Communist parties of the respective republics, the situation of the minorities might suddenly become much worse.

As things stand, there has been some tendency in quite recent years toward greater participation in public life at the lowest levels and toward greater restraints on capricious intervention from above, so that in the opinion of some outside observers, Yugoslavia has moved closer to the Western type of democracy (McClellan in Vucinich, 1969:147). The importance of the administrative organs at the lowest levels should not be underestimated; according to McClellan, the communal peoples' committees are in a sense the most important decision-making bodies in Yugoslavia (ibid.:143).

*Religion* has traditionally been at the very base of nationalism in Yugoslavia. Since Serbian and Croatian are essentially one language, the main distinction between the two nationalities, aside from the matter of residence, has been that the Croatians were Roman Catholics while the Serbs adhered to the Orthodox Church persuasion. The Moslem community in Bosnia-Herzegovina was not differentiated from the Serbs and Croatians except by religion; they were Slavs, speaking Serbo-Croatian. They were nevertheless recognized as a separate nationality. The Orthodox Church has traditionally been organized on the basis of national states. But the Roman Church was much more highly centralized, and its Archbishop Stepinac became a storm center in the postwar period.

Tito at first proposed that the Roman Catholic Church in Yugoslavia should sever its links with Rome. When this idea was rejected, the government set about to deprive Stepinac of his perquisites and emoluments. It was years before a modus vivendi was worked out. The Church, in response, played upon Croatian nationalism. For example, an obscure Croatian monk, Nikola Tavelic, who had been martyred in Jerusalem a thousand years ago, was rediscovered and canonized, thus giving Croatia its first saint. It was said that fifteen thousand Croatians journeyed to Rome for the canonization ceremonies.

Recently, good relations between the Roman Church and Yugoslavia have been facilitated by the fact that the highest authority (the Vatican) now uses the vocabulary of the socialist countries on the national question. The Decree on the Missionary Activity of the Church proclaimed by the Vatican Council in 1965 states that Christians should practice "true and effective patriotism" in their respective countries and at the same time "altogether avoid racial prejudice and bitter nationalism" (Abbott, 1966:603). The Church's definition of patriotism is similar to that of Rousseau.

The exercise of religion is today freer in Yugoslavia than in any of the other East European countries. On a purely formal basis church-state relations have never been better (Petrovich, 1972:20).

The churches are, however, still a problem to the government in that they have assumed a special protective attitude toward their respective nationalities, and have thus tended to accentuate the divisive trends that have reappeared in recent years. Both the Greek Orthodox Church and the Roman Catholic Church stress local republican nationalism. In Serbia, the Orthodox Church emphasizes that it is the historic guardian of the Serbian nation and of that nation's cultural heritage. The Roman Catholic Church of the Croats and Slovenes is probably more national today (says Petrovich) in an ethnic sense than ever before in its modern history. However it denies having links with the Ustasha or the émigrés (ibid.:121, 130, 132).

Religion is protected like race and nationality by the Criminal Law of 1951. Article 148 makes it an offense punishable by up to five years' imprisonment to limit the rights granted citizens in the constitution or to grant favors or advantages on the basis of nationality, race, or religion. Article 119 makes punishable by up to fifteen years' imprisonment the exciting or inflaming of national, racial, or religious hatred (Shoup, 1968:110).

While the government is quick to counter any attempt by a religious sect to exercise political power, the government still occasionally interferes in church matters where its national policies so direct. Thus the CPY had long advocated a national church for Macedonia, and in 1967 this project was carried through by the unilateral action of the Macedonian church, although the Serbian Church did not approve (Petrovich, 1972:125-27).

## SOCIAL ORIGINS OF NATIONALISM
## IN THE SOCIALIST STATE

What caused the reappearance of nationalist rivalries in 1971–1972? The writer made a visit to Yugoslavia in the autumn of 1973. A number of important leaders were interviewed, and they were nearly unanimous in their belief that it was the economic crisis—the combination of mass unemployment, galloping inflation, and difficulties with the system of workers' self-management—that had caused the revival of nationalism. The lone dissenter emphasized long-run factors, but did not have any answer to the question of why nationalism reappeared at this time and not at some other.

Who are the nationalists? The traditional answer to this question would quite likely be in any country at any time: the peasants or the lower middle class. Some would say that the peasants were nationalists because they were conservative. Indeed this was the answer given by one informant, Jovan Georgevich of the Serbian constitutional court.

But peasants do not themselves create a nationalist movement. Who does set it up in the first place? Was it the "intellectuals," as Dean Vukadinovich put it?

Several informants denied that it was the intellectuals as such, the top intellectuals, who had picked up and propagated the nationalist slogans as a cure for the country's economic ills. The nationalists were, in the first instance, "anyone eager for power," in Georgevich's phrase. Other informants described the nationalist leaders as demagogues and careerists, those ready to revive old antagonisms if that would advance their own political fortunes.[7] The analogy with Moczar in Poland in 1968 came readily to mind.

Mihailo Mihailovich, a dissenting professor, attributes the resurgence of republic nationalism to the single-party monopoly, which he says "by its very existence brings out all kinds of separatist movements" (*New York Times*). He did not discuss why separatism suddenly became a burning issue in 1971.

What then should be our conclusion as to the relation between socialism and nationalism in Eastern Europe? Has socialism solved the national problem?

Plainly, it has not. Socialism has not furnished any automatic answer to the economic problems of the area, and, partly for that very reason, nationality problems have persisted.

However, neither the industrial working class, which represents the basic constituency of the present regime, nor the peasants are particularly nationalist, in the sense of traditional republican nationalism. Indeed traditional nationalism has, in the opinion of one informed observer, "only sporadic and very limited support." It is kept alive by a section of the intelligentsia and by the respective churches (Denich, 1976:6-7). During the war the peasants were Yugoslav nationalists as against the invaders, but there has been no reason since then to put the peasants down as nationalist-minded. Indeed the observer just quoted thinks that after their period of supremacy during the war, the peasants have been, in effect, outside the political system, neither hostile nor particularly supportive of it (ibid.:4-5).

Whether excessive repression of dissent set the stage for extreme nationalist agitation is a point that must remain open. But it is clear that in Yugoslavia such agitation assumed crisis proportions before being summarily checked. There was danger of civil war among the several nationalities, especially of Croatia against Serbia. The lives of the Serbs living in Croatian territory were once again endangered. Nationalism of the chauvinist variety penetrated the several parties, showing that the lesson of Leninist policy had been learned only imperfectly.

However incomplete the application, Leninist nationality policy, correctly interpreted, remains the hope of the world, and the nonsocialist nations, which do not even pretend to an ideal of national equality and still lag in allowing freedom to minorities, have much to learn from the example of the socialist nations. Marxists, who have stressed class exploitation as almost the only form of exploitation, have come to recognize at long last that national exploitation can be just as serious and long-lasting as class exploitation. However, this does not mean that every claim that the rights of a nationality have been infringed must be accepted at face value.

From Yugoslavia we learn that nationality policy cannot be considered apart from the other policies a country is following. Even the best policy regarding the relations among several nationalities may break down if a crisis develops in the polity for reasons not connected with nationality. In Yugoslavia, the recent unmannerly squabbling over scarce resources among the several regions seems remote from a Marxist nationality policy, and the virtual abandonment of the idea of giving preference to the development of the backward areas is not Marxist at all.

## KARDELJ AND THE THEORY OF NATIONALISM

Edvard Kardelj, the theoretician of the Communist Party of Yugoslavia (League of Communists), wrote a book on the national question among the peasants in his native Slovenia, and the introduction contains some remarks on the conditions for the rise of nationalism which are important for our purposes. This is especially the case because Kardelj does not assume that socialism will bring an end to nationalism, either immediately or in the foreseeable future. His ideas on the origins of nationalism are most interesting.

National consciousness, we know, has political consequences; it is itself a political and cultural phenomenon. But consciousness is determined, in the last analysis, by the sum total of the relations of production that constitute the economic structure of society. "It is not the consciousness of men that determines their being," said Marx, "but, on the contrary, their social being that determines their consciousness."

If, then, we wish to explain national consciousness, we have first of all to examine what it is in the modern relations of production that gives rise to the nation-state as the most appropriate political form.

Kardelj called attention to the *social division of labor* which is characteristic of the epoch of capitalism. It was precisely this social division of labor, he said, and not the operations of the bourgeoisie as such, that created nations as the framework of economic and cultural self-assertion. In the presence of capitalistic competition and the concentration of capital, he argued, the social division of labor involves also a struggle for the distribution of the surplus which would favor the cultural self-assertion of the nation. People have always fought, said Kardelj, for that part of the world to which in their social consciousness they belong. The differing degree of the social division of labor has determined the scope of the struggle for the surplus, from tribes and ancient city-states through medieval communes and feudal provinces to modern nations (Kardelj, 1958:58-63).

It is thus the function of the nation, in Kardelj's view, to enable people to successfully vindicate their claim to an appropriate portion of the social surplus, within an area that is determined by the social division of labor. When the social division of labor has proceeded to a certain point, it may be possible for people to become citizens of the world directly in a manner similar to that contemplated by E. H. Carr (who, however, was not familiar to Kardelj); meanwhile, the nation remains the most appropriate unit for people to use in order to vindicate their rights and resist oppression.

As to just how big a unit the nation presupposes, Kardelj remained vague. But it is significant that he, along with Tito, always avoided pressing the claims of his native "nation" (Slovenia, in the case of Kardelj) as against Yugoslavia as a whole; he will have no part of narrow nationalism in that sense.

Kardelj criticizes Stalin for misunderstanding the nature of the peasant problem. Stalin saw that in many lands the peasants were the mass army of the national liberation movement and for this reason he proclaimed the national question to be "essentially a peasant question." This assertion is correct only in one sense, says Kardelj. The peasant remains the main army of the national liberation movement regardless of the role played by the bourgeoisie. But the peasant joins national demands with social and economic demands. In this sense, the peasant's fight for national liberation is largely a fight for the control of power. In its essence, says Kardelj, the national question is doubtless a question of the whole society. Organically, it is connected with the social relations of capitalism and also with the transitional period from capitalism to socialism (ibid.:62-63).

Kardelj's criticism of Stalin is more than a mere matter of definition. For Stalin, in common with Lenin and the other Marxists of the period before the Russian Revolution, looked on nationalism as a specific outgrowth of capitalism, and expected it to disappear with the international proletarian revolution. When nationalism did not disappear, but rather intensified, and was shown to be affecting not only capitalist but socialist states, it became necessary for Marxists to re-evaluate Stalin (and Lenin) and find some other roots that might account for nationalism in both epochs: the epoch of capitalism, and that of competition between socialism and capitalism. Kardelj found the key in the social division of labor, and the institutional framework set up to effectuate it.

But since a "socialist nation" is simply a result of the change in the nature of power and property in that nation, and since this change does not greatly affect the social division of labor, at least directly, it would follow from Kardelj's approach that nationalism is quite likely to persist into the period when socialist nations are struggling for existence (ibid.:63). And indeed, Kardelj in his later writings does not even contemplate that the state will ever wither away completely. It follows that loyalty to the state — that is, nationalism — would also persist indefinitely.

Suppose, says Kardelj, that there were another world war which eventuated in the disappearance of capitalism as an economic system. Then, there would be a "world socialist system." Would that be a world free of national oppression and war?

Not so, says Kardelj. For such a war would be so destructive that one precondition for world socialism—a generally high level of well-being—would have disappeared in the war. Vestiges of hegemonic nationalism, inequalities among nations, and so forth might still linger on, and one nation might oppress others even under socialism (Kardelj, 1960:180). "There will always 'remain' contradictions in socialism which will continue to appear as the elemental pressure of the objective facts of the social conscience" (ibid.:192).

Kardelj sees the future of the world in decentralized terms. All the processes of development of socialism "will unfold the less painfully and the more democratically and so much the more rapidly, the more freely every nation is in a position independently to choose the ways and forms of its own socialist development." Any attempt by any socialist nation to impose specific forms of socialism by force or even pressure would mean a setback to the whole movement (ibid.:193-95).

Kardelj is far more successful than Stalin in tying up the superstructure (psychological elements in the composition of the nation: national consciousness) with the base (production relations). The nation, as he sees it, has two functions with respect to the social relations of production. On the one hand, the nation (the state) assumes greater and greater importance as the integrator and manager of the economic process. And on the other hand, the state (or the nation) is the agency used by the people who make up the nation for the purpose of capturing the economic surplus that the economy generates. Implicit in this latter idea is defense against any attempts by others to make off with that surplus. Both of these functions of the nation will continue and even increase when socialism succeeds capitalism as the prevalent system of property ownership.

Kardelj's definition of the nation is an historical one and is far superior to Stalin's static, schematic approach. Kardelj brings in the struggle against national oppression as coordinate with, and by no means inferior to, the struggle against class oppression. Stalin, as we have seen, left the implication that national oppression would disappear with the death of capitalism. Kardelj was wise after the event no doubt, but his correction of Stalin is no less indispensable on that account.

Kardelj was furthermore on solid ground when he criticized Stalin for talking about "internationalism" without defining his terms. Stalin's "internationalism," said Kardelj, meant whatever Stalin wanted it to mean. As a concrete criticism of Stalin's policies, this contention can hardly be disputed. However, when Kardelj himself wanted to talk about internationalism, he fell into the same trap.

Kardelj was unable to explain just how the shift in the social relations of production in the epoch of capitalism gave rise to specific aspects of national consciousness. He left the impression that the relations of production may themselves create national consciousness, whereas this is, as we know, an illusion.

Kardelj's concept of the social division of labor remains somewhat vague, although one is tempted to see in it the same kind of tendency that we have described as integration—social, economic, political, and cultural integration. He has also been described as contradictory (Vucinich, 1969:392). But his insistence that nationalism may not be overborne by strictly economic considerations—his preference for decentralization—and his furnishing a rationale for the continuance of nationalism into the era of socialism are excellent reasons for taking him seriously.

The struggle between a centralizer such as Lenin and a decentralizer such as Kardelj is not one that is likely to be settled by abstract reasoning. It may be that this particular struggle, with which the future of nationalism is intimately bound up, is not likely to be settled at all in any permanent way. According to Kardelj's own reasoning, the size of the unit within which the social division of labor operates is destined to increase in the long run. It has been the contribution of countries such as Yugoslavia and Vietnam to stress that a forced increase in the size of the political unit, through colonialism or conquest, is reversible; such matters are not settled by military preponderance, even when that is seemingly backed by economic forces as well.

In seeking a formula that will explain nationalism as something more than the result of bourgeois needs, Kardelj is plainly on the right track. Whether his "social division of labor" is the key to the solution depends on just what he means by the term. Mere "division of labor" is not enough. It is an economic concept. It may set the broad limits within which nations can be formed, but a nation is primarily a political and cultural phenomenon. Much more elaboration is needed. It may be that in his other writings Kardelj has furnished such elaboration. In any case he emerges as a Marxist of real distinction.

# 6

## Nationalism
## and the Chinese Revolution

Nationalism had everything to do with the success of the Chinese Revolution. The foreign imperialists had to be defeated and ousted. China, which had disintegrated into a congeries of largely independent provinces, each dominated by a warlord, had to be reintegrated and consolidated, before an all-inclusive socialist republic could be set up. Mao Tse-tung was a nationalist before he was a socialist.

To give a full account of the relation between nationalism and socialism in China would require nothing less than a full history of the country in the modern period. It is not our intention to write such a history. But certain issues have been debated with reference to China which have relevance elsewhere, and these we do have to face and resolve as best we can, if we are to have a rounded theory of nationalism.

It may seem obvious that no revolution can be directed from a distance of 9,000 miles. Yet the Communist International did attempt to give directives to the Chinese Revolution. When, in the 1920s, the Revolution suffered near-fatal reverses, the blame had to rest largely on the out-of-country leaders who had made the many wrong decisions. Apportioning the blame for these decisions has been a matter of partisan politics within the international Communist movement ever since. For our part, we have no intention of entering into this debate; our position is that the attempt to run the revolution from Moscow was doomed from the outset. The Chinese Revolution had to be made by Chinese, using what advice they found helpful, and depending as little as possible on outside supplies or experts. And that is the way it was eventually done.[1]

## SOCIAL CLASSES, NATIONALISM, AND THE REVOLUTION

If we ask who made the Chinese Revolution, the answer must be the peasants and workers. Making all allowances for the importance of leadership, it was the peasants of Hunan who, by their attitudes and actions, convinced Mao Tse-tung that peasant militancy was a reliable factor. It was the workers who seized the British concession in Hankow and the city of Shanghai in 1927, and the workers who remained militant, though suppressed, in the long years until the final victory. It was of course the workers and peasants who conducted guerrilla warfare and joined the Red army.[2]

The students are not a distinct social class, but their collaboration as a group was crucial. The Chinese Revolution really got under way when urban workers and students began helping with each other's struggles, in the period immediately following World War I. The special factors conditioning the student psychology are well summed up by Eric Wolf:

> Caught between the conflicting standards of the old and the new; between East and West; between the world of their parents with their more particularistic loyalties, and their own involvement with fellow students drawn from all over China; faced often with uncertain economic conditions and threatened by unemployment and ever more conscious of the impotence of China in the face of the growing foreign threat, the students reacted to their situation with an accentuated nationalism. (Wolf, 1969:138)

Nationalism, taking the form of a revulsion against the semicolonial status of China in the world, was a factor in the psychology not only of students and intellectuals but of the masses of the workers and peasants who actually made the revolution, and even of some of the bourgeoisie.

In the early years of nationalist and revolutionary agitation the city workers played a leading role. China, unlike some colonial countries, had a proletariat. The bulk of the population consisted of peasants, but the wage-earning class, though small relative to the peasants, was large absolutely, as in pre-revolutionary Russia. Moreover, it was strategically located: the workers in the treaty ports and some inland cities were very conscious of the privileges enjoyed by foreigners and of the exploitation that these visited on the Chinese workers.

Even before World War I, but especially just after it, big strikes that had started for economic reasons turned into antiforeign demonstrations. A nationwide boycott of British goods grew out of the general strike of May 4, 1919. (On the early period, see Wales, 1945.) By 1925 a million workers had gone on strike in support of political causes, largely nationalist (Wolf, 1969:137).

The Communist Party of China (CPC) at this time was overwhelmingly urban. In 1926 only 5 percent of its members, reportedly, were peasants. In 1925 the biggest iron mines in China, the Hanyehping mines near Wuhan, had been shut down, throwing one hundred thousand miners out of work. Mao's original Red army in Hunan was recruited from these miners, from peasant guards, and from mutinous Kuomintang (KMT) soldiers.

But this original army was decimated in futile urban uprisings, and the center of gravity of the revolutionary movement shifted to the country, where the peasantry had a big backlog of unresolved grievances. By 1930 the overwhelming majority of the CPC were peasants. Fifty-eight percent of the army in Kiangsi were said to be peasants and another 38 percent came from the "rural proletariat." The remaining 4 percent came from the petty bourgeoisie and were usually the younger sons of small landlords, intellectuals, and the like (Wales, 1939:56-57).

There is some justification for regarding the Red army soldier as having been more than a simple peasant, even when he came from a peasant family. The broadening of view and the political indoctrination transform him, to a degree. But it is well to remember that the turnover in any such popular army is large, with soldiers frequently retiring from active combat, and their places being taken by new recruits. A special study established that the Red army at any given time was actually composed for the most part of men from local peasant families.

There is no question that the Communist regime that eventually took power was overwhelmingly of rural provenance. By 1951 80 percent of the six million Party members were of peasant origin, and former peasants were in key posts, from Mao Tse-tung down (Wright, 1951:258). Mao in his *New Democracy,* issued in 1940, emphasized very strongly the peasant composition of the population and the peasant base of the Party. The leaders were intellectuals, but they too were predominantly of rural origin, the sons of landlords and rich peasants (North, 1965:395).

Chalmers Johnson has attributed the success of the Chinese Communists in building a mass base among the peasants to the fact that the Communists appealed to the nationalist sentiment of the peasantry as against the Japanese (C. Johnson, 1962).

> *Popular* Communism without a basis in nationalism does not exist. . . . The reality underlying the creation of the independent Communist states is the social mobilisation of their masses. (C. Johnson, 1962:179)

Johnson downplays the successes of the Party prior to 1937. He argues that it was the mobilization of the *nationalist*-minded peasants in the face of the Japanese invasion that enabled the Communists to seize the leadership of a mass movement and ultimately to establish themselves in power. Specifically, he insists, it was the Japanese advance southward from the Peking area in 1937 that saw the Communists emerge as leaders in guerrilla warfare, mobilizing the peasant for the anti-Japanese resistance.

No one disputes that the Chinese Communists did mobilize the peasants for guerrilla warfare against the Japanese. However, they had a foothold among the peasants before this. Donald Gillin has shown that the Communists had established solid bases in Shansi as early as 1936 (Gillin, 1964:272). It is of course well known that the Communists had bases before 1935 in Kiangsi and elsewhere (later transferred to the Northwest), and that the Long March would have been impossible without peasant sympathy along the route.

With regard to Johnson's implication that the Communists bore the brunt of the defense against the Japanese, Gillin does not deny that this was true as regards guerrilla fighting, but he points out that the main fighting in North China was done by the forces of Chiang and Yen (ibid.:280-81).

In one respect, certainly, the Japanese invasion simplified the task of the Communists. The peasants were by no means a homogeneous mass; there were marked class differences among them. The welding of the poor, middle, and rich peasants into an effective fighting force is a story in itself. The nationalist motive had everything to do with the surmounting of what otherwise could have been an impossible task. The victory of the Chinese Revolution was made possible by the anti-Fascist world war. But it is going too far to call Communist success in China "a triumph of nationalism" (Chang, 1950:554, 556). It was a triumph of statesmanship in handling a difficult problem.

It is perhaps significant that Johnson's basic data are taken largely from the files of the Japanese War Office. If the Japanese War Office overemphasized the role of the Communists in the resistance, which is possible, that would fit in with the overall Japanese official philosophy according to which Communism was the main enemy.

Johnson has also argued that the Communists took over the power in the rural areas of China by default: the landlords fled when the Japanese approached, and the Communist-led guerrillas, said Johnson, moved into the vacuum.

This point of view is sharply rejected by Selden, who pointed out that absentee landlordism began long before the Japanese invasion. The decline of central authority had left the rural areas largely unpoliced, except by self-seeking warlords, whose soldiers were considered by the peasants as being little different from bandits. Whoever succeeded to power in the countryside had to overcome the warlords' stubborn resistance. It was under these conditions that the Communist program of local initiative and local control captured the imagination of the poorer peasants, and also of the middle peasants. The result was no "vacuum" but rather a new power mix (Selden, 1969:361-63).

Johnson says that in the period after 1947 the landlords were attacked "not solely as rentiers but also as collaborators with the enemy" (Johnson, 1962:198). Of course they did collaborate with the foreign invaders—out of class interest. Was it a mistake for the Communists to point out the connection? Johnson overstates his case. But we must still concede a major place in our theory to the wartime solidarity which has drawn rural as well as urban classes together and led them to sink their differences, to the point where socialism seemed the only way out of their difficulties.

In China, as in Yugoslavia, peasant resistance to the invader was solidified under Communist leadership. But the moblilization of the peasants had begun before the invasion. The Communists contributed a rationale and a social program which were absolutely vital to the peasant mobilization.

The flexibility of the approach to the different strata of the peasantry had everything to do with the success of the Communist appeal.

There is of course a question as to *which* strata of the peasantry nationalist movements appeal to. Anouar Abdel-Malek does not believe that it is the *bottom* layer of the rural population that will lead the national liberation movement and make the socialist revolution. He writes:

> Contrary to the common idea, it is not the least equipped peasants, the most ignorant and backward ones, who carry on guerrilla warfare; it is the peasant small-owners, the agricultural laborers, the former in touch with the rural intelligentsia and the latter with that of the cities. It is this more developed sector of the peasantry which, in alliance with the industrial proletariat, constitutes essentially the socialist battle force in the Third World countries. (Abdel-Malek, 1972:321)

Eric Wolf also finds that it is not the landless peasants, or agricultural laborers, or even the tenants, who make up the bulk of the participants in the peasant uprisings in the twentieth century; it is the small owner, fighting to save his land and to get some more. "A rebellion cannot start from a situation of complete impotence; the powerless are easy victims" (Wolf, 1969:290).

With regard to China, Wolf makes the interesting observation that it was not in the areas of greatest tenancy that the revolution first made headway but precisely in the areas of least tenancy (Wolf, 1969:134). Here, as in Russia, the small *owner* proved to be receptive to left-wing slogans.

When the revolution had been defeated in the cities, in 1927, and the Communist Party took to the countryside, there was much talk and some action aimed at radical land reform which would confiscate all land and pool it in newly established collectives (ibid.:146). But it was soon realized that this policy would alienate the middle peasants and isolate the poor peasants. There was a radical shift. The Party played up not only to the middle peasants but to the rich ones, who received land along with the others in the distribution and who presently eased into leading positions in the villages and even in the Party. The policy was again changed. The abolition of the landlord class was a long process (ibid.:153).

In the later stages of the revolution, with the Communist armies in full control of the situation, the tactics became somewhat different. Referring to the final victorious march to the south by the Chinese Red army, Mao recalled much later:

> We roused the poor and middle peasants to launch class struggle and seize all the land of the landlord class and distribute the surplus land of the rich peasants, apportioning land on a per capita basis. (This was a tremendous revolution in the rural areas.) Immediately afterward, we followed up with the mutual aid and cooperative movements. And from that point, steadily advancing step by step, we led the peasants on the road to socialism. We had a massive party and army. When our forces went south a full complement of cadre squads had been set in place in every province to do local work. . . . As soon as our forces would arrive they would penetrate deeply into the agricultural villages, "paying calls on the poor to learn of their grievances," "striking roots and pulling things together," and getting the active elements of the poor and lower-middle peasants organized. (Mao, 1977:17)

After the war, the peasants were organized first into cooperatives and later into communes. But rent continued to be paid to those who had pooled their lands voluntarily. Everything possible was done to avoid a sharp break. So, productivity in Chinese agriculture has been maintained and increased; the "high and stable yield" regions in China have yields almost as high as those of the most modern areas of the world, and the production of food staples per caput for the whole of China is above that of any Asian country except Thailand (Stavis, 1974).

In China, as in Russia, the middle peasant alone could not have been relied on to bring socialism to the countryside. Still, in the late 1960s, Mao's followers were insisting that rural political power be placed in the hands of the underprivileged poor and lower-middle-class peasants. The long-run priorities of the Revolution were evidently still in the minds of the leaders.

Wolf makes a similar point with respect to Vietnam. Following the final French defeat at Dienbienphu, between 1954 and 1958, the Vietminh attempted to bring the class struggle to the villages in North Vietnam, with the poor peasants taking the lead in a war on the rich peasants and landlords. The classification of the population into various groups was carried out, says Wolf, with the "utmost ferocity"; the attempts to spur the class struggle in the villages nearly wrecked the agrarian reform (Wolf, 1969:191). Thereafter a middle ground was found between complete collectivization and individual ownership.

The mass of the peasantry, the "middle" peasants, had to be convinced of the rightness of the NLF cause; and this was done by a patient process, extending over years, of education at the grassroots. The final triumph of socialism in Vietnam was not caused by the foreign intervention alone; but it was the NLF with its socialist program that proved best able to resist the invader, and thereby gave cogency to socialism's economic appeal. Once convinced, the peasants participated actively in the liberation struggle, which was clearly a democratic struggle too. The three great movements—nationalism, socialism, and democracy—were working together, and they proved to be irresistible. In spite of the incredible odds against the NLF, it used its help from the socialist countries to defeat first the French and then the Americans, without calling in the Chinese army.


## MAO AND THE "NATIONAL BOURGEOISIE"

Social categories developed in the West sometimes do not fit the conditions in the developing countries with any exactitude. The psychology and even the definition of a particular group in China may be quite different from what one would expect if working with European models and concepts. Similarly the experience of China may not be applicable to colonial and semicolonial countries where the stratum in question is differently composed and oriented or perhaps absent altogether. This point must be recalled repeatedly when studying Mao Tse-tung's policies with regard to the "bourgeoisie."

Mao favored cooperating with the so-called national bourgeoisie, and at the time of Chiang's northern expedition it was Communist International policy to do so, in spite of its own earlier (1920) warnings about this group. Why did Mao, whose judgment of the political capabilities of the various social elements was in general so sound, favor working with the national bourgeoisie?

His observations in his own native Hunan may have influenced him. For Hunan was a center of antiforeign nationalism on the part of local financiers, as well as of opposition to Peking which it thought was subservient to foreign interests. Already before World War I, money for the North-South railway had been put up by local capitalists, who opposed this railway being incorporated into the Peking-controlled Hankow-Canton and Hankow-Szechwan lines on the ground that Peking would be a cover for England, France, Germany, and the United States. Hunanese officials also opposed the entry of foreign capitalists into mining during World War I (Landis, 1964:159). Hunan had some industry that was locally financed.

The national bourgeoisie, in Mao's definition, included "the enlightened gentry and individual landlords with democratic leanings." (Would such a group be called a "bourgeoisie" at all in Europe?) This element, he said, gave considerable political help during the War of Resistance. Most of the national bourgeoisie, according to Mao, had ties to the land.

Mao was always an advocate of a flexible policy toward the national bourgeoisie; he described the ultra-Left policy of fighting against it as "adventurist." The correct policy was to try to win it over. The Manifesto of the Chinese People's Liberation Army called in October 1947 for uniting "workers, peasants, soldiers, intellectuals and businessmen, all oppressed classes, all people's organizations, and other patriots" to "form a national united front." As explained by Mao, the expression "businessmen" in the manifesto means all the national bourgeoisie who are persecuted and fettered, that is, the middle and petty bourgeoisie (Mao, 1954:150, 207, 209).

Mao even included the national bourgeoisie in the popular coalition during the period of national liberation. In the areas controlled by the Communists there was for some time a policy of limiting the Communists in the governing political bodies to one-third of the total number of representatives.

The political risk in this course of action was not especially great. Where the power rests in the hands of the revolutionary workers and peasants, the bourgeoisie, which is a remnant in the process of extinction, can do no serious harm even in positions of (joint) leadership. The direction and the driving force of the revolution will not be impeded and the transition may be facilitated (see Schram, 1967:236-44, 247).

Mao thus found it possible to work with (1) businessmen who were themselves victims of imperialism, at least to the extent that they were willing to oppose it and work against it; and (2) businessmen and others who were willing to unite against the foreign invader for patriotic reasons.

Fortunately, Mao did not trust the national bourgeoisie too far. When the big bourgeoisie went over to the counter-revolutionary camp, the national bourgeoisie followed suit (Mao, 1954:55). Mao remarked: "The Chinese national bourgeoisie is extremely flabby politically and economically, and is prone to compromise with the enemy of the revolution" (ibid.: 20).

## "INTERNATIONALISM": CHINESE VERSION

"Internationalism" in the West having been so long identified with the national interests of the Soviet Union, one turns to the Chinese writings on the subject with special interest. Has Mao Tse-tung or have the Chinese produced an overall theory that would find a function for "internationalism" in an operational sense?

The question was discussed by Mao in 1938. He wrote:

Can a Communist, who is an internationalist, at the same time be a patriot? We hold that he not only can be but must be. The specific content of patriotism is determined by historical conditions. There is the "patriotism" of the Japanese aggressors and of Hitler, and there is our patriotism. Communists must resolutely oppose the "patriotism" of the Japanese aggressors and of Hitler. The Communists of Japan and Germany are defeatists with regard to the war being waged by their countries. To bring about the defeat of the Japanese aggressors and of Hitler by every possible means is in the interest of the Japanese and German people, and the more complete the defeat the better . . . China's case, however, is different, because she is the victim of aggression. Chinese Communists must therefore combine patriotism with internationalism. We are at once internationalists and patriots, and our slogan is, "Fight to defend the motherland against the aggressors." For us defeatism is a crime and to strive for victory in the War of Resistance is an inescapable duty. For only by fighting against the aggressors can we defeat the aggressors and achieve national liberation. And only by achieving national liberation will it be possible for the proletariat and other working people to achieve their own emancipation. The victory of China and the defeat of the invading imperialists will help the people of other countries. Thus in wars of national liberation patriotism is applied internationalism. (Mao, 1967:110)

This is the argument made familiar by the Russians.

The same argument, but emphasizing the international obligations of the Chinese proletariat along with those of the proletariats of Japan and the West, was made in the following year in these terms:

We must unite with the proletariat of Japan, Britain, the U.S., Germany, Italy and all other capitalist countries, before it is possible to overthrow imperialism, to liberate our nation and people, and to liberate the other nations and peoples of the world. This is our internationalism, the internationalism with which we oppose both narrow nationalism and narrow patriotism. (Ibid.:111)

The argument that internationalism consists in defending the interests of the Soviet Union was presented in an impassioned form in a pamphlet of November 1948 against Tito and the Yugoslavs by Liu Shao-chi. The pamphlet was entitled *Internationalism and Nationalism*. It author, Liu Shao-chi, was at the time a member of the Political Bureau of the Central Committee of the Communist Party of China, and stated the official position of the Party:

> If ... the Communists ... reject the international solidarity of the proletariat and the working people and oppose the Socialist Soviet Union, then all this is a betrayal of the proletariat and of Communism. ...
>
> To declare as the Tito-ites do that the same attitude should be adopted toward the Soviet Union and the New Democracies, led by the Communist Parties, as is adopted in relation to imperialist countries—this is but the outcome of betrayal of the principles of Marxism-Leninism, a betrayal of proletarian internationalism and of switching over to a bourgeois-nationalist position. (Liu, 1948)

Yet Peoples' China had perforce adopted the position here described as bourgeois, of putting its interests ahead of those of the world revolution, from the time that it emerged as an independent government. The fact that the attitude toward the Soviet Union has changed, and the definition of patriotism and internationalism also, merely underlines the point made by Mao that the definition of patriotism (and internationalism) varies according to the time and place. Mao still insisted that there are moral principles in international relations. He wrote: "The people who have triumphed in their own revolution should help those still struggling for liberation. This is our internationalist duty" (ibid.:111). The principle here enunciated is one that Marxists must endorse; they must however also recognize, if they wish to be realistic, that there are limits to the implementation of this principle by any particular socialist state, limits imposed by considerations of national interest.


## THE PROBLEM OF THE MINOR NATIONALITIES
## SINCE LIBERATION

Sun Yat-sen, the "father" of Chinese nationalism, was at first inclined toward the assimilationist point of view; he thought of the Han, the preponderant nationality group in China, as the "big brothers" of the minor nationalities. However, when he established relations with the Russian revolutionaries and the Communist International, he took over the idea of the equality of nationalities, and this idea is found in the 1924 Manifesto of the Kuomintang (KMT).

Sun, to be sure, was not any more rigorous in defining

self-determination than his opposite numbers in the West—if anything less so. He believed that peoples are arranged in natural families, and that the weaker peoples should be protected by the central government "to make them capable of self-determination and self-government." This provision was retained in the KMT manifesto (Herrfahrdt, 1950:134-35).

Whether Sun would have showed the same restraint in dealing with the minor nationalities inside China as Lenin did in Russia is doubted by some. But it is certain that the kind of government Sun advocated was not as highly centralized as that which the Kuomintang later tried to introduce. Loyalty to the nation, as Sun saw it, did not take precedence over loyalty to the family and the clan; he saw all three loyalties as desirable, in contrast with the situation in the West, where loyalty to the nation was put ahead of everything.

Communist rule appeared in Mongolia (then called "Outer Mongolia") when the Bolsheviks established control over the old tsarist Empire. Bands of counter-revolutionary cavalry retreated from Siberia into Outer Mongolia and continued to conduct raids onto Soviet territory. The government at Peking could not control the situation, so Red army cavalry units were dispatched into Outer Mongolia. Having cleaned out the nests of counter-revolutionaries they then proceeded to set up a government in Outer Mongolia, which was in fact independent of the rather shadowy authority of Peking. Later this independence was recognized by the Soviets and eventually by other countries, including China.

The Chinese Communists in the 1930s accepted the Russian point of view on the border provinces. In 1931 the First All-China Congress of Soviets, at Juichin, still strongly under the influence of the Communist International and the Soviet Union, declared that the Chinese Soviet Republic "categorically and unconditionally recognizes the right of national minorities to self-determination"; they should have the option of joining the Union of Soviet Republics, or forming an autonomous area within the Chinese Soviet Republic, or being an independent state. The independence of the Outer Mongolian National Republic must be defended, continued the resolution (Moseley, 1966:165). At the same time Sun Yat-sen's "so-called 'nationalism'" was repudiated, on the ground that it fully satisfied the interests of the landlords and bourgeoisie (ibid.:164).

After Liberation, the question of the national minorities was of great importance to People's China. They formed only 6 percent of the population, but the area they inhabited was over half of the total extent of People's China.

With regard to minority nationalities within China, the CPC from the beginning adopted a Leninist policy. At its Second Congress (1922) it issued a manifesto proposing to set up China proper, including Manchuria, as a single republic, and the three regions of Mongolia, Tibet, and Turkestan as autonomous regions; all of these would then unite voluntarily in a federal republic of China (Moseley, 1966:48). Later the number of autonomous regions was increased to five by the inclusion of the Hui (Chinese Moslems in Ningsia, in the Northwest) and the Uighurs (Turkic tribes in Sinkiang).

National regional autonomy was practiced perforce during the Anti-Japanese War (ibid.:54). Chang Chih-i, the Party specialist on the national question who produced the first systematic discussion of the subject in 1956, states that the minorities at first were not fully integrated into the Chinese nation, but became so integrated as the result of the aggressions of the imperialists (ibid.:42-44). This statement is questioned by Chang's translator and American editor, George Moseley, who says that on the contrary the border peoples rendered no assistance during the War of Resistance, but retained a profound distrust of the Han (ethnic Chinese); they showed an almost complete lack of revolutionary enthusiasm (Moseley, 1966:16, 44).

The Constitution of 1955 declares war on both "dominant-nation chauvinism" and "local nationalism," recalling the long-standing, double-barreled policy of the Soviet Union (Para. 5 of Preamble). It restates that all nationalities are equal, but does not specify any "right of self-determination"; instead we read that the national autonomous areas are "inalienable" parts of the People's Republic of China. Discrimination against, or oppression of, any nationality, and acts that undermine the unity of the nationalities, are prohibited (Art. 3 of Ch. 1, General Principles of the Constitution; see Moseley, 1966:169-70).

How large should the unit be in which nationality rights are exercised? It was at first thought that each *hsiang* (township) should practice regional autonomy. Only after some 1,000 of these nationality *hsiang* had been established was it realized that the unit was too small. So, the *hsiang* no longer exists as a formal administrative unit (ibid.:95-96).

The Central Institute for Nationalities was established in Peking in 1957. Its task is to train students from the minority areas for leadership and to instill in them a sense of their own cultural identity (*New York Times,* July 31, 1972). Some forty-eight minorities are represented in the institute. About ten similar institutes have been set up in other parts of the country.

The largest single non-Han nationality in China, by far, are the Chuang of Kwangsi, in Southwest China. They number more than ten million, nearly half of the population of their autonomous region. There appears to be no special effort to build up the Chuang as a separate culture. Schools are conducted in the language of the Chuang, but Chinese is the second language even in elementary school (*New York Times,* Oct. 28, 1973). At the same time there is no intention of having the Chuang die out. As is the case in other minority regions, the government is not pressing in Kwangsi the birth control policy generally encouraged in the rest of China, and the Chuang population is increasing rapidly.

The Mongol language and culture are being carefully preserved. Although the Mongols themselves are only a very small minority in the population of the Autonomous Region of Inner Mongolia (420,000 out of more than eight million; the total number of Mongolians in China outside of Mongolia is about 1,600,000) (*New York Times,* Oct. 28, 1973), they are guaranteed 18 percent representation on all administrative bodies. This quota is set in accordance with the general policy of according appropriate representation to each national minority at every level of state administration (Moseley, 1966:96).

Some of the minority peoples had lived in highly stratified societies, and the policy of the Communist Party of China was not to attack the ruling strata with premature demands for equality and the introduction of socialism, but to win the cooperation of the religious and nationality leaders while recruiting for the Party at the mass level (Moseley, 1966:17). As Chang put it, the people must take their own time; "if the time is not ripe, then it must be awaited."

It is interesting to compare the Chinese policy regarding Tibet with the Soviet policy on Kazakhstan. It will be recalled that the Central Committee of the Soviet Communist Party had originally favored a go-slow policy for the Kazakhs. Stalin insisted on rapid denomadization and precipitated a major crisis in the area. The go-slow policy rejected by Stalin for the Kazakhs was actually followed in the 1950s in Tibet. The Chinese government agreed in 1951 that reforms would be carried out solely on the initiative of the Tibetan government (Moseley, 1966:153). But the crisis came anyway.

The Dalai Lama in 1959 attempted to force the issue and get rid of Chinese suzerainty altogether. This move, which was presumably encouraged from abroad, was resisted by the Chinese, who then decided that the time had come to modernize Tibet. The Dalai Lama was quickly defeated and took refuge in India. The Panchen Lama, who also enjoyed some religious authority, returned from Peking where he had been studying and announced that feudal serfdom would be abolished and other reforms introduced. Under the direction of the Peking government the lamaseries were closed, trade was stimulated, roads were built, and Tibet became integrated into the People's Republic of China. In 1959 there had been no schools at all in Tibet. By 1965 there were 1,600 primary schools in operation (Moseley, 1966:109).

Sinkiang has also been the scene of unrest. From the victory of the Chinese Revolution down to 1957 there was little friction, but in that year a campaign against localism was launched by Premier Chou En-lai. Economic development speeded up, and many Chinese (Han) immigrated to Sinkiang, so that by 1974 the Han reportedly comprised a majority of the population. Pressure for assimilation increased, and met with some resistance (Moseley, 1966:2-3, 23). Finally in 1962, after an uprising in the Ili area, some 60,000 Kazakhs crossed the border into the Soviet Union (*New York Times*, Aug. 16, 1970). This group had initially migrated to Sinkiang in the aftermath of the 1916 uprising in Kazakhstan and during the upheavals attending collectivization in the 1930s. The Chinese authorities are said to have known about the mass migration in advance, and to have favored it up to a point.

Some years later, the Cultural Revolution brought a new situation (Sheehy, 1969:271-83). The Soviet press has carried stories at various times about the "discrimination" in Sinkiang not only against the Kazakhs, Kirghiz, and other peoples living mainly in Soviet territory, but also against the Uighurs, a Turkish people who at first were supposed to have constituted a majority of the population in Sinkiang. The Chinese have taken note of the accusations of the Russians, and a conference of the Sinkiang Revolutionary Committee, the administrative body of the autonomous region, called in 1970 for vigilance in combating the splitting activities of the Russian "counter-revolution-ists"; the goal, it declared, should be to "promote the great revolution-ary unity of people of all nationalities" (*New York Times,* Aug. 15, 1970). Taken in context, this would appear to mean more pressure for assimilation.

The Chinese have made one cardinally important discovery—on paper. A spokesperson wrote in 1956: "Only where big-Han nationalism has been energetically resisted and fundamentally overcome can the tendency toward local nationalism be satisfactorily overcome" (Moseley, 1966:153). But it was admitted that "Great-Hanism" per-sisted almost everywhere (ibid.:139-40). And the effect of this big-culture chauvinism has been to provoke resistance on the part of the local patriots (ibid.:37).

In China, as in the Soviet Union, carrying out the social revolution and modernization has involved terrific strains on the minority nationalities. The strains have been all the greater where the innovations were introduced on the initiative of the majority nationality. The fact that the social reorganization was accepted, that the border nationalities did not in the end break off from or create insurmountable problems for the center, is a measure of the acceptability of the innovations. Socialism has worked; and that fact has enabled the great socialist republics to avoid the fragmentation that has overtaken the exploitative capitalist empires.

In China, the Leninist nationality policy has been an outstanding success, but the road has sometimes been rocky. Resistance to the upheaval of social revolution and modernization sometimes took the form of organized nationalist obstruction and even of emigration or attempted secession. The revolutionary priorities of the larger state could not countenance either.

# 7

## Latin America:
## Nationalism or Revolution?[1]

Writers on Latin America have usually assumed that Latin America was going through the same stages of development traversed earlier by Europe, with respect to the development of nationalism and economic life in general. The long period of mining and plantation agriculture, during which the landowners dominated the state, is often referred to as Latin America's "feudal" period; this era is thought by some to have continued into the nineteenth century and even the twentieth century (see de Castro in Horowitz et al., 1969:243).

In support of the idea that Latin America had a feudal period it is possible to cite the Andean highlands (Peru and Bolivia), where certain customs grew up that were suggestive of feudal conditions. Peasants had to work the land of the landlord three to six days a week; they were obliged to perform certain services for the landlord without compensation; there was a corvée, under another name, for road work, and even a droit du seigneur, also under another name (see Patch in Silvert, 1963:114-15). The socioeconomic system in the Andean highlands was also similar to that in medieval Europe, as far as agriculture was concerned, in that there was little internal trade: transportation was so difficult that only a limited number of items were produced for a national or world market.

But the Andean system exhibited important differences from the European, too. The European serfs were tied to the land; they could not be evicted, and supposedly they could not leave. They enjoyed the protection of certain age-old customs that were supposed to be observed. The Andean peasants, by contrast, could be evicted, and had little or no protection in the form of customary rights. They were free to leave in theory, but could be brought back if they owed the landlord money, as they frequently did. This system is known as "peonage," or "debt slavery." It may be arguable whether the status of the peon was superior or inferior to that of the serf, but it was certainly not the same.

In another important respect, the system in all the Latin American colonies was far from feudal. European feudalism as a system was decentralized, whereas the colonies, although economically decentralized (except for the products of the mines and plantations), were highly centralized politically. During the period of Spanish rule, appointments had to be cleared all the way back to Spain (Véliz, 1968:69). This centralization persists today.

Conditions in the Andean highlands were semifeudal at most.[2] In Brazil and the Caribbean, where sugar plantations were worked on the basis of slavery, the system could not be called feudal at all, any more than in the South of the United States before the Civil War. The products of the mines and plantations were typically tied into the world market and the capitalist system in a most unfeudal way.[3]

The analysis of Latin American history as a rerun of European history continues with a supposed transition to a nation-state on the European model. For example, Kalman H. Silvert sees a middle sector in the class structure emerging with the growth of cities and some industrialization. "Where there are middle groups, there is nationalism," says Silvert. Industrial urbanism, he continues, implies stability and a high degree of interdependence. The various ethnic groups move toward greater integration with each other at the same time as their economic interdependence increases. Thus there emerges eventually the "truly national society" on the European model, with democracy as its favored political system. Needless to say, what is meant is capitalist democracy. Surprisingly, Silvert lists Cuba, along with Uruguay, Argentina, Costa Rica, and Chile as one of the countries that is "closest to nation-state standing" (Silvert, 1966:16-18; one suspects that the passage in question was written before 1959 and not revised in the 1966 edition).

If Latin America were really duplicating the development gone through earlier by Europe, we would expect to see the rising bourgeoisie in the cities, first commercial and later industrial, taking over the political power from the landed interests. We would expect to see this bourgeoisie use the nation-states to consolidate its control over the respective internal markets and to defend its interests abroad, in the manner described by Lenin. We would expect to see the emerging proletariat support the efforts of the bourgeoisie (up to a point) and follow its lead in abolishing "feudal remnants." We might even visualize Latin America entering a period of "take-off" into rapid industrial development and mass consumption, as contemplated by Walt Whitman Rostow. The bourgeoisie would meanwhile have consolidated its status with the masses by adopting social legislation as in Europe, and by extending the vote to the working and peasant population—the democracy contemplated by Silvert. Something like this model has evidently been in the minds of South American Communist parties that have followed the lead of what they take to be the "national class" (the bourgeoisie), and even in the minds of some further Left groups who thought they were following Lenin's analysis.

It is of course true that the formerly absolute power of the landed interests, the *latifundistas,* has been curbed and superseded, in a struggle still not fully concluded. It is true that certain popular leaders have emerged—such as Cárdenas in Mexico, Perón in Argentina, and (for a time) Vargas in Brazil—who have played up to the masses of the people and even adopted some progressive laws. Latin America is not the hopelessly backward, totally undeveloped area that is sometimes pictured. And these developments had quite evidently been connected with urbanization, with the rise of the middle classes and the emergence of a kind of proletariat. Nationalism, both in the sense of loyalty to a particular nation-state and in the sense of economic and social integration, has arisen and will rise still further, by all indications.

One cardinally important element is all but lacking in Silvert's analysis, however: the role of the imperialists. The real power in Latin America was exercised from abroad in the days of Spanish and Portuguese domination, and still is so exercised in these days of economic colonialism, though by a different imperialist power or powers. There can be no nationalism worthy of the name that does not challenge this foreign rule and seek to return to the people control over their own resources and participation in the administration of their respective countries and economies.[4]

Aníbal Quijano has argued that there is no nationalist anti-imperialist bourgeoisie in Latin America, and there is not likely to be one in the absence of a strong anti-imperialist movement on the part of the dominated masses (Quijano, 1971:115). And Claudio Véliz asserts that the "industrial bourgeoisie" relied on by Silvert to lead the nationalist movement does not exist, or in any case, cannot or will not oppose the wishes of the foreign industrialists (Véliz, 1968:74, 81-83). James Petras suggests that Latin American bourgeois nationalism once had a "moral fibre" that sustained it for half a century. But Petras agrees with Véliz and Quijano that for the Latin American bourgeoisies today, the "national question" is subordinate to the "class question": for most Latin governments it is preferable to accommodate U.S. paramountcy in the hemisphere rather than risk any popular mobilization that might undermine their own social hegemony (Petras, 1966:63).

Silvert is on fairly safe ground when he says that nationalism has been the work of the middle class. But what is this "middle class" in Latin America? It includes the traditional small shopkeeper group and any number of petty traders and probably white-collar workers as well as the upper bourgeoisie, the professionals, and the intellectuals. In the absence of any considerable concentration of industrial workers, this petty bourgeoisie is likely to furnish the mass base of the Latin American demagogues. To look on the "middle class" as an undifferentiated whole can lead to nothing but confusion.

Instead of confining ourselves to generalizations, we should describe briefly the experience of certain key countries where the nationalist and socialist movements have arisen in recent years, with varying results—Brazil, Cuba, and Bolivia.

## BRAZIL:
## DISASTROUS RESULTS OF WRONG POLICY

The Brazilian Communist Party (PCB), founded in 1922, was at first committed to a revolutionary policy. In 1935, it attempted to seize power by a coup, but popular support was not nearly great enough. The Party has been illegal throughout most of its history, except in 1945–1947, but has long since abandoned its revolutionary line. As the only national political party appealing directly to labor, its policies have a certain importance.

The PCB, and the Brazilian Left generally, have showed a persistent tendency to follow the lead of various nationalist groups that were not anticapitalist, though they sometimes appeared so. It is revealing, we believe, to recapitulate some of the history of these nationalist groups, while showing why they could not be expected to offer a real challenge to neocolonialism.

Brazil's economy depended for many years on the export first of sugar and cacao, produced with slave labor, then, after slavery was abolished in 1889, of coffee. As late as 1930 the economy was semi-colonial, with little manufacturing and no heavy industry. Since then, manufacturing has grown by leaps and bounds, and has even come to include a heavy industry based on local ores. By 1965 over half the population lived in cities, compared with 20 percent in 1930. The industrial working class numbers two and a half million, and there are five million other wage earners (Morray in Petras and Zeitlin, 1968:104).

Manufacturing was established partly with local capital, contributed by the old landed interests, and partly with foreign capital. Industry has also grown through the reinvestment of earnings.

There was no traditional rivalry between the landowners and the rising bourgeoisie (Petras, 1968:162). After the abolition of slavery, the plantation owners even participated in the early beginnings of manufacturing industry, putting up the capital for the establishment in the Northeast of cotton mills for the fabrication of the cotton that was produced there, and in São Paulo of jute mills to make the jute sacks in which the coffee was packed and shipped. Thus, Caio Prado, points out, "The agrarian and industrial sectors of the Brazilian economy, and hence the managers and beneficiaries of these sectors, the bourgeoisies of each, are intimately interlaced, and their respective interests are united" (Prado, Jr., 1966:182).

The rural plantation owners are similar to urban industrialists in that the large operators, the ones who produce the bulk of the marketable crop, are actually employers of labor on a large scale. They are a subdivision of the *same class* as the big traders and the industrialists of the city. The raising of the sugar cane, for example, and its conversion into sugar at the "central," are all under the management of a single enterprise, frequently employing hundreds of workers. It is true that in some of the backward areas, relations between the patrons and the working force can be found that recall the early master-and-slave relations out of which they have grown (peonage, company towns, and so forth). But such phenomena are found under capitalism elsewhere, too, and are due to the isolation of the enterprises concerned rather than to a difference of system (ibid.:162-63).

The landed proprietors frequently join occupations other than those of agriculture and stock raising; they are bank directors, merchants, and small manufacturers, thus illustrating in their own persons the intermingling of the rural and urban bourgeoisie in a single class (see Cohn in Ianni, 1965:132).

The big landowners are usually pictured in the literature of the Left as being reactionary—which no doubt they are as a group, though not more so than the urban bourgeoisie proper—and as being linked in some special way with imperialism (Ianni, 1964a:51-52). But there is no good reason in theory for singling them out in this regard. They are not especially tied in with imperialism; for the most part they are ignorant of it, or if they come in contact with it they are inclined to be hostile to it rather than otherwise. The coffee planters or the cattle raisers who sell their output to the English and American firms are not more favorably disposed toward them for that reason—on the contrary (Prado, 1966:164-72).

The traditional rivalry between the landowners as exporters, eager for cheap goods to be imported from abroad for them to buy, and the manufacturers, seeking to protect themselves against foreign goods competing with their own products, can be noted in Brazil, but the manufacturers do not speak with a single voice; many of them are agents or fabricators for foreign firms, and do not dare to oppose the imperialist interests. Hence they are against the protective tariff. They are also against government regulations of business; hence they are known as the "non-interventionists."

The extent of the foreign control of Brazilian business is greater than appears on the surface. Not only have there been heavy direct and portfolio investments in industrial and commercial enterprises, but a substantial amount of domestic capital has been mobilized in foreign-controlled investment trusts. Already before the military takeover of 1964, which consolidated the position of the "non-interventionists," it was estimated that foreign interests controlled 40 percent of Brazilian industry, and the proportion has since become substantially higher (see Prado, 1966:135; Galeano, 1969:11-30).

While foreign investment as such has been welcomed by the Brazilian bourgeoisie, there has always been an element which was opposed to too great foreign control of the economy, and which sought to counter it by building up the influence of the state as such. This interest included businessmen who got orders from government departments, or who carried out construction on government contract, or who used their connections with the government to carry out financial trans-actions—people who generally sought to increase the degree of public intervention in the economy. This group, known as the "bureaucratic capitalists," had enlisted some popular support under the leadership of Getulio Vargas, until that statesman took his own life in 1954. In the decade that followed, the speaker for this point of view was the Instituto Superior de Estudos Brasileiros. Their approach may be studied in the writings of Celso Furtado, Helio Jaguaribe, and others; some of their works have been translated into English (Martins, 1970:IV:156). They were nationalists but not socialists; they would perhaps be clasified as state-capitalists. The PCB, and the Left in general, carried on their own respective campaigns against imperialism. As between the "non-interventionists" and the "bureaucratic capitalists," they were strongly in favor of the latter, but overestimated the extent of the "bureaucrats' " anti-imperialism.

The leftists' policy of strengthening the "national bourgeoisie" which was supposed to be opposing the entry of foreign capital could not succeed as long as there was no effective group of domestic businessmen ready to substitute themselves for the foreigners, and there was none. The alliance with the "bureaucratic capitalists" confused the proletariat and brought no gains to the Left (Cohn in Ianni, 1965: 147-48, 150-52).

The complete inability of any section of the middle class to take a stand against the reactionary military was demonstrated in 1964. The workers and the poor peasants have received no benefit from the spectacular "development" that has since taken place. They continue to suffer in grinding poverty.

Yet the massive unrest among the peasants of the Northeast in the 1960s showed that the perspective of a coalition of workers and peasants to bring about socialism on a national, anti-imperialist basis in Brazil was by no means unthinkable. This is the solution advocated, from various angles, by writers as different as Gunder Frank (1969), Caio Prado, Jr. (1966), and Régis Debray. Excessive concentration on the nationalist objective has so far blurred the necessity of building a firm basis in the class interests of the workers and peasants.

## NATIONALISM AND SOCIALISM IN CUBA

Fidel Castro, like Friedrich Engels and Mao Tse-tung before him, was a nationalist before he was a socialist. While he was training for the law, and until long after the assault on the Moncada Barracks (July 26, 1953), Castro's hero was not Marx or Lenin but José Martí, the Cuban patriot who helped organize the revolt against Spain in the early 1890s and was killed in action in 1895. Martí was a staunch anti-imperialist and had a program of reform that would perhaps be called populist, but without a Marxist class analysis. Similarly, Castro's famous speech "History Will Absolve Me," delivered in court on the occasion of his trial after the July 26th movement had failed, refers repeatedly to "the people" but not at all to the working class. This terminology was still used by Castro even after his adoption of Marxism as a philosophy (Fagen, 1972:35).

But of course both Martí and Castro had plenty to say about the workers and peasants as revolutionaries. Castro said, in his 1953 statement:

The people we counted on in our struggle were these:
Seven hundred thousand Cubans without work . . .
Five hundred thousand farm laborers . . . who work four
months of the year and starve during the rest . . .
Four hundred thousand industrial laborers and stevedores . . .
One hundred thousand small farmers . . . working on land that
is not theirs . . .
Thirty thousand teachers and professors who are so devoted,
dedicated and necessary to the better destiny of future genera-
tions and who are so badly treated and paid.
Twenty thousand small business men . . .
Ten thousand young professionals: Doctors, engineers,
lawyers, veterinarians, school teachers, dentists, pharmacists,
newspapermen, painters, sculptors, etc. . . . (Castro, 1968:41-42)

The Cuban Revolution was not a class revolution in the traditional
sense. According to James O'Connor, the program under which Batista
came to power (for the second time) in 1952 was not very different
from the program of the July 26th movement. Land for the peasants,
protection for the workers, redistribution of the wealth in favor of the
underprivileged, industrialization, the development of education—these
were announced aims of the demagogic Batista, on the basis of which
he was able to secure the support not only of middle-class elements but
of the Communist-led labor movement, whose leaders actually participated in the Batista government. Later, when it became apparent
that Batista had no intention of carrying out those parts of his announced program that were distasteful to the United States, the labor
leaders had been compromised in the eyes of the masses. But they still
retained their grip on the unions and Castro had to deal with them and
eventually even take them into his own government.

Neither in his program nor in the people to whom he appealed was
Castro oriented to a real social revolution, at first. But whereas Batista's
followers were grafters and opportunists, ready to compromise on
principle for the sake of retaining power, Castro meant business. And
when it turned out that his announced aims were not attainable within
the limits of Cuba's neocolonial status, Castro insisted on pushing
through not only the previously announced objectives but a still more
radical program, without which the earlier, more modest aims could not
have been won.

It was the middle peasant, not the poor peasants or kulaks, who gravitated to the Castro movement. Let Che Guevara describe the peasantry encountered by the revolutionists in the Sierra Maestra:

> The Sierra Maestra . . . is a place where peasants struggling bare-handed against latifundism took refuge. They went there seeking a new piece of land—somehow overlooked by the state or the voracious latifundists—on which to create a modest fortune. They constantly had to struggle against the exactions of the soldiers, who were always allied to the latifundists; and their ambition extended no farther than a property deed. Concretely, the soldiers who belonged to our first peasant-type guerrilla armies came from the section of this social class which shows most strongly love for the land and the possession of it; that is to say, which shows most perfectly what we can define as the petty-bourgeois spirit. *The peasant fought because he wanted land* for himself, for his children, to manage it, sell it, and get rich by his work. (Guevara, 1967:29; emphasis added)

Castro and Guevara began with Cuban nationalism and a program that was democratic in the conventional sense. Socialism was added later, forced on them by the logic of the situation, as Leo Huberman and Paul Sweezy with rare prescience predicted would be the case. If the peasantry followed their lead, this was partly for the reason just cited, because they wanted the land. But it has to be remembered also that Cuba as a whole was a country with a relatively high level of political sophistication, so that elements which had not been reached at first responded later to the nationalist, socialist, and democratic slogans. Also, an important part of the rural population, the cane cutters, who were significant in the later if not in earlier stages of the revolution, were wage earners and not either large or small landowners.

But of the eighty-two men who sailed in the *Granma* to conquer Cuba (1956) not one was from a proletarian or peasant background (Guevara, 1969:28). The little group that survived the landing and took refuge in the Sierra Maestra had at first no agrarian program, and did not understand the psychology of the city workers either. The latter for their part did not understand or follow the Castro movement; the general strike called by Castro for April 9, 1958, was a failure, at least in Havana. The July 26th movement included some members who were in favor of making concessions to the United States in order to get and retain power for themselves—an orientation reminiscent of Batista. The movement had indeed no clear policy with regard to the rich. Even Guevara, who had some acquaintance with Marxism, was at first in favor of leaving the rich alone while helping the poor (ibid.:30).

The U.S. State Department, in adopting a hands-off policy when Castro was taking power, evidently hoped and assumed that the right wing within the July 26th movement would win out, and that U.S. interests in Cuba would not be disturbed.

Guevara, of course, had other ideas. He noted that the movement had at first no agrarian program, and really no mass base. But its contacts with the peasants presently led it to base itself on the peasants, for whom a real program was adopted. The peasants, completely disenchanted with the treatment they were receiving from Batista's regime, began to join the guerrilla army. It was then that Guevara worked out his philosophy according to which the vanguard of the people was the Rebel army, composed mainly of peasants. The army could be used to politicize and mobilize the people (ibid.:15).

The July 26th movement had thus a mixed class base, and the division between it and the Batista forces was not along clear class lines. Nearly every organized economic class was divided. In 1962, after his forces had taken power, Castro said that no rich people had supported the revolution, which may have been true, but when he continued with the statement that the participants in the revolution were workers and peasants, he was on more questionable ground. In Santiago de Cuba the movement was indeed predominantly working class; in the Sierra Maestra it was dominated by middle peasants; but in Havana it was more middle class. The sugar workers, Cuba's numerically strongest group, were not in the base of the rebellion at all; and the small sugar producers who were producing more than half of Cuba's cane in 1958 had hardly been touched by the movement (O'Connor, 1970:28, 42-43). "In town and country, revolutionary-minded intellectuals, students and professionals constituted the leadership" (ibid.:44).

The element in the July 26th movement that was ready to compromise with U.S. interests lost ground during the period in the Sierra. In the end, it was the nationalist issue that most clearly divided the forces led by Batista and Castro, respectively. Batista was clearly not going to take a stand for Cuban independence from U.S. influence. The forces of Cuban nationalism rallied to Castro. "Nationalism was one issue that bound together the diverse elements engaged in the struggle with

Batista" (ibid.:52). Guevara was a proletarian internationalist, but as against U.S. capital he was a Cuban nationalist (ibid.).

The class struggle, which had not been clearly evident in the early phases of the revolution, now emerged after Castro's victory. The moderates in the revolutionary government would have liked to see the leadership in the fight against U.S. domination taken by a unified, progressive national middle class; but there was no such class. The political initiative shifted to the Left, and the anti-imperialist struggle was conducted with the backing of the elements most interested in preserving and extending the gains of the revolution, namely, the workers and peasants (ibid.:53). The Cuban Revolution, which had begun as a kind of palace revolution as far as the masses of the population were concerned, now became a bona fide social revolution.

There ensued a confrontation with U.S. interests and with the U.S. government, in which the independence of Cuba was preserved by the intervention of the Soviet Union. Cuba, from having been an economic colony of the United States, became associated with the Soviet Union diplomatically and economically. When the Soviet army occupied Czechoslovakia in 1968, Castro put out a statement endorsing the step, a move that some European Communist parties refused to follow. In 1972 Cuba became a full member of the Soviet-sponsored Council for Mutual Economic Assistance (Comecon). Cuba thus pledges itself to a long-range program of economic integration with the Soviet bloc; economic plans will be fully coordinated within fifteen or twenty years.[5]

Under Russian advice, the export of cane sugar, which had been de-emphasized perforce when Cuba lost its principal customer, the United States, has been resumed full scale; over six million tons are produced annually, mostly for export, with the Soviet Union as the principal customer.

Internally, the stresses of the various crises of the 1960s would have disrupted a regime not firmly bound together by strong popular support. Socialism was a major element in securing this solidarity. Cuba's national independence was preserved by its socialist system. At the same time, the survival of the socialist system in Cuba was possible only because of the people's passionately felt nationalism.

The unity displayed by the Cubans, after the departure of some tens of thousands of counter-revolutionists (*gusanos*) was indeed remarkable, especially when it is remembered that the country is racially heterogeneous. The number of persons of African descent in Cuba is a matter of dispute; perhaps Raúl Castro's figure of two million Afro-Cubans (in a population of seven million) will do as well as any. (Other estimates say that as many as two-thirds of the population have some African ancestors.)

The black slaves have been called the original Cuban nationalists. Like the whites, they revere the memory of José Martí, who was strongly against any kind of racism. In the struggle within the Castro movement after the assumption of power, race was an issue; Castro's firm stand against discrimination won out and what segregation there had been was eliminated. The army, and also the national militia, formed in the missile crisis of 1962, have been predominantly black. There are some who maintain that there are too few blacks in the top leadership of the regime, but this point of view is disputed by others. The most that can be said in criticism of the Castro leadership on this point is that it has not been as insistent on building up the self-esteem of its ethnic minority as some followers of Lenin in Eastern Europe. (For two points of view on the position of the blacks in Cuba see More, 1964; Depestre, 1965).

Castro and the Soviet leaders differed sharply on the possibility of bringing about a social revolution quickly in all of Latin America. Guevara took a rather extreme line on this issue. In 1963 he was saying that liberation would be achieved only by a continental struggle. Four years later the whole underdeveloped world had to be won if socialism was to survive anywhere. In Guevara's last statement, his message to the Tricontinental Congress (April 1967), he said that the anti-imperialist revolution would be forced on one country after another, and after "two, three, many Vietnams" final victory would be achieved.

He did believe that continental revolution in South America was the order of the day, and he set out to launch it in Bolivia. The tragic consequences of that venture are well known. The question is, did Bolivian nationalism (as some contend) frustrate the enterprise? Or were there other reasons for the failure?

## BOLIVIA: NATIONALISM AND REVOLUTION

Late in 1966 Guevara and a small group of Cubans arrived in Bolivia and set up a base camp on the Nancahuazú River, which flows down the eastern slope of the Andes.

By the following June, the guerrilla movement had been completely defeated and dispersed, and Guevara himself had been captured and killed.

According to a widely disseminated interpretation of this episode, the failure of the movement was due primarily to the nationalist sentiment provoked in Bolivia by the fact that the leadership of the movement was Cuban. In our opinion this version does not correspond to the facts, and it is important that it be refuted. In order to understand the real reasons for Guevara's failure, we must glance at the background of Bolivia, with an eye to the nature of Bolivian nationalism. Some aspects of this nationalism illustrate a type, and are highly instructive. Other aspects are unique, which gives the study of nationalism in Bolivia a special importance.

Bolivia is a landlocked area in the high Andes. It has long been known to possess great mineral riches. Its mines—first of silver and then of tin—have yielded fortunes to a few; the silver city Potosí was at one time the largest city in South America. But with the decline of silver mining, the area fell far behind the rest of the continent in economic development. The infertile, remote territory, although twice the size of France, has a population well under 4,000,000.

Perhaps more than anywhere else in Latin America, conditions in the Bolivian hinterland smacked of feudalism. The dominance of the landlord in Bolivia was a comparatively recent development. The traditional method of farming was by *ayllus* or village collectives, which lasted in certain areas from pre-Columbian times down to the 1880s; the *latifundia* were not fully developed until well into the twentieth century (Malloy and Thorn, 1971:124).

Before 1952, Bolivia was not a nation in the usual sense of the term. Too large a proportion of the population was isolated, unself-conscious; deep class and cultural differences precluded national solidarity (Malloy, 1970:339; Asturias, 1968:52). Such nationalism as existed was an affair of the ruling class, or at most of the middle class. For the peasants, the government and the army were hostile elements, in league with their exploiters.

Daniel Salamanca became President of Bolivia in 1930, as the world-wide depression was setting in. Frustrated in his attempt to reactivate the economy by inflation and manipulation of the currency, he turned to external war, against Paraguay, with the idea (among others) of using the patriotic outpouring to keep himself in power.

The result was entirely unexpected. Paraguay proved to be more than a match for the Bolivian troops, who had been forced into the army and showed little interest in the fighting. But the Bolivian Indians came in touch, in the army, with a whole new set of ideas. The Quechuan-speaking Indians developed a sense of ethnic solidarity which they had not known since the days of Túpac Amaru (1780). On returning to their respective *fincas* (estates) as laborers and tenants, they did not forget their new-found solidarity. They maintained contact with one another and began to set up *sindicatos,* somewhat similar to unions but devoted to the struggle for land (see Patch in Silvert, 1963:111-12). The Chaco War brought the Bolivian Indians into the twentieth century. The war was lost and national patriotism was forgotten but ethnic and class solidarity survived, and crystalized around the struggle to break up the big landed estates.

When, in 1952, a movement under the leadership of a section of the elite set out to take over the government and organized a National Revolutionary Movement, *Movimiento Nacional Revolucionario* (MNR), with an advanced land-reform program, the peasants participated eagerly. The tin miners furnished radical leadership and important cadres, and a real revolutionary movement developed, based on the peasants and miners. Peasants occupied the *latifundia,* which were broken up and turned into small peasant properties. The tin mines were nationalized. Incredibly, the workers and peasants defeated and abolished the army. Observers were amazed at the way the workers and peasants developed their own competent leadership (Malloy, 1970: 334). A new electoral law enfranchised all citizens without regard to their literacy.

But the workers and peasants never really controlled the government, which remained in the hands of the middle-class *mestizos* (27 percent of the population); and these in turn remained closely tied to the United States. Bolivia continued to receive U.S. "aid" all through the period of the agrarian revolution and the nationalization of the tin mines. Presently the army was reorganized with the aid of U.S. advisers. The tin miners, perceiving what was happening, fought back with guns; but they were cut off from the rest of the country and defeated. By 1965, the waves of revolution had ebbed. The government even engaged the CIA to train a force of "Rangers" with the special task of guarding against leftist guerrillas.

Castro was following in 1966 a policy of fomenting anti-U.S., anti-imperialist revolutions throughout Latin America. The Cubans sought to establish guerrilla *focos* in the Andean countries. The guerrillas, they believed, would win the peasants to their side and set up revolutionary governments in one country after another; the revolution, starting in the south, would sweep north. It would have an international character. The natural leaders of the movement would be the Cubans, who had already showed the way with their own revolution.

It had originally been the Cuban intention to start the guerrilla movement in Argentina, but when difficulties developed there, the base of operations was shifted to Bolivia. The movement in Bolivia was originally organized by two Bolivians, the Peredo brothers, "Coco" and "Inti." They were internationalists, as was the whole movement. According to the French radical journalist Régis Debray, the Peredos invited Guevara to be their leader in the field. Guevara, who came originally from Argentina, had been in touch with the Communist movement in Bolivia for years and had friends in all of the several revolutionary groups. He accepted.

Guevara assumed that the glamor attaching to the Cuban Revolution would serve to overcome factional differences and that all groups would accept his leadership. As a result of this assumption, which turned out to be false, and of other miscalculations, Guevara lost his life.

It is axiomatic that a guerrilla movement, to succeed, must have the sympathy of the population. It must also have urban contacts that will assure it the necessary supplies. Guevara's expedition was in difficulties from the start because it did not have either of these prerequisites.

The peasants were not in a revolutionary mood—for reasons that we have outlined. The urban contact on whom Guevara most relied was Mario Monje. The Communist Party of Bolivia had just split. Monje was the leader of one group, which retained a pro-Soviet orientation, while a pro-Peking faction was led by Zamora. Monje and the Russians from whom he was taking advice were lukewarm about the whole idea of guerrilla warfare, as Castro and Guevara should have known. Monje also objected to the theory that a guerrilla movement, the *foco,* develops its program as it goes along, and this objection was well-founded.

It is evident that these reasons for Guevara's failure are related only distantly to Bolivian nationalism. That such nationalism did exist in the Bolivian Left is undoubted. Debray, who barely escaped with his life, has changed his theory. Socialism, he now says, must be combined with nationalism if it is to have meaning in Latin America today. At the same time, says Debray, nationalism without socialism is a snare and a delusion, and has nothing to offer the workers and peasants.

However, the real difference between Cuba, where the revolution succeeded, and Bolivia, where it failed, had to do not with Bolivian nationalism but with the counter-guerrilla forces, meaning the CIA. The mistakes of Guevara in Bolivia were no more serious, on balance, than the mistakes of Castro and Guevara in Cuba. If Guevara had been able to function on the Ñancahuazú with the same degree of freedom that Castro's group had enjoyed in the Sierra Maestra, these mistakes might have been overcome and an effective movement developed. As Inti Peredo put it:

> The first phase of any guerrilla struggle consists in the guerrillas being able to survive until they have taken deep roots among the people, mainly among the peasants. . . . In our own case, the newly established guerrillas were not able to surmount the first phase. (Peredo, 1968:80)

The Bolivian government, traditionally procrastinating and frequently corrupt, was under pressure from the U.S. government and the CIA. It dispatched 600 U.S.-trained Rangers to the Ñancahuazú district when it had been reliably reported that Guevara was there. Richard Gott, who was in the area when Guevara was killed and saw his body before it was buried, thinks that the Bolivian military intelligence would have been incapable of uncovering even the loosely organized urban network of the revolutionaries, and doubts that the Bolivians would have thought up the idea of sowing the guerrilla zone with soldiers dressed up as peasants (Gott, 1967:529). The CIA was much in evidence when Guevara was taken. It was even said that the order for his execution had come from the White House. Had the Yankees deliberately sought to stir up the peasants against the "foreigners," that is, the Cubans and Peruvians? If not, their astuteness was less than they have been credited with.

The importance of this anti-foreigner component in the peasants' outlook was probably not great. Even in the remote Ñancahuazú, the country people had begun to learn political sophistication, and if there was xenophobia in their psychology, in all likelihood it was against the CIA and the Americans who had reestablished the army and were working to introduce into Bolivia a regime in league with the international corporations.

The big difference between the situation in Bolivia and that in the successful Cuban movement was pointed out, by implication, in Guevara's own writings. Cuba, he said, benefited from "exceptional circumstances," and among these he listed first of all the fact that the United States misjudged the situation. They expected Batista to fall, but they did not expect to have any special difficulty in corrupting and managing Batista's successors. "When we were marching through the streets of Havana, it was already too late" (Guevara, 1967:28). Contrast the hands-off attitude of the United States toward the Castro movement in its early stages with the implacable antagonism of the American-directed antiguerrilla movement in Bolivia nine years later, and you have surely the key to the difference in the outcome.

The Communist Party of Bolivia (CPB) had been formed only in 1950. It took the position that the oppressed nationalities were the chief revolutionary force. The CPB included in its program a demand that the Quechuans, Aymarás, and other oppressed nationalities (it identified five large and several smaller ones) be set up as free nations (Ovando, 1961:103, 106-07).

Actually there was little sentiment among the Indians for the formation of separate nations. The several tribes cooperated well with one another. The Quechuans (36 percent of the population) took the lead in the movement to secure the land, and the Aymarás (24 percent of the population) joined the movement under the leadership of the tin miners. The peasants sought recognition as *campesinos* or rural people, not primarily as Indians (Patch in Silvert, 1963:111-12).

The CPB, having launched a policy of basing itself on the several nationality groups, naturally included in its platform a demand for education in the vernacular. Ironically, the Jesuits who dominated southern Paraguay in the seventeenth and eighteenth centuries had also stressed this policy. They were absolutely opposed to cultural assimilation and wanted to teach the Indians in their own language, Guaraní (Ovando, 1961:148). To assist this effort, they wrote down and standardized the Guaraní language, thinking that this step would help the Indians to learn the catechism and so aid in keeping the Indians under control (Baudin, 1962:48).[6]

The MNR government, too, has not opposed education in the vernacular. It seeks to integrate the Indians into the (capitalist) culture, a movement which it calls "castellization." The MNR sponsored a study of the several nationalities by Ernest Beaglehole of New Zealand, a strong advocate of integration. Literacy in one's own tongue, he found, does not interfere with integration since the literate Indians can learn Spanish much more readily (Ovando, 1961:151). The North Americans are alive to the possibilities of infiltrating the culture by way of castellization. So, a text in Quechuan for teaching children to read and write was developed at the University of Oklahoma (ibid.:140, 146). What then should be the Communist attitude toward an education which is national in form and capitalist in content?

The CPB, in concentrating its attention on ethnic issues, in which the peasants were less interested than in economic and political issues, was thus out of touch with the masses. The Party failed to furnish leadership in the 1952 revolution, and later took a lukewarm attitude to the Guevara guerrilla movement. Did its concentration on the issue of local nationalism have the effect of diverting its energies, such as they were, from more important things?


CONCLUSION


Latin America furnishes proof that Lenin's analysis—adopted by Stalin—of the class basis of nationalism is in need of reformulation. Nationalism, in the form of anti-imperialism, is widespread in Latin America. Imperialism in Latin America is, and has been for over a century, primarily *economic* imperialism rather than direct political control. The leadership in the campaign against this form of exploitation cannot be taken by the semicolonial bourgeoisie, which is deeply involved in the exploitative process and fears to jeopardize its own privileges. The rank and file of an anti-imperialist movement in Latin America must be the proletariat and sections of the peasantry. But the large, inchoate middle class in the cities contains elements which are probably also indispensable for a successful socialist-nationalist movement, and further analysis of this class is a must for Latin American Marxists.

In order to free itself of semicolonial exploitation, the anti-imperialist movement must be at the same time a socialist movement. Only for such a movement will the masses of the population make the necessary sacrifices—and only when they are satisfied that they will not be exchanging old masters for new ones. Hence the enormous importance of the Cuban Revolution.

# 8

## Social Classes and the Formation of Nations: Fanon, Cabral, and the African Liberation Struggle

It is when we turn to Africa that we feel most keenly the lack of an adequate theory of nationalism. Here were literally dozens of countries, with political independence already won or in the offing, with minimum integration and little consciousness of themselves as nations, seeking to establish an independent and (above all) self-conscious existence in a none-too-friendly world. Where should they look for guidance?

### COLONIALSM AND NATION-BUILDING

The problem of building nations was, for the Africans, in large part, a problem of amalgamating and eventually superseding tribes. The tribe is a kinship group, including typically a number of clans or gentes; it has as a rule a common language and a putative or magical common ancestor. A tribe may consist of only a few hundred members.[1] In primitive economic conditions, a tribe may increase until segments of it become independent of one another, and even fight one another. But a consciousness of common origin may persist, and in times of crisis, tribes with a common language and tradition often come together for joint action to meet the emergency.

The federation of tribes so formed has been variously denominated. J. S. Coleman, for instance, called each of the three large supertribal groups of Nigeria a "nationality," the term still used in East Europe for a linguistic group that is not constituted as a nation-state. But the African tribal federation is not the same as a European nationality, though it has points of similarity. French anthropologists, speaking of these federations, have leaned to the term *ethnie,* which is also descriptive of an ethnic group. Anthony Smith uses the same terminology (see A. Smith, 1971:162). The Soviet Africanist I. Potehkin, finding the field open, used the Russian term *narodnost,* and suggested that all tribes pass through the *narodnost* stage on the way to becoming nations (Potehkin, 1957-1958:62).

To be sure, some writers try to avoid the question of how a tribe becomes a nation by simply equating the tribe with the nation, or, perhaps we should say, equating tribalism in Africa with nationalism in Europe (Argyle in Gulliver, 1969:41-58). However, this approach breaks down on the question of size: a nation does have some minimum size (see ibid.: Intro., where the editor takes issue with his contributor). There is also a more decisive difference between a nation and a tribe: the nation is organized on the basis of territory, while the tribe is a kinship group.

The amalgamation of related tribes into a federation may take place under military pressure or by conquest. Thus, in South Africa in the 1820s Chaka, chief of the Zulu tribe, set out to bring all the Natal tribes under his rule. As A. T. Bryant described it:

> Independent tribes . . . ceased to be independent, the governing families were hounded out or exterminated, all the tribes without distinction were amalgamated and together they could be called the Zulu nation with Chaka at their head. (Cited in Wallerstein, 1966:564)

This "nation" or empire was indeed extensive; the Zulu army that took the field against the Dutch in 1838 was said to have included a million warriors.

It is also possible that the federation of tribes may be assembled peacefully. The Fang had been defeated and scattered by the Zulus in south central Africa; but they retained a common language and a common ancestry. At a certain point a number of leaders banded together to bring about a regroupment of the Fang. Their weapon was not military force but folklore.

Every one of the more than hundred and fifty Fang clans traced its origin to *Adzap Mboga,* the pierced Adzap tree. At first, concerned with certain questions of exogamy and other complications, the regroupment leaders were content to regroup no more than six clans into one unit, with a new name. Every clan had a migration legend, in which the pierced tree occupied a key position. This legend was revised and brought up to date, and in its revised form penetrated into every hamlet of the Fang area (northern Gabon and southern Cameroon). The authorities of Gabon and Spanish Guinea of that period (early 1950s) were well aware of what was happening, and would have liked to prevent their subject peoples from getting together, but it was too late (Fernandez in Wallerstein, 1966:587-90). The Fang had already become a self-conscious tribal federation—although this was one case where the federation, or *ethnie,* did not become the basis of a new nation.

Where a single *ethnie* (we shall use this term for the tribal federation) is large enough to constitute a nation, the old customs are not broken down to the same extent as they are in a multitribal state, and the persistence of such customs may be a drag on progress. The Somalis are a case in point. Somalia was constituted out of two colonies, Italian and British Somaliland. The *ethnie* inhabiting Somalia is indeed so extensive that it includes also large sections of the population of neighboring Ethiopia and Kenya. The very uniformity of the culture has given stability to the old tribal structure, in which the lineage is an important feature. The rivalries of various lineages have been a complicating factor in social and economic life; nepotism is rampant. Thus Somalia remains far from being a modern, integrated state (Lewis in Gulliver, 1969: 359 passim). It was partly on the ground that modernization was not proceeding fast enough that a military group took over the government in 1969.

I. M. Lewis goes so far as to argue that a state having a multiplicity of tribes may have a *better* chance to achieve a unifying, modern, national culture than monocultural Somalia (ibid.). But this is pushing the idea too far. The disastrous results of the imperialist policy of divide-and-rule in other colonies are plain for all to see. And even in the absence of direct imperial control, frictions among different cultural groups have resulted in a vast amount of bickering up to the point, in some cases, of civil war. Nigeria, which was wracked by an intertribal civil war in 1967–1970, is the most important illustration.

The tribal organization of African society also sets limits on the applicability of Western class theory. The tribe itself is classless in its internal organization; and since the tribe was the prevalent form of social organization in most of Africa until recently, it is perhaps not surprising that the myth of a "classless Africa" should have taken root.

Samir Amin, in an article that deserves to be more widely known, has challenged this idea (Amin, 1963). Amin points out that in many areas certain tribes held other tribes in subjection, the result being a caste system. Wherever an economic surplus emerged, some local group moved to appropriate it and institutionalize its flow into the group's own hands. According to Amin, great numbers of peasants in West Africa worked under conditions of semi-servitude; in Fouta at the bend of the Niger and in northern Nigeria, he puts the number in the millions (ibid.:53).

The land in Africa was usually held in common, but there still were great variations in the distribution of cattle among individual families. The cattle breeders formed a little aristocracy among the Moors, the Tuaregs, and certain Peuls.

The classless village community that is still found in certain areas has misled students of the African scene, says Amin. In some areas the village community was already in process of decomposition as early as the tenth century. Small states tended to form and to institutionalize a system of exploitation (ibid.: 51, 54). Some of the preconquest African states were based on slavery; a number are said to have been as ruthless in their exploitation as the Europeans who replaced them.

The appearance of the Europeans, their establishment of trading posts on the coast, and the growth and spread of the slave trade introduced new elements of inequality into "classless" Africa. In the rising cities, such as they were, free enterprise brought in its wake the incipient growth of classes. The ethnic groups also tended to develop class structures.

The African economy never developed feudalism in the European sense. When the Europeans started to exploit Africa as a source of raw materials and foodstuffs, they resorted to various kinds of forced labor to assemble the manpower for their mines and plantations. But these laborers were not serfs. They were not attached to the soil; on the contrary, the purpose of the forced labor arrangements was to pry them loose from the soil, in the interests of capitalist exploitation.

It is high time that historians, Marxist and otherwise, stop trying to fit Africa into the Procrustean bed of European development. African history has to be studied in its own terms. Nations have appeared in Africa as elsewhere in the world; but the modalities of their development and those of the Europeans are different. This is particularly the case because the African development has been perverted from the outside, by the very Europeans whose own development is so persistently held up as a model for the "backward" Africans.

Apologists for imperialism have put forward a whole series of specious arguments to prove that imperialism was really a benefit to the people of the colonial territories. Specifically with regard to the establishment of nations, Martin L. Kilson, Jr. has argued that colonialism prepared the way for the emergence of nations in three ways: the colonial powers established rigid political boundaries; they supplied a lingua franca; and they furnished a common culture. Let us see whether these claims can be substantiated.

With regard to the "rigid political boundaries" established by the colonial powers, these have proved to be rigid in certain cases only because they were backed by the armed forces of the colonial powers; even after "independence," some of the former French colonies have continued to rely on the French to protect their boundaries. Such boundaries, said Julius Nyerere, president of Tanzania, in a speech in 1963, are "ethnological and geographical nonsense." The Somalis, on the "horn" of Africa, won their independence in 1960. They found that their territory did not include Somali-inhabited areas in neighboring Ethiopia, Djibouti, and Kenya, areas to which they proceeded to lay claim. Nyerere, in the speech just quoted, did not mention that lack of religious unity complicated the problem of building a unified nation in areas like the Sudan and Chad, where civil wars broke out after independence and dragged on for many years. Religion was a factor in the large-scale Nigerian civil war of 1937–1940.

Even where a colony did possess some ethnic unity, this might be disrupted by shifts in the power relations of the Europeans. The Cameroons were at first a German colony; but after World War I the colony was split, with one part being assigned to France and another to England. The wishes of the natives were not consulted. The Cameroonians carried on a long campaign for reunification, partly by armed movements; but it was 1961 before they secured the setting up of Cameroon as a state.

The claim that the colonial power supplied a lingua franca must be judged in light of the fact that this lingua might change, as in the case just cited.[2] Some of the colonies already had a lingua franca of their own, as in East Africa; Swahili became the official language of Tanzania soon after independence, although it is not a tribal language but a hybrid import that had taken hold in the precolonial period. The language of the colonial power has been continued in most of the former colonies faute de mieux; if it provides a measure of unity to the new state, it also gives a big advantage to the imperialists who seek to perpetuate the Europeans' privileges in the system of neocolonialism.

As for the "common culture" that Kilson supposes the Europeans to have provided, we note that two of the colonial powers, Belgium and Portugal, made no effort to share their cultures with the colonized. On the contrary, they sought to keep European culture from the indigenous people of the colonies. The attempts of the British and French to substitute their culture for those of the African peoples have given rise to some of the bitterest denunciations of the whole colonial system.

Kilson's claim that colonialism prepared the way for the emergence of nations is altogether misleading. Indeed, it can be argued that the irruption of the Europeans into African affairs *postponed* the development of modern, integrated nations.

> The development of African peoples was abruptly cut short and their civilisation (which, in several places, had reached a highly advanced state) was most completely destroyed. These nations were later declared pagan and savage, an inferior race, destined by the Christian God to be slaves to superior Europeans. (From the resolution on the Negro Question of the First International Congress of the League against Imperialism and Colonial Oppression, held in Brussels, Feb. 10-15, 1927; quoted by Hodgkin in Owen and Sutcliffe, 1972:100; for historical data see Davidson, 1970)

Actually, political instability is to be expected in countries emerging from colonialism, argues James O'Connell of Ahmadu Bello University in Nigeria. Colonialism, he says quite justly, transmitted an authoritarian tradition: it shaped the institutions of power in such a way as to continue privileges and interests of the colonial power and its nationals. It had little regard, on the other hand, for the power relations among the groups that would take over on independence, when a period of testing of strengths was bound to supervene (O'Connell, 1967:182-85).

In some areas, exploitation of one tribe by another had existed before the coming of the Europeans. This continued right through the period of colonialism, to emerge with renewed force on the coming of independence. For example, the Belgians, when they took over the administration of Rwanda and Burundi, in Central Africa, found a minority tribe, the Tutsi, lording it over the Hutu majority. When independence came, in 1962, the Hutus in Rwanda managed to secure control of the government; but in Burundi the Tutsi put down a series of Hutu revolts and slaughtered uncounted thousands. Elsewhere class antagonisms that had existed before colonialism continued through the colonial period. O'Connell sees "tribalism" as the competitive struggle for the jobs in state bureaucracy.

The imperialists not only did little to alleviate intertribal hostility; they frequently created it. Jomo Kenyatta's Kenya African National Union (KANU) was founded on the principle of intertribal unity. Quite different was the Kenya African Democratic Union (KADU), which kept tribalism in the center of its focus and in effect perpetuated it (Mboya, 1963:66-67). KADU was said to represent the British approach. (On British revival of divisive tribalism in the Gold Coast—Ghana—see James in Miller and Aya, 1971:127).

In the economic field, not especially stressed by Kilson, imperialism delayed and impeded the integration which, as we have seen, is an essential element in nation-building. The imperial powers did, typically, develop a considerable export trade, with corresponding imports, but the trade within a colony remained small indeed.[3] The mines and plantations are integrated more closely with the economy of the "mother country" and the other advanced countries than with the domestic economy, which remains decentralized and largely untouched by Western civilization. Thus in most of the new states of Africa the process of internal integration has only begun.

## THE THEORY OF NATIONAL LIBERATION:
### FRANTZ FANON

Marxism, to be useful, must be a living doctrine, capable of being modified and brought up to date. People who have been in the middle of the fight for national liberation have developed concepts which, while not necessarily inconsistent with traditional Marxism are certainly not identical with it. Two of the foremost theorists of the African liberation struggles were Frantz Fanon and Amilcar Cabral, the one a West Indian black who worked for the independence of Algeria, the other a native of Portuguese Guinea (now known as Guinea-Bissau) who helped to found the party of Guinea's liberation, the Partido Africano da Independencia da Guiné e Cabo-Verde (PAIGC). Both were revolutionary socialists, Cabral a Marxist, Fanon not. Fanon used some categories unfamiliar to Marxists; Cabral, the more penetrating thinker of the two, though he recognized the value of traditional Marxism, also departed from it at times. We shall examine the analysis of each of these men at some length.

Marx and Lenin, who assumed that the social revolution would take place in Europe ahead of the rest of the world, naturally assumed also that the European proletariat would lead the rest of the world to socialism. Fanon challenged this concept, and discarded the whole analysis that put its hopes in a revolutionary proletariat and an anti-imperialist colonial bourgeoisie. Fanon also studied the psychological impact of imperialism on both the colonized and the colonizers.

Fanon was born in Martinique, in the West Indies, in 1925. He went to school in Martinique, and was strongly influenced by Aimé Césaire, the West Indian poet. Césaire preached *race* pride for the blacks; nationalism was for him a secondary consideration (Fanon, 1967b: 21ff). Martinique was indeed not especially conscious of political grievances. It sent deputies to the French Parliament, and its inhabitants, including Césaire and (at first) Fanon, considered themselves loyal Frenchmen.[4] However, the French population, a small aristocracy at the top of the colonial pyramid, was always to some extent racist, and the resentment of the Martinique population against the French was greatly intensified in 1940, when the Vichyites sent racists and Nazi collaborators to administer Martinique.

While the war was still in progress, Fanon went to France. He hoped to "make some sense out of the shocking contrast between his own self-image and how he discovered that others, especially white Frenchmen, looked at him." He joined the Free French and fought valiantly with them, but was shocked to find among their ranks the same color consciousness that had been so conspicuous among the Vichyites.

Fanon remained in France to study medicine. There he met blacks from Africa who were engaged, like himself, in a quest for a self-image that they could live with; and though he came to differ sharply from men such as Léopold Senghor (later president of Senegal) and Alioune Diop of *Présence Africaine,* he always retained a warm personal regard for them. In Lyon he associated with Trotskyist groups and absorbed some of their disrespect for "official" Marxism. He learned something of economic exploitation and became a revolutionary socialist, though he did not consider himself a Marxist. He did still consider himself a Frenchman. In 1952 he wrote:

> We [blacks] refuse to be considered "outsiders"; we have full part in the French drama. . . . I am a Frenchman. . . . I am personally interested in the future of France, in French values, in the French nation. (Fanon, 1967a:203)

Fanon did very well in his studies and upon their completion he should, according to the rules of the game, have fitted into French institutional medicine at a high level. But difficulties were raised, and it became evident that these were due to his color. Eventually he accepted a position in charge of an Algerian hospital.

Fanon's special field was psychiatry, and he applied his interest to the problem of dominated and dominator. He undertook a series of studies that showed how this relationship poisoned the individual psyches of both. Fanon perceived that overcoming the feeling of inferiority which the white man had instilled in him was for the dominated colonial a matter of great importance. Fanon did not at first stress the effect of participation in a nationalist (national liberation) movement in building up the self-respect of the individual. Instead he emphasized the value as he saw it, of individual acts of violence against the oppressor. Violence, he said, has a cathartic effect on the psychology of the individual; it has a positive value in and of itself. But his study of individuals did not produce evidence to substantiate this contention (Gendzier, 1973).

Different from Fanon's analysis of the psychology of the individual, though not necessarily inconsistent with it, was his description of the need for mass violence in the social revolution if anything serious was to be accomplished:

> Violence committed by the peoples, violence organized and educated by its leaders, makes it possible for the masses to understand social truths and gives the key to them. Without that struggle, without that knowledge of the practice of action, there is nothing but a fancy-dress parade and the blare of trumpets. There is nothing save a minimum of readaptation, a few reforms at the top, a flag waving: and down there at the bottom an undivided mass, still living in the Middle Ages, endlessly marking time. (Fanon, 1967b:117)

The emphasis on violence in Fanon of course reminds one of Sorel; but Irene Gendzier, who studied Fanon's work, did not find any evidence linking Fanon's thought with that of Sorel, who in any case was not an authentic interpreter of French working-class ideas, much less of colonialism (Gendzier, 1973).

In estimating Fanon's defense of violence, middle-class pacifists and others who abhor violence must recall that violence is the everyday fare of the poor and oppressed, of the blacks in Caucasian-dominated mixed societies, and of the colonials, especially during an anti-colonial war. The typical member of the white ruling group in such situations is not aware of the violence that is used to maintain his privileges, nor of the discriminatory way in which it is applied. Fanon was to comment bitterly in 1960:

> Soon we shall have had seven years of crimes in Algeria, and there has not yet been a single Frenchman indicted before a French court of justice for the murder of an Algerian. (Fanon, 1966:72)

For a trenchant statement of how the French maintained their repressive regime *under color of law* while still resorting to torture of liberation fighters *in Paris* the reader may examine *The Gangrene* (Alleg, 1960).

A series of events both in and outside of Algeria weakened Fanon's loyalty to France and emphasized the gulf between his thinking and that of the "official" French Marxists.

The weakness and vacillation of the Communist Party of France

(PCF) in the face of colonialism after World War II is a matter of record. In May 1945, after nationalist riots broke out in the Constantine Department of Algeria, the PCF called for punishment of the instigators and set its face firmly against Algerian independence. It also attempted to keep Vietnam within the French Union.

Then for a period, beginning in 1949, the PCF, being outside of the government, was in the forefront of the opposition to the war against the Vietnminh. General Secretary Maurice Thorez saluted the dockers who refused to load arms bound for Indochina, and railway sabotage was actively encouraged. Ho Chi Minh sent messages of greeting and appreciation (Caute, 1970:48-49).

When peace came to Indochina, as far as France was concerned, in 1954, the war of colonial liberation broke out in Algeria, and this time the PCF's hesitation was marked and long lasting. It called for "peace," but not for independence. In March 1956 the Communist deputies voted for special powers that enabled the government to do virtually as it liked in Algeria. The PCF did not come out for Algerian independence until 1957. Some small left-wing organizations, by contrast, had demanded Algerian independence all along. For example, Francis Jeanson, Sartre's disciple and Fanon's friend, led a pro–National Liberation Front resistance network that was not finally crushed by the police until 1960.[5]

Césaire was outraged by the PCF's attitude, and he resigned from the Party. He wrote to Thorez of

> some of the very evident faults which we notice in the members of the French Communist Party: their inveterate assimilationism; their unconscious chauvinism; their conviction—which they share with the European bourgeoisie—of the superiority of the West on all counts; their belief that revolution as it has developed in Europe is the only one possible, the only one desirable, that it is that evolution which the whole world will undergo; to sum it up, their belief rarely admitted but real, in civilization with a capital C, in progress with a capital P (note their hostility to what they disdainfully call "cultural relativism"). (Quoted from Owen and Sutcliffe, 1972:110; our trans.)

The fact that the inhuman treatment meted out to the colonials was accepted in France meant, said Césaire, that France—and this applied to the whole continent of Europe—had been barbarized by colonialism;

the humiliation of man as man that had been visited on white Europe by Hitler was nothing but the application to Europe of the treatment accorded to the blacks over the years by the smug European whites in the colonies (ibid.:111).

The idea that the working class in the imperialist countries is the natural ally of the colonial peoples goes all the way back to Marx and Lenin; it was still held after World War II by certain writers, with respect to France if not to the Anglo-Saxon countries.

Césaire challenged this belief. Reviving an idea that we have previously associated with Sultan-Galiev, he charged the French workers with participating in the spoilage of the colonial countries. The natural allies of the colonized peoples were other colonized peoples, he wrote:

> There are no allies by divine right. There are allies who are chosen for us by the place, the time and the nature of things. And, if the alliance with the French proletariat is exclusive, if it tends to make us forget or to pass up other necessary and natural alliances, perfectly legitimate and fruitful, if Communism breaks up our most life-giving friendships, those which unite us (Martiniqueans) to the other Antilles, to Africa, then I say that Communism has served us very poorly in having us exchange a living fraternity for what runs the risk of appearing as the coldest of cold abstractions. (Ibid.:113; our trans.)[6]

For Fanon, too, the turning point had come. He had no further use for Europeans.[7] He resigned his position in the medical service and worked for several years in the Algerian resistance movement, largely from bases in Tunis. He wrote for the paper *El Moudjahid* and also completed a number of essays of his own, including the highly significant study *The Wretched of the Earth*, published in 1960. He died in 1961.

Fanon is known largely for his violent diatribes against the white man. (See articles later reprinted in *A Dying Colonialism*, 1965). However, he always maintained cordial relations with European white members of the Algerian resistance movement. And the position of the Algerian independence party, adopted at Soummam in 1956, was to welcome cooperation with all Frenchmen accepting its principles. Fanon even acted as spokesperson for this policy.

Fanon's principal contributions, those which conern us here, have to do with the role of the several classes in bringing about the social revolution under conditions of colonialism. Fanon broke with the then-orthodox theory of Marxism according to which the standard-bearer of the revolution would be the proletariat, in association with the peasants and led by the Communist Party.

For Fanon, the proletariat was not a revolutionary class. The French workers, both in the metropolis and in Algeria, were the enemies of the Algerian liberation struggle (Fanon, 1967b:65).[8] Even the native African workers, while they were by and large a part of the movement for national liberation, were not a revolutionary force, Fanon asserted (Fanon, 1966:47). They were, on the contrary, a pampered, privileged group. By means of their unions they had been able to secure an income far above the average of the whole country; they also had gained special laws to protect them. Thus, these workers, and the nationalist movements in which they took part, were at best reformist. Did this mean that the social revolution which Fanon considered essential would have to wait until the workers as a group were ready? For Fanon this meant waiting too long; it meant postponing the revolution indefinitely.

Fanon believed that the revolution would develop out of the simultaneous fight against two kinds of privilege: economic privilege and national privilege. The social group which would take the lead in this revolution would be, not the proletariat as such, not the intellectuals (although they would be necessary too), but the peasantry and (in the cities) the lumpenproletariat.

As employed by Marx, the term "lumpenproletariat" referred to the pimps, the prostitutes, the gangsters, the drug pushers and addicts, the demoralized elements of society who are for sale to the highest bidder. When the Army of National Liberation, which had operated chiefly in the countryside, was defeated and obliged to become a group of guerrillas, it moved to penetrate the cities, and did succeed in establishing a base in the Casbah, the Muslim quarter of Algiers, with a population of some eighty thousand. Here it set up a shock force of some four thousand persons, around a core of lumpenproletarians, who were described as "hooligans with a pure heart" (Ouzegane, 1962: 253-54).

That some of the previously demoralized lumpens were indeed remoralized, or moralized for the first time, is undoubted. The nationalist struggle caused the regeneration of some, and had a significant psychological impact on the whole community. Nor should this development surprise Americans, who are used to the idea that Black Muslims have reclaimed many despairing blacks, some actually in prison, both before and after Malcolm X, with black nationalist slogans.

However, for Fanon to base his hopes so largely on the lumpenproletariat was unfortunate. The military results of urban terrorism were not great; the terrorists were quickly contained by the French troops under General Massu. Fanon may have intended to include in the concept a substantially larger group, not only the slum dwellers but the city-bound migrants who had congregated in the *bidonvilles* at the edge of town. Members of this group, which is familiar to students of the colonial and semicolonial setup, are frequently underemployed, and are only a step away from the village, to which they may return at any time (Caute, 1970:80; Fanon, 1966:109). Fanon is rather vague on this point. But these deracinated peasants, or neo-urbanites, do indeed furnish a potential reservoir of liberation fighters.

One special reason for emphasizing the lumpenproletariat was that Fanon realized how much of a danger they constituted to the nationalist movement. If the lumpenproletariat, traditionally for sale, were not inducted into the service of the revolution, they might well be used against it (Fanon, 1966:109).

Fanon idealized the peasants, who furnished the bulk of the liberation fighters, in Algeria as in China and Yugoslavia.[9] But even he had to admit that the peasants do not gravitate to the movement until city workers and intellectuals have shown the way and worked out the procedures. The fact that the first armed resistance in Algeria emerged in a rural environment was due to special circumstances; the cities were so sharply policed that it was not possible for an organized military movement to start anywhere except in the countryside.

Fanon was clearly in error when he found the main source of peasant revolutionary power in the *starving* peasant. When the Badissia religious reform movement began to spread in the Algerian hinterland around the middle of the twentieth century, and nationalist agitation followed in its wake, it was the *middle* peasantry who responded, while the agricultural laborers and poor peasants clung to their traditional holy men and resisted the reformers (Wolf, 1969:229-30).

It may be suggested that Fanon, in describing the class that, in his view, would lead the revolution, had in mind not the demoralized elements so much as the unorganized. Rosa Luxemburg, in her pamphlet *General Strike, Party, and Unions,* written in 1906, pinned her hopes not on the unions, which she was convinced would *not* lead a revolutionary general strike, but on the *unorganized* workers, who she thought were numerous enough and potentially possessed of enough spontaneous revolutionary spirit to accomplish the task. Indeed the whole philosophy of syndicalism presupposes the possibility of such a semiorganized, semispontaneous uprising. Fanon's thinking is much closer to certain Western models than he himself was perhaps aware.

Fanon has, to some extent at least, taken the curse off the term "lumpenproletariat," so that Bobby Seale and Eldridge Cleaver have used it without apology to refer to the black urban community in the United States (see Worsley, 1972:230).

Fanon is important for our purposes, finally, because of his incisive critique of "bourgeois" nationalism as it develops in the colonies and excolonial countries. He points out that the middle class in the colonies are not a bourgeoisie in the classical sense. They include no industrialists, no captains of industry, no financiers. They are not engaged in production (in the technical Marxist sense), nor invention, nor building; they come from the fields of trade, agriculture, and the liberal professions.

> [They favor nationalism] in order to transfer into native hands those unfair advantages which are the legacy of the colonial period. . . . [They follow] the Western bourgeoisie along its path of negation and decadence without ever having emulated it in its first stages of exploration and invention. (Fanon, 1966:122, 124)

Writing before Algeria or the bulk of the African colonies had actually secured their independence, Fanon stated that the native "bourgeoisie" would not build up their respective countries, would not industrialize them or launch them on the road to prosperity and progress. The "bourgeois" nationalists, he said, are literally good for nothing. Power will continue to be exercised by the metropolitan countries, operating through their chosen instrument, the new "bourgeoisie," and through the army and police forces which they build up and train. Fanon saw Africa traveling along the road to becoming another Latin America (ibid.:139-41).

The only way to create an alternative to rule by a new class of native exploiters working with the foreigners, in Fanon's view, is of course to rouse to consciousness the hitherto-submerged classes. Fanon has no doubt that the national liberation war plays a highly important part in creating such consciousness (ibid.:154).

In the whole literature of nationalism there are few more eloquent pleas for a humanist nationalism than those of Fanon. Fanon rejected Western culture because of its attitude toward the blacks and to colonial peoples generally. Not at all in the spirit of the Nazis who opposed all culture, he wrote:

> When the native hears a speech about Western culture he pulls out his knife—or at least he makes sure that it is within reach. (Ibid.:35)

At first, Fanon did not find it necessary to discover any African cultural heritage (Caute, 1970:105). However, in 1956 he wrote that "the plunge into the chasm of the past is the condition and the source of freedom" (Fanon, 1967b:43). He made the important distinction between the native culture as it actually is, after the colonialists have degraded and perverted it, and the native culture as it was developing before the colonialists got hold of it. He evidently had Africa in mind when he wrote:

> The setting up of the colonial system does not of itself bring about the death of the native culture. Historic observation reveals, on the contrary, that the aim sought is rather a continued agony than a total disappearance of the preexisting culture. This culture, once living and open to the future, becomes closed, fixed in the colonial status, caught in the yoke of oppression. . . .
>
> Thus we witness the setting up of archaic, inert institutions, functioning under the oppressor's supervision and patterned like a caricature of formerly fertile institutions. . . .
>
> These bodies appear to embody respect for the tradition, the cultural specificities, the personality of the subjugated people. This pseudo-respect in fact is tantamount to the most utter contempt, to the most elaborate sadism. (Ibid.:34)

For the natives, an important part of the nationalist movement is thus to get back their culture as it was before it became perverted—to reacquire their history. Fanon asked, Does the rise of nationalism and the throwing off of the colonial yoke have a rejuvenating effect on the psychology of the indigenous population? Does it lead to the ending of alienation?

Fanon's answer to this question was that alienation derived not only from national but from class oppression, which is not necessarily ended by national liberation. Fanon thought that the Negroes' inferiority complex had economic origins; black people had internalized that economic inferiority. In the end, Fanon took the position that alienation on the world scale was rooted firmly in the imperialist division of the world into poor countries and rich, exploiters and exploited, rulers and ruled (Caute, 1970:32).[10] But the beginnings of self-respect do not need wait for the ending of either class or national oppression (Fanon, 1967b:21; Caute, 1970:64-65).

Fanon presents a model of the way a nationalist revolt may be expected to develop. Although the model is supposed to apply generally, we may assume that he has first in mind Algeria.

First, the nationalist movement takes root in the towns, where it affects the native middle classes and also the proletariat: tram conductors, taxi drivers, dockers, interpreters, nurses, and so on. (Fanon also includes miners, although these could hardly be considered urban.) This proletariat is not like Marx's proletariat, which had "nothing but its chains to lose"; the colonial proletariat is on the contrary a pampered class, which has a great deal to lose: wages higher than the national average income, and protective legislation.

The colonial authorities meanwhile have established their rule in the countryside, based on the traditional hierarchy of "marabouts, witch doctors and customary chieftains."

Second, the native traders from the cities, the young bourgeoisie, seek to penetrate the country districts for purposes of trade. They are resisted by the "feudal" elements (Fanon's term), which form a screen between the young Westernized nationalists and the bulk of the rural population. The landless peasants move to the towns and, finding no jobs, congregate in the slums and *bidonvilles* at the edge of the city. They are part of the lumpenproletariat.

The colonialists stir up antagonism against the towns in the rural districts, which the nationalist parties have not succeeded in penetrating. Tribalism is fostered and sometimes carries over into the phase of independence.

Third, the peasants become aware of the nationalist movement in the towns, and sometimes organize uprisings of their own, like the famous rebellion in 1947 in Madagascar. The nationalists in the urban area are put under pressure by the authorities. They split; some go over to the colonial authorities, and the true revolutionists are driven out of the city. The latter take refuge in the countryside, where the peasants welcome them.[11] The city nationalists begin to educate the peasants. During this period the peasant uprisings are not motivated by any common program, only by a vague antiforeign feeling. This is the period of spontaneity.

Fourth, the peasantry gradually acquire national consciousness; military leaders develop and decide to carry the struggle to the towns. A national program and organization emerge. The rebellion finds its urban spearhead in the *bidonvilles,* among the lumpenproletariat.

Fifth, the colonialists counterattack and the revolt is quickly suppressed. A prolonged period of peasant education and organization begins. Unless the rebellious forces pay special attention to the lumpenproletariat, these may be organized as shock troops for the colonialists, as they were in the Congo, in Algeria, and in Angola.

Sixth, the colonial authorities may make concessions, while salvaging the most important part of their privileges, by the grant of a pseudo-independence (Fanon, 1966:88f.).

Fanon did not emphasize sufficiently the fact that the divisions between exploiter and exploited in Algeria were not primarily racial but economic and cultural, even religious; the Arabs who made up most of the resistance were, after all, not black, but very many of them were Muslims, so that the revolt necessarily had strong Muslim overtones.

Further, Fanon's analysis of the politics of Algeria, while of course mentioning the presence of a large group of French settlers, did not differentiate Algeria from other colonies on this basis, though, as Arghiri Emmanuel has recently showed, this factor can be crucial. The white settler element is completely unscrupulous in pushing its own interests, even to the point of setting up an independent state if the occasion offers, as in South Africa and Rhodesia. This element also exercises surprising political influence in the imperialist country; it will be recalled that the Algerian settlers almost succeeded in overthrowing the government in France at one point (Emmanuel, 1972:40).

Fanon also pays little attention to another distinctive feature of the Algerian struggle, namely, the Algerian workers in France, who num-

bered 600,000. These contributed significantly to the struggle with
money and manpower, particularly after the Algerian liberation army
had been forced across the border into Morocco and Tunisia. The
Algerians in France also organized mass demonstrations in French
cities, and helped to bring home to lethargic French opinion the fact
that a colonial war was raging on their very doorstep. (It was in
metropolitan France, we might note, that the first modern nationalist
Algerian movement had taken shape: the Étoile Nord Africain, formed
in Paris in 1925. Later, this movement developed into a conservative
nationalist group, which fought the militant revolutionary Algerians
both in Algeria and in metropolitan France, where it is estimated that
close to 1,000 Muslims died in internecine warfare (see Wolf, 1969:
236).

Fanon's model is much too restrictive; it would indeed be surprising
if we encountered all the steps he mentions in the order specified in any
one country. But before discussing in detail the question as to whether
any general model at all can be drawn up, let us examine the contributions of another major thinker from Africa who, like Fanon, died at an
early age—though not early enough to satisfy his imperialist assassins.
We refer to Amilcar Cabral.


## THE THEORY OF NATIONAL LIBERATION:
## AMILCAR CABRAL


A pioneer both in practice and in theory was the hydraulic engineer
Amilcar Cabral, from the little country known formerly as Portuguese
Guinea, then as Guiné, and now as Guinea-Bissau, situated next to the
Republic of Guinea at the western end of sub-Saharan Africa. In
Lisbon in 1948, Cabral and a small group of other students from the
Portuguese colonies in Africa organized a study group, the Center for
African Studies, with the perspective of (1) bringing modern civilization
to their countries; and (2) as a necessary means to this end, getting rid
of the Portuguese dominion over those countries.

Cabral was one of only eleven college graduates from Guiné. He
returned to his native country in 1952 and was commissioned to make
an agricultural survey of the whole country. This assignment occupied

two years, and took him into every corner of the country, which is about the size of Switzerland. He learned to know the peasants personally and to understand their psychology and their problems.

In 1956, on another visit to Guiné, Cabral helped found the Partido Africano da Independencia da Guiné e Cabo-Verde (PAIGC).[12] This group petitioned peacefully for political and social change, but the appeal was met with silence. They then resolved to resort to "all possible means, including war" (Davidson, 1969:Ch. 1).

Cabral's analysis of the class structure of Guiné is of the greatest interest for our purposes. He distinguished only two classes in the towns proper: the whites (Portuguese) and the Africans. The whites included, besides the administrators, a small group of workers who were even more bitterly opposed to the demands of the Africans than were some of the officials.

As for the Africans, Cabral classified all the town dwellers as "petty bourgeois." These were subcategorized not so much according to their relation to the productive process as by their attitude to the independence movement. Generally opposed were the few higher officials and certain members of the liberal professions, a small group at best because of the Portuguese policy of restricting educational opportunities for Africans. At the other extreme were the active workers for the PAIGC, with the balance, those unable to make up their minds, somewhere in between. It will be seen that Cabral's analysis is more political than sociological or economic (Cabral, 1969:56-76).

Most of Guiné's eight hundred thousand population was rural, and Cabral, while aware that they had resisted the Portuguese for hundreds of years (the final "pacification" did not take place until 1936), did not expect the peasants to take the lead in the national liberation struggle. Cabral and his group, as revolutionary Marxists, sought to base their movement on the working class. But here a difficulty arose: there was no working class as such. There were only a few thousand wage earners and some salaried workers, many of whom were white and bitterly opposed to the aims of the PAIGC. "We looked for the working class," Cabral wrote later, "and did not find it."

The PAIGC did nevertheless concentrate its initial efforts on the relatively few native workers, and succeeded in organizing a union among the longshoremen. However, when these went on strike for higher wages and union recognition in 1959, the Portuguese police fired on the strikers and killed about fifty, smashing the movement. Cabral, who had been in Angola, returned to Guiné, and the PAIGC, forced to operate underground, decided on a complete change of tactics.

The workers, the PAIGC now determined, were too few, and their movements were too closely watched by the police for them to make or lead the revolution. Instead, the PAIGC set out systematically to organize the peasants. To train organizers, a party school was established in Conakry, in the neighboring Republic of Guinea, which had just won its independence from France.

What program would attract the peasants? There was no land problem; land was not in short supply; land was not privately owned (interview with Cabral, *Guardian* [N.Y.], Jan. 12, 1972). But the peasants did have grievances against the Portuguese overlords, and they were aware of the need to introduce modern methods of cultivation. It was decided after discussion that cooperatives would be the best basis for the organization of economic life, and some of the early PAIGC recruits were sent abroad to study methods of agricultural cooperation in such places as Czechoslovakia (Davidson, 1969:35).

Who was to do the organizing of the peasants? The urban wage earners and intellectuals were available, and were of course used, but their number was small. Also, they did not at first understand the psychology of the peasants. It was then that Cabral and his friends discovered the neourbanites.

As Cabral later described them, this group—called by him the "Nameless Group"—lived on the outskirts of a town, not demoralized, but also not working regularly, living on their relatives in the town for the time being in accord with long-standing tribal custom. They were literate as a group, and receptive to new ideas. They had enough contact with the country to be able to talk to peasants. They had also enough contact with the city to be aware of its advantages, of the possibilities for them of modern civilization, and also of the obstacles in the way of native advancement (meaning especially the imperialists, with their scorn of native Africans and their discriminatory practices).[13] Cabral, then, proposed to use this Nameless Group to spearhead his attack. In Conakry between 1961 and 1963, close to one thousand young party workers were trained in the methods and social philosophy of the PAIGC. There they learned the necessity not only of getting rid of the Portuguese but of reorganizing society, of carrying out a social revolution. The national struggle and the class struggle were one. But in the first stages, the national struggle had priority.

Consistent with the idea that national consciousness must be built up, Cabral emphasized that any successful liberation movement must be preceded by a cultural revival, which would provide a grounding in African (not necessarily distinctively Guinean) tradition. Intensive study of cultural origins preceded the period of indoctrination. Cabral, like Fanon, looked on national liberation as a process of restoring to a people its history—of putting a people back on the road to the independent development from which the colonialists had tried by every means to divert it. Cabral rejected the idea that peoples have no history before they become differentiated into classes; the Balante tribe had no classes, but they had had a history, said Cabral, before they were overtaken by imperialism.

This approach involves a rejection of one of the favorite dogmas of Marxism, that the class struggle is the motive force of progress. Not so, says Cabral; the level of the productive forces is the true and permanent driving power of history (Cabral, 1970:4). The implication of this very interesting argument is that the class struggle serves to adapt the mode of production to the attained technique. Where the fetters on production are maintained not only, or principally, by class exploitation, but also by imperialist domination, then the removing of these fetters is no less a contribution to raising the level of production than is breaking the bonds of class domination.

Cabral's formulation disposes of one difficulty that some scholars have seen in the conventional rendition of Marx and Engels: If the class struggle is the driving force in history, what will become of progress in the classless society? Cabral puts his faith in posterity; and indeed where else is there to put it?

Cabral did not formulate his theory of the motive force of history with care and completeness. He refers sometimes to the level of productive forces, sometimes to the mode of production, or just the productive forces, as the driving power (Cabral, 1969:77, 82; 1970:4). However, his meaning is clear throughout: it is people themselves, people in their ceaseless striving for improved methods of production, who are the motive force. This indeed is the unspoken major assumption without which the *Communist Manifesto* fails to make sense.[14]

Cabral does not deny that under certain circumstances the class struggle may be the driving force of history. He merely denies that this is the only, or the main, driving force.

The education of the peasants was not looked on as a one-way process; it was a process of give and take. Let Cabral describe it himself:

> The leaders of the liberation movement, drawn generally from the "petite bourgeoisie" (intellectuals, clerks) or the urban working classes (workers, chauffeurs, salary-earners[15] in general), having to live day by day with the various peasant groups in the heart of rural populations, come to know the people better. They discover at the grass roots the richness of their cultural values (philosophic, political, artistic, social and moral), acquire a clearer understanding of the economic realities of the country, of the problems, sufferings and hopes of the popular masses. The leaders realize, not without a certain astonishment, the richness of spirit, the capacity for reasoned discussion and clear exposition of ideas, the facility for understanding and assimilating concepts on the part of population groups who yesterday were forgotten, if not despised, and who were considered incompetent by the colonizer and even by some nationals. The leaders thus enrich their culture —develop personally and free themselves from complexes, reinforcing their capacity to serve the movement in the service of the people.
>
> On their side, the working masses and, in particular, the peasants, who are usually illiterate and never have moved beyond the boundaries of their village or region, in contact with other groups lose the complexes which constrained them in their relationships with other ethnic and social groups. They realize their crucial role in the struggle; they break the bonds of the village universe to integrate progressively into the country and into the world; they acquire an infinite amount of new knowledge, useful for their immediate and future activity within the framework of the struggle; and they strengthen their political awareness by assimilating the principles of national and social revolution postulated by the struggle. They thereby become more able to play the decisive role of providing the principal force behind the liberation movement. (Cabral, 1970; see Fanon, 1966:150-54)

Cabral anticipated that the class struggle would emerge as soon as the anticolonial struggle was won. He argued that the only class which was in a position to take power and organize an independent government was what he had called the "petty bourgeoisie," meaning specifically the group usually called "the intelligentsia": people in the liberal professions and in government service, teachers and writers, and after liberation some workers and peasants, all infused with a sense of national mission (Cabral, 1969:85).

If this class followed its "natural" interests, said Cabral, it would make its peace with imperialism and settle into a condition of neo-colonialism, as in the other African countries; it would "betray" the revolution, and become what he called a pseudobourgeoisie, evidently meaning agents of the foreign imperialists—compradors and exploiters.

What reason is there to think that the revolutionary vanguard will carry the struggle through to socialism, supported by the peasantry and the rising working class? Cabral told the seminar at the Frantz Fanon Center in Milan in 1964 that he believed the revolutionary petty bourgeoisie was honest (ibid.:59). But if the revolutionary vanguard is to live up to its duty as custodian of the conscience of mankind, it has the obligation not to rely on a few courageous individuals, but to educate the propertyless elements to demand socialism, and to see to it that later "petty-bourgeois" intellectuals do not renege on the commitment of the early leaders, nor transmute what was to have been a socialist commonwealth into a personal dictatorship or a self-perpetuating oligarchy.

Cabral did not give any very convincing *economic* reason why the class of "petty-bourgeois" leaders of the nationalist movement should "commit suicide," as he put it, by joining with the workers and peasants to introduce real socialism. But he cited Cuba as an example to prove that it could be done. For Cabral it was a question of leadership (ibid.:89-90). Such a decision would be based on moral, not narrowly economic, grounds—an outlook by no means inconsistent with Cabral's approach to Marxism.

It is significant that Cabral suggests that the petty bourgeoisie may have some members who are actuated by motives of "patriotism," meaning anti-imperialism plus social reorganization. Patriotism emerges as the highest possible motive, from Cabral's point of view, or at least as part of such a motive. Thus, the nationalist elements in his thought remain intertwined with the socialist and the moral in a way quite new to Marxism and very suggestive.

Cabral and Fanon agreed in their low estimate of the proletariat in the imperialist countries, but the two men assigned very different roles at all stages of the national liberation struggle to the native colonial workers. This difference was clearly due in the first instance to the different degrees of development of Algeria and Guiné respectively. Whereas the workers in Algeria had achieved a certain degree of organization and had secured some protective labor legislation, so that Fanon could refer to them as pampered and nonrevolutionary, the workers in Guiné had not won any concessions; they had nothing but their chains to lose; they were real proletarians, potentially militant and receptive to socialist ideas—close to Marx's conception of the proletariat.

Cabral did not think, however, that the workers would develop a revolutionary leadership alone, out of their own entrails so to speak. Cabral reverts to Lenin's conception of a revolutionary vanguard, with this difference: that it is *national*-minded as well as *socialist*-minded. Cabral drops the Leninist phraseology of vanguard of the proletariat, especially in view of the fact that when this vanguard is forming, in the early stages of the anticolonial struggle, there really is no proletariat as such in a place such as Guiné, nor any revolutionary peasantry either. Cabral's revolutionary vanguard is "firmly united, conscious of the true meaning and objective of the national liberation struggle which it must lead." It leads the movement in the early days; later, a developing proletariat and an aroused peasantry can exercise vigilance over the liberation movement and make sure that it keeps on the path to full social emancipation.

To turn once more to the peasants, Cabral was conscious of great diversity in the character of the several tribes. The Fulas, he knew, had a semifeudal type of organization, with the chiefs, nobles, and religious figures at the top, supported by the Portuguese; the artisans and itinerant traders in the middle; and the peasants at the bottom. Among the Fulas, the women did not even own what they produced. By contrast, the more numerous Balantes had no class divisions, and the women owned what they produced. The Balantes were the backbone of the revolutionary forces.

The PAIGC's approach to the Fulas was made in the end with the aid of the itinerant traders (ibid.:47).

PAIGC analysis concluded that the animosity of one tribe against another would not produce major difficulties, and in fact at first it did not; although later, in 1974, it was reported that the Portuguese had managed to recruit a force of commandos from tribes hostile to the Balantes (*New York Times,* Mar. 19, 1974).

It was not until late in 1963 that the PAIGC moved into open opposition, and when it did so it was able within four years to achieve de facto control of two-thirds of the area of Guiné. This was not a guerrilla force; it administered the land that it conquered. By 1967 the Party had set up 159 schools with 220 teachers and 14,386 pupils, and sent fifty young men and women to Europe for training in various technical fields (Davidson, 1969:125). It had established clinics and hospitals, though its headquarters were still abroad, in Conakry. Arms were obtained mainly from East Europe, especially from the Soviet Union (Gibson, 1972:260). Independence was won in 1974. But Cabral had been assassinated earlier, in 1973, in Conakry.

The PAIGC has been outstandingly successful as a nationalist movement. But concentration on the nationalist slogans has tended to distract attention from the socialist objectives, as Cabral feared. The problem now is to carry through the socialist revolution in a pre-industrial country—no mean task. But without the attainment of the nationalist objective, the socialist objective could not even have been contemplated.

The close connection between socialist objectives and the nationalist movement emerges in the other Portuguese African colonies, Mozambique and Angola, too. These are much larger in size than Guinea-Bissau, and in the protracted war of liberation, it was absolutely essential that guerrillas should be able to move freely from one part of the area to another and find a warm welcome. Thus a sense of national consciousness was a necessary condition of success. But further, the peasants (and workers) had to have, in Cabral's view, a sense of participation, a stake in the operation; they had to feel that it was *their* war of liberation. The involvement of the masses of peasants had to be brought about by a real grass-roots popular movement. The people involved needed to feel that power was passing to them—that they would not merely be exchanging a group of foreign exploiters for a domestic elite who would continue the old exploitative institutions (interview with Cabral, *Guardian* [N.Y.], Jan. 12, 1972; Arrighi and Saul, 1973:378-405). Especially where the Portuguese had taken severe measures of reprisal against guerrilla activity, destroying villages and removing whole communities, the setting up of new, popularly controlled institutions on a democratic basis was to make the war into a peoples' war.

Outside of Algeria and the Portuguese colonies, the leadership of the national liberation movements was for the most part not socialist, although there was not the same prejudice against socialism (communism) that one finds, for example, in the United States. Some of the leaders, like Kwame Nkrumah in Ghana, preached socialism but did not practice it. The liberation movements were led by political parties that were organized in the cities, based on a variety of voluntary associations: some social, based usually on tribal origin; some economic, including not only unions (where permitted) but burial societies and immigrant aid societies; and some political, seeking redress for certain obvious wrongs (Rothberg in Wallerstein, 1966:508-12). The members of the liberation parties acquired national consciousness in the struggle; they were not class conscious either before or after the granting of independence.

An exception should be made for the Republic of Guinea (not to be confused with Guiné, or Portuguese Guinea, or Guinea-Bissau), which became independent in 1958. Alone among the former French colonies, Guinea at first left the franc zone and created its own currency. The government also took over much of the economy. The socialist ideas of the leadership were taken into the back country; the government, headed by a former trade union organizer named Sékou Touré, accomplished the remarkable feat of signing up 1,800,000 persons (of a total population of 4,000,000) for the independence party, the Democratic Party of Guinea (PDG).

However, the disinterested help that would have been needed from abroad to make Guinea's experiment succeed was not forthcoming, although some individuals did come and offer their services. The Soviet ambassador was accused of meddling and given his walking papers. Touré's associates, not imbued with any egalitarian ethic, proceeded to enrich themselves. Mismanagement was colossal. The agricultural program was a failure. Eventually Guinea was obliged to rejoin the franc zone, to contract a loan for "development" from the World Bank, with all the economic restrictions that that implies, and in general to forget its socialist dreams.

## CLASS AND NATIONALISM IN SOUTH AFRICA

In the African countries studied thus far, no particular social class can be said to have contributed exclusively to the creation of the new nations: certainly not the bourgeoisie. We take it that the same is true generally throughout Africa as far as the national liberation movements are concerned: the class formation is quite different from what classical Marxist theory assumes, and so that theory does not apply. There is another aspect of Marxist theory that we have touched on briefly and on which we should comment further: the attitude of the white proletariat, the wage earners of the white community in Africa, to the national liberation movement.

In general, as is well known, the white wage earners oppose the liberation struggles. We do not need to confine ourselves to Algeria and Guinea-Bissau to make this generalization or to understand its roots. The Union of South Africa has a fairly large white wage-earning class, and it is white-nationalist to the core. Its psychology is middle class. White wage earners ape the ways of the middle class; they are upwardly mobile. Social standing is correlated with the number of (black) servants that a family has. So, white wage earners, such as the railroad workers, who are at the lower end of the income scale, have more servants than families with higher incomes; it is a status necessity (Munger, 1967:26). Wage earners actually do move up in the social scale; there are no obvious barriers, though the paths of advancement are well defined, and there are few short cuts (ibid.:27). "South African society lacks a true middle class. . . . Class in its fullest sense has become synonymous with color" (ibid.:32).

White labor depends on politics to maintain its privileged position. This was not always the case. The white unions staged a general strike in 1922, which was smashed by the employers and the government (the so-called Rand Revolt). The white workers then turned to political action, and became allied with the Nationalist Party, which needed a mass base. This unholy alliance was able to set up a government in 1924, which enacted a series of measures securing the position of white labor against competition from the blacks.

Whites in lower-paid state jobs are given a special "cost of living" allowance which brings their wages up to what are considered "white" standards. High minimum wages are set for a whole series of occupations that are in effect reserved for whites. In setting tariff rates and in awarding government contracts, the government discriminates in favor of those industries and firms having a high percentage of white workers. The Department of Labor caters to white labor and protects it against competition from the blacks. Finally, a law enacted in 1926 reserves by law certain categories of skilled and semiskilled work for whites (Davies, 1973:45).

When white workers want to perform labor that is actually in the hands of blacks, they are able to take over those jobs and a wage is set for them higher than was being paid the blacks. This happened in the 1930s when white workers took over the pick-and-shovel work on the government railroads (Munger, 1967:32).

The Nationalist Party was temporarily eclipsed in the 1930s and 1940s, but the special laws for protection of white labor were not repealed. Since 1948, the Nationalist Party has ruled South Africa. The Labor Party has disappeared; the opposition is formed by the United Party, supported mainly by the English-speaking whites. Most of the white workers support the Nationalist Party, though some vote for the United Party. No progressive white working-class organization exists today in South Africa (Davies, 1973:55). The apparently liberal statements of the Trades Union Council of South Africa (TUCSA) are not to be taken seriously. Even the slogan of "equal pay for equal work" means nothing as long as blacks are effectively barred from all of the desirable employments.

There is continual pressure from the black majority to get education, to organize unions, and to enter the skilled and semiskilled occupations. In spite of all the obstacles placed in their way, in 1966 3,000 Africans had graduated from a university, while 14,421 had passed Standard X or high school. In spite of the opposition of the Afrikaners, there has been some movement of blacks into the civil service, and police and educational work. The government has also hired some coloreds and Africans as letter carriers, and in the government-owned railways, the iron and steel corporation, and so on. The expansion of manufacturing has opened up a whole range of semiskilled operations, some of which inevitably have been filled by blacks (Munger, 1967:33-35).

The legal barriers to employment of Africans in skilled jobs are evaded in several ways. A skilled African may do skilled work in a small shop and get a bonus under the table. In factories skilled jobs are reclassified as unskilled so that Africans can do them (at lower wages). Afrikaner clothing manufacturers locate near the African reserves and escape the ceiling on skilled African work (ibid.:37).

Practices such as these of course threaten the alliance of white workers, employers, and government. But the last still needs its labor base and has shown a willingness to heed any new demands of white labor for special protection against African competition.

Attempts of Africans to protect themselves by union action have met with no support from the whites. The few struggling black unions that had been set up and affiliated with the Trades Union Council of South Africa were thrown out in 1969. The international union movement (the ICFTU) is aware of the situation in South Africa, and considers it something of a scandal, but is unable to influence the situation. The British Trades Union Congress has done nothing for the blacks, and has even advised the TUCSA on how best to maintain the privileged position of the whites (Davies, 1973:54).


## NATIONALISM AND PAN-AFRICANISM

When it became evident in the early 1960s that the end of political colonialism in British and French Africa was at hand, the heads of the new governments at first thought it might be possible, by federating their several efforts, to set up a unit that would have the strength to stand up to the fading imperialist powers. Many of these leaders were pan-Africanists before they were nationalists. Nyerere said:

African nationalism is meaningless, is dangerous, is anachronistic, if it is not at the same time pan-Africanism. (Sigmund, 1972:293)

Kwame Nkrumah stated:

The independence of Ghana is meaningless unless it is accompanied by the total liberation of Africa. (Mboya, 1963:207)

In the early days of Ghana's separate existence, Nkrumah gave almost as much time to campaigning for a federation of African states as to building Ghana as a separate nation. Sentiments similar to those just quoted were expressed by heads of state who varied in their political leanings all the way from the extreme Right to the extreme Left. The PAIGC in Guinea-Bissau set as its goal "the construction of a strong and progressive African nation," not merely a confederation. The conservatives, Tom Mboya in Kenya and Hastings Banda in Malawi, expressed similar sentiments.

As independence for the colonies approached, there seemed to be no good reason for creating as many different states as were at first projected, and proposals for federations filled the air.

Sometimes the aim sought in federation was the advantage of the imperialists, and the federation was quite properly resisted from within and from without, as in the case of the short-lived Central African Federation of Northern Rhodesia (Zambia), Southern Rhodesia (now just Rhodesia), and Nyasaland (Malawi). Sometimes the heads of the new states sought to pursue quite different policies; the Mali Federation could not continue to include Léopold Senghor, the anti-Communist, and Sékou Touré, the revolutionary socialist. When Touré did find a head of state who shared his views, Kwame Nkrumah, the two states were hundreds of miles apart and there could be no thought of uniting them.

Of all the federations proposed, that in East Africa seemed to have the best prospects for success. Kenya, Tanganyika, Uganda, and Zanzibar had a common language (Swahili) and the way to federation had been prepared in the colonial period by the establishment of uniform currency and tariffs and a unified communications system. The leaders, especially Mboya in Kenya and Nyerere in Tanzania, worked hard for federation; Nyerere was willing to postpone his country's independence if that would have helped federation (Klein, 1971:349). In 1967, Tanzania, Kenya, and Uganda established a common market and administrative union called the East African Community. It operates four independent corporations that run East Africa's airlines, railways, harbors, and telecommunication services. But real federation remains remote. In the end, the only unification that took place was that of Tanganyika and Zanzibar, which came together to form Tanzania in 1964.

Nyerere continues to believe in the advantages of federation; he deplores nationalism as leading to Balkanization. He says:

As each of us develops his own state we raise more barriers between ourselves. We entrench differences which we inherited from the colonial period, and develop new ones. Most of all we develop a national pride, which could be inimical to the development of a pride in Africa. (Nyerere, 1968:211)

When, after numerous unsuccessful attempts at regional federation, most African states met at Addis Ababa in May 1963 and set up the Organization of African Unity (OAU), the charter that was adopted was based on the proposition that "It is the inalienable right of all peoples to control their own destiny." The "essential objectives" were stated to be "freedom, equality, justice, *and dignity*" (emphasis added; text in Sigmund, 1972:218). In the classic formula of the French Revolution, "dignity" was thought to be included in the idea of equality; it has remained for Africa to spell out this explicit attack on racialism and on the whole idea, implicit in most European dealings with Africa, that one race or one civilization is *innately* superior to another. Dignity is a contribution of the Africans to the world vocabulary dealing with the objectives of nationalism.

The political objectives of the OAU included the support of national liberation movements in the remaining colonies in order to end colonialism in Africa. The machinery set up was by no means adequate for this task, which involved, as was realized, a long and grueling battle against a stubborn foe; the Portuguese and the white settlers in South Africa and Rhodesia would not give in easily. A second objective was the settling of disputes among the members; a separate treaty established a Commission of Mediation, Conciliation, and Arbitration.

The resolution on economic cooperation provided for the exploration of economic problems such as free exchange of commodities between the African countries and the adoption of standard foreign tariffs in order to protect African industry; the establishment of an African currency zone; the coordination of development programs; and the creation of all-African institutions—a development bank and an Institute for Economic Development and Planning (Potehkin, 1964: 18-20). Unfortunately, some of the countries still prefer to operate through their former imperial masters and to use such access as they have to the European Common Market, in which they can never hope to be more than junior partners, if that. Thus the 1963 resolution has remained a paper one.

The economic argument against fragmentation ("Balkanization") is just as strong now as it ever was (see Seidman and Green, 1968). The

African states are not complementary to one another, could not form a self-sufficient economic unit; they are all at a relatively primitive stage of economic development, and the trade among them is bound to remain small for some time to come. There is, however, an excellent opportunity for each one to specialize and not duplicate another's efforts in trade, or, if more than one produces a given article, to pool their bargaining power and get a better price for such articles.

Pan-Africa is, finally, a rubric under which could be included not only common economic and political activity, but common cultural and research activity, similar to that now being done by the United Nations.

The Charter of the OAU provides for continuing the building up of Africa as a cultural unit, through education and research. The vindication of Africa as an historical entity worthy of respect has always been recognized as a major task, ever since W. E. B. DuBois called together the first Pan-African Congress in 1900. (A good review of the Pan-African Congress movement from 1900 to the founding of the OAU is given in Woddis, 1963:114-17.) Some of the claims made on behalf of Africa have indeed been exaggerated; but it is not necessary to resort to any exaggeration in order to prove that Africa was a leader in world civilization at a not too remote time in the past. The man who has been the most attacked for alleged exaggeration has no doubt been Cheik Anta Diop (see Diop, 1955; Balandier, 1957). Diop's contention that all civilization derived from the Nile Valley may have originated with an Englishman, Grafton Elliot Smith (see G. Smith, 1923). But nothing in the African literature can at all compare, for sheer brazenness and unscientific audacity, to the racist diatribes that long passed for science in the West!

For the moment, the effective political unit in Africa continues to be the nation-state, with a sovereignty as limited as its very modest political and economic clout.

The failure of the OAU to take a stand in favor of the genuine national liberation movement in Angola, the Movimento Popular de Libertaçao de Angola (MPLA), in 1975, raises a question as to whether the OAU can be expected to furnish much help to the several member nations in their coming struggle with neocolonialism. Water cannot rise higher than its source.

ATTITUDE OF THE UNIONS
TO NATIONAL LIBERATION IN AFRICA

Trade union organization in most African countries dates only from the twentieth century. The incipient unions in the colonies had to learn the techniques of organization and of collective bargaining where these had been legalized. They turned naturally to the unions of their respective imperialist countries, which responded in a friendly way, and a continuing relationship was established; the unions in the French colonies were mostly affiliated with the Confédération Générale du Travail (CGT) of France.[16]

When the national liberation movements were organized, the colonial unions participated eagerly, though not in a leading position.[17] The relation of the unions to the parties of national liberation varied. Some union movements became an integral part of the nationalist parties, as in Tunisia, Guinea, and later Tanzania; while in Morocco, Nigeria, and Cameroon, the unions, though strongly nationalist, were at the time of the granting of independence on the outs with their respective nationalist parties, which had come under the leadership of an antilabor elite. In general, the unions were at the peak of their influence. Fanon, writing in 1961, did not doubt that the psychology of the workers and peasants, which had been moving to the left during the immediately preceding years, would continue to move still further to the left. To others also it seemed that social revolution was beginning (Geiss, 1965:20; Lynd, 1968:34-35). It was not. Only by exception, as in Zanzibar in 1964, did the African unions become part of a revolutionary force.

The leaders of the colonial unions naturally hoped that the metropolitan unions with which they had enjoyed friendly relations would sympathize with their aspirations for self-determination. They were disappointed. The unions in the several imperialist countries were, at best, a drag on the liberation movements in the colonies of their respective nations, although they had no objection to seeing the colonies of *rival* imperialist countries become independent.

The French CGT and the British Trades Union Congress (TUC) were in 1949 both affiliated with the World Federation of Trade Unions (WFTU), along with all the leading union centrals of the world except the American Federation of Labor (AFL). In 1949 a number of union centrals, including the British TUC, seceded from the WFTU and joined the AFL in forming the International Confederation of Free Trade Unions (ICFTU). This body was anti-Communist but not necessarily against the independence of the colonies.

The British TUC continued to talk about the virtues of democracy and self-determination, but did not actively assist the colonial liberation movements. Kenya is an example of its attitude. During the "Mau Mau" crisis in 1954, when the commercial press had poisoned the minds of workers and others in the West with a cascade of vilification of "Mau Mau violence," the ICFTU sent a representative, a Canadian named Jim Bury, to Kenya. At this time the unions alone were carrying on the fight for independence, all other organizations having been banned. Bury aided the unions, and helped to get the story out to the world about the true situation in Kenya. He was threatened with deportation, and was saved only by the intervention of a special envoy from the British TUC, Sir Vincent Tewson. This was about the extent of the TUC's aid to the Kenya unions in this period.

The AFL (after 1955 the AFL-CIO) was able to expose the hollowness of the demagogic protestations of the TUC; it helped to destroy the British influence in the African nations during the independence struggle. Some of the resolutions passed by the ICFTU sounded quite radical (especially in 1957; see Davies, 1966:197). Sympathy for the national liberation movements was quite in line with U.S. State Department objectives, up to a point. It was believed that the colonies of France and England, if independent, would be more readily accessible to penetration by American capital.

The French CGT was under Communist leadership, but it was not any more active in pushing the independence demands of the African unions than was the British TUC. An example was Tunisia, which was one of a number of countries where the CGT had affiliates in the period before 1950. A group of unions, which were collaborating very closely with the Tunisian nationalist organization, the Neo-Destour Party, found that the CGT affiliate was not pushing their demands adequately. They seceded from the CGT affiliate and applied for direct admission to the WFTU. Their application was refused; they were told to rejoin the CGT affiliate. They then affiliated with the ICFTU, in 1951.

The WFTU lost one after another of its African affiliates, which were pulling out of the CGT in protest over its pro-colonial policies. In 1957 a number of the African union centrals, now independent of any international affiliation, decided to affiliate with each other in a regional African union federation. They formed the Union Générale des Travailleurs d'Afrique (UGTAN), with Sékou Touré of Guinea at the head. The WFTU, having seen which way the wind was blowing, even assisted in the creation of UGTAN, and advised its remaining African affiliates to join (Davies, 1966:200). The UGTAN was succeeded by the All-Africa Trade Union Federation, formed at Casablanca in 1961.[18]

Once the British and French colonies were "independent," the AFL-CIO pulled out of the ICFTU and resumed its direct appeal to the African unions, using all kinds of blandishments. It was at this time that the American unions supplied $200,000 (perhaps obtained sub rosa from the CIA) to build a big trade union center in Kenya for the unions headed by Tom Mboya. The U.S. backing eventually became so embarrassing to Mboya that before his death he publicly dissociated himself from his overseas sponsors. Indeed, American labor made no secret of the fact that it was working jointly with employers and the government; all three contributed to the American Institute for Free Labor Development (AIFLD), set up to train leaders who would bring the principles of anti-Communism and "business" unionism to the Third World.

The AFL-CIO has been so open and brazen in helping the imperialists to make profits at the expense of colonial and neocolonial labor that we sometimes forget that the British TUC really initiated this process in some areas where the AFL-CIO was later active. When Guyana was still a British colony, the dominant industry was sugar; the sugarcane cutters were—and still are—the most numerous body of workers in the colony. The British TUC assisted in setting up a company union for the cane cutters and thus thwarted bona fide trade unionism in this area for a generation. The British TUC also collaborated with the AFL-CIO, the CIA, and the secret services and foreign offices of both the United States and England in an elaborate conspiracy to oust the popularly elected (and socialist oriented) government of Cheddi Jagan and substitute the racist Forbes Burnham as prime minister of Guyana when it was becoming independent. In the process, a near civil war and a general strike wracked the country. It was not until 1975 that two long and bitter strikes of the cane cutters finally forced the sugar planters to hold an election to determine the workers' bargaining agent, and to recognize the union of their choice.

It is clear enough by this time that the traditional Marxist proposition that labor "tends" to be internationalist is not correct. In fact, much to the displeasure of some Marxists, we have to note that organized labor in the socialist countries, too, goes along with the foreign policy of its respective country, even when this puts it in opposition to the interests of labor in some other country. The international solidarity of labor then becomes a bitter charade. We need only cite the actions of the Soviet trade union leaders in welcoming with open arms the delegation appointed by military dictator Marcos to represent the Philippine "unions" at the World Congress of Peace Forces which met in Moscow in 1973. The bona fide unions in the Philippines were not even invited, and their representatives could not have got out of the country anyway. (Marcos has had the surprising diplomatic success of getting favorable treatment and recognition from the Soviet Union and People's China at the same time!)

So, it was to be expected that anti-Marxists would hail the collapse of labor internationalism as proving that "nationalism has a much deeper and more profound influence on men than do class interests" (King, 1973:256). It is a matter of common observation that class differences are sunk in a common national effort during a war; but when the crisis is past, class differences reassert themselves. Marxists are correct in stressing the importance of the class analysis on the home front, but are in danger of being considered doctrinaire if they cite authorities from an earlier period of the labor movement to prove the existence of proletarian internationalism today.


CONCLUSION

Marxist theory regarding the underdeveloped countries must explain how it is that revolutionary socialism and revolutionary nationalism can come to a country which does not have a revolutionary proletariat or a progressive bourgeoisie. Indeed a country that was lacking altogether in either a working class or a bourgeoisie would seem, according to traditional Marxist theory, to be poor material for either revolutionary socialism or revolutionary nationalism.

But Lenin, while recognizing that there could be no question of a purely proletarian movement in a precapitalist environment, emphasized that if the masses of the people were really aroused, they could accomplish miracles (Lenin, CW, XXX:153-54; XXXI:242-43). It was the contributions of Fanon and Cabral that showed how in their particular environment the masses might be aroused, and just who might give the necessary leadership.

Cabral accepted Lenin's proposition that the leadership of the socialist revolution must come from individual members of the intelligentsia. Fanon, though less explicit, could not but accept this idea. But both explicitly challenged a favorite dogma of traditional Marxism, that the leading class in the revolution must be that of the city workers. Both also denied that the European proletariat would furnish leadership or even support for the anti-imperialist revolution.

Cabral's discovery and utilization of the Nameless Group (the neo-urbanites, as we have called them) must rate as a contribution of the first importance.

The emergence of Third World thinkers such as Mao and the Africans shows that the center of gravity of nationalist theory has shifted away from Europe. The problem of exploitation is more acute, and the need for an up-to-date theory of how to fight it is more urgent, in the parts of the world long exploited by Europe (and, now, by the United States).

# 9

## Conclusion

Nationalism is still a movement possessed of great vitality. Yet a surprising number of students of the subject have predicted an imminent decline in the power and influence of present-day nations and thus of nationalism.

E. H. Carr, at the close of World War II, contemplated a world which would be dominated by a limited number of multinational superstates, which might be able to come to an understanding with one another. Individual rights would be guaranteed not by the several national states but by the superstates directly (Carr, 1945:67).[1] This prediction was offered before the organization of the United Nations but is not to be taken as involving that body in any way. It was quickly rendered out of date, in any case.

At about the same time Hans Kohn opined that nationalism might become "de-politicized" and "retreat into the intimacy and spontaneity of the individual conscience" as religion did in the eighteenth century (Kohn in Sulzbach, 1943:viii).

Karl Deutsch, twenty years later and twenty years wiser, thought in 1967 that most national boundaries were not due to change, and that at the end of the century the nation-state would still be the main social engine for getting things done (Deutsch, 1967:661). Harvey Perloff, director of the Regional Studies Program at Resources for the Future, Inc., challenged this idea. He wrote:

> For much of the world, and especially for some of the new countries, the nation is incapable of organizing the kinds of public policies that are needed. For example, the very small countries of Africa are basically nonviable.

Of the various possible reactions to this situation, he suggests that several nations might organize on a regional basis to form a common market. Thus, the year 2000 "might very well be dominated by political units that do not look at all like the nations of today" (Perloff, 1967:671).

Carr's proposition that nationalism interferes with the formation or perpetuation of large states is sometimes true, sometimes not; after all, it was the intensive nationalist propaganda of the Fichtes, Herders, and Mazzinis in the nineteenth century that conditioned, if it did not exactly cause, the emergence of the large, viable states of Germany and Italy. But where empires break up and small states emerge, it is forcing the facts to attribute this development to nationalism alone. Nationalist movements in several countries of sub-Saharan Africa were weak indeed, not enough to account for the emergence of all of the new African states.

Whether due to nationalist movements or not, the claims of the smaller nationalities have one general cause that is persistently overlooked but is still perfectly obvious: exploitation.

When Carr contended that small states are nonviable and are due to be absorbed or dominated by larger ones, he overlooked one important factor: the small state may exercise an option as to which orbit it favors. The fact that Cuba could not live in isolation did not prevent its shifting its allegiance from one great power to another in the 1960s; and Vietnam has spent most of its independent existence resisting domination by some larger state to which it did not choose to be subordinate.

## THE FUTURE OF UNDERDEVELOPMENT

The position of the underdeveloped countries in the world economy, as described by Andre Gunder Frank and others, is grim (Frank, 1969 and 1971). But Frank's analysis has been challenged.

Although most of the underdeveloped countries are now free of overt political domination, as the Latin American countries have been for many years, their economic status remains subordinate to that of the advanced industrial countries. Not only that, but they are said to fall further behind every year; their industrialization, long retarded by deliberate action of the advanced countries, is too slow. The terms of trade, it is said, turn further against their primary products. They have indeed, in this view, little to hope for as long as capitalism continues.

The argument about the deterioration in the terms of trade is by now so sacrosanct that even to discuss it seems superfluous to some. It has apparently solid material foundations, which were described in some detail in a 1949 UN study that drew on an earlier League of Nations report. This analysis, on which the theories of a whole school of economists in the Economic Commission for Latin America, and after 1963 at the United Nations Commission on Trade and Development, are based, has been summarized as follows:

> The income elasticity of demand for primary products is low. The increases in population in the poorer countries will force new entrants into primary production, thus expanding output at low wages ... Technical progress has resulted in economies of raw material usage while at the same time a number of petroleum-based synthetic fibres have been developed, which have made severe inroads into the markets for natural fibres. Finally, most primary products are produced by or sold to large oligopolistic business groups who are "price-makers" rather than "price-takers." (Hone, 1973:90)

To round out the analysis, figures are usually presented on the growth of the multinational corporations and of their influence in the underdeveloped countries. If political power is really the handmaid of economic power, as is usually maintained, then the picture of domination of all the backward areas by the big monopolies is complete.

A recent issue of *New Left Review* (no.81, 1973) contains articles which if they do not refute the conventional analysis altogether, at least suggest the limitations of it. The deterioration in the terms of trade which has been a standing complaint of the underdeveloped countries for so many years, is not necessarily a secular trend. Countervailing forces may reverse the trend, and indeed seem to have done so already. The price of primary commodities nearly doubled in the year 1972-1973, and it seems likely that the downward trend in the terms of trade will not be resumed until after 1980, if then, especially if the producer countries learn how to organize and maintain the prices of their products as has already been done effectively in certain key fields (e.g., oil) (Hone, 1973:82ff.).

The international corporations through their subsidiaries may compete with one another, and all are subject to the laws of the several countries in which they operate. No doubt this statement assumes that the governments of the underdeveloped countries in question are not completely dominated by the multinational corporations, and some clearly are. But with the expected increase in nationalism in these countries, such domination cannot be assumed to continue indefinitely.

The trend toward ownership of natural resources by the country in which they occur is probably irreversible, barring temporary setbacks, as in Chile. Even where resources remain in the hands of foreigners, the terms of their concessions have been getting stiffer; provisions for long-run recapture of the properties are encountered on an increasing scale. The advanced countries are well aware of the psychology of the newly emerging countries, and some of the speakers for imperialism have been calling for greater flexibility in the policies of the international enterprises in both the extractive and the manufacturing sectors.

It is no longer true that the advanced countries offer a united front opposed to the industrialization of the Third World. Indeed, industrialization has begun on a large scale in a number of formerly backward countries, led by Brazil. Brazil already exports quantities of manufactured products to Argentina, and is looking farther afield. Brazil exported $81.2 million-worth of shoes to the United States in 1973, and is reported to be exploring markets in Africa and the Soviet Union.

It is true that the advanced countries have know-how that the Third World lacks; but this ascendancy cannot be maintained indefinitely, as the example of the Soviet Union shows. Independence of the former colonies has stimulated the demand for a scale of living comparable to that of the advanced countries.

Bill Warren points out that the nationalism of the new countries, which he finds to be on the increase, is not necessarily associated with any particular political leaning; there are progressive nationalist countries and also reactionary ones, but all (he says) are agreed on the need for development (Warren, 1973:11). Warren fully agrees that it is not the national industrial bourgeoisie but the petty bourgeoisie that adds especially to the drive for national development. "Just as a national bourgeoisie is not necessary for industrial development, so it is not necessary for nationalism," says Warren (ibid.:43).

A point that needs to be stressed in this connection is that the emphasis on manufacturing industry as the measure and substance of development, which was so widespread just after World War II, has been modified somewhat with the rise of international economic blocs such as the Common Market and Comecon. The experience of Cuba is in point. Cuba had been known as a country whose economy was dominated by sugar production. After 1959 it sought first of all diversification; but when it became part of the Soviet bloc it reversed its policy and specialized in sugar more than ever. While monoculture is frowned on, the way out for underdeveloped countries is now seen to be in the joint action of a number of such countries, as in the OPEC, rather than in self-sufficiency.

Another point stressed by Warren is that the per capita increases in Gross National Product have been relatively low in the underdeveloped countries because of the very rapid population increases in those countries. But the absolute increases in production have been fairly large, and per capita increases stand to become larger faster when (1) the economies are reorganized and an infrastructure is created; (2) the rate of population increase tails off, as it will; and (3) the resources of modern science begin to be applied in a serious way to the problems of the less developed countries, instead of exclusively to the problems of the temperate zone, as in the past.

The underdeveloped countries cannot be prevented from developing; their new-found dignity and self-respect, a function of their rising nationalism, will not permit them to pay tribute indefinitely to the advanced countries. The example of the socialist countries, plus the political and economic assistance from the same source, will create a groundswell of popular resistance to imperialist-sponsored military dictatorships.

## CONCLUSION

We take it that nationalism which represents resistance to exploitation is the manifestation of a healthy tendency. Writers of all persuasions, from Acton to Lenin, have advised members of minor nationalities to remain in larger polities or consent to be absorbed by them for the sake of the economic benefits. It was many years before people realized that in the case of colonies the benefits were largely illusory and were counterbalanced by disadvantages. But even where the economic benefits were real, the advantages of political independence have seemed superior to very many small nationalities, and in our view, they are the ones to decide.

The main task of the socialist revolution in the period of monopoly capitalism is to attack the power of the international capitalists at its weakest point, and this point has been shown by recent experience to be the less developed countries which are just winning consciousness of themselves as nations. It is time to drop altogether the idea that the "international working class" will bring about the revolution. There is no such thing as an international working class. Rather, there are many national working classes. In some countries there is not even a working class at all. In many others the working class, or the bulk of it, is not anti-imperialist or socialist.

The main force to rely on is then not class consciousness on an international scale; this has proved to be a broken reed. The power to win freedom for the underdeveloped countries and ultimately for the whole world resides in the nationalist strivings of those countries fighting economic imperialism (neocolonialism) as they recently fought colonialism.

For a movement like this to bring permanent gains, it has to be socialist oriented; otherwise the gains of the struggle may be expected to slip away—as has happened in most of Africa. Thus for Marxists to participate in the national movements against economic imperialism is not enough; they must continue to hold high the banner of socialism, for otherwise they are in great danger of being absorbed in the nationalist movements and losing their distinctive identity.

In the advanced imperialist countries, the main task for Marxists may be for a time the struggle against aggressive, expansionist nationalism. But capitalism is incapable of organizing the world, or any particular country, for peace and prosperity, and this fact will become more and more apparent, to the point where the people will become aware of it and demand a change. At such a time, it will no doubt be the proletarians of city and country who will have the most to gain and on whom reliance must be placed for mass support. Submerged and exploited ethnic groups and age groups and women will lead the way because of their specific grievances. Eventually, socialist and class consciousness may be expected to spread, if the partisans of socialism have not become discouraged and have maintained a running fire of criticism of capitalism and all its works. There are sections of the so-called middle class which may be more receptive to the socialist message than the working class.

A Marxist theory of nationalism in this day and age is thus nothing less than a theory of society as a whole on an international scale. Instead of treating nationalism as a side issue, a nuisance that distracts attention from the main task, Marxists have to reorient themselves on the new nature of the struggle, which in the first instance is often nationalist more than anything else. In so doing, they will be carrying on in the spirit of Lenin, who took the crucial step of incorporating national exploitation alongside of class exploitation as a basic part of Marxist theory.

# Notes

## CHAPTER 1: INTRODUCTION

1. The country whose interests they serve may of course not be their own. Communists in countries outside the Soviet Union who follow the lead of the Soviet Union in foreign policy should perhaps be put down as Russian nationalists.
2. This was the opinion of the Polish scholars Walecki and Markiewicz (Wiatr, 1969). Lepkowski, another Polish scholar, criticized his countryman J. J. Wiatr, who he said took 200 pages to define the nation and then did not use his own definition! (Lepkowski, 1971:96).
3. Coleman in effect does this when he discusses the early resistance movements in Nigeria; see Coleman, 1958:169.
4. Of course, some Third World countries do have an industrial bourgeoisie. In India, it was primarily the industrial bourgeoisie who first organized a viable nationalist movement (Desai, 1948: 141-42).
5. Jairus Banaji argues the opposite, and cites Lenin's reply to the manifesto of the League of Armenian Social Democrats (1903) to prove that Lenin thought there were two kinds of self-determination: a principle of democratic self-determination that applied to nationalities within a given state, and a principle of

national self-determination that covered subjugated or oppressed nations (see Banaji, 1974:1539). This is too deep for us. The idea of self-determination for nationalities within a given state is absurd, and was so labeled by Marx, Engels, Lenin, and Banaji himself. (Lenin's reply to the manifesto is to be found in Lenin, CW, I:329-39.) The Armenian Social Democrats were demanding national-cultural autonomy on the Bauer-Renner model.

On the interchangeability of the terms "nation" and "nationality" in Lenin, we cite a sentence from "Critical Remarks on the National Question" (1913): "The proletariat . . . supports everything that makes the ties between nationalities closer, or tends to merge nations" (Lenin, CW, XX:351-56).

6. Most dictionary definitions of the nation are defective. The one in *Webster's New World Dictionary* is patterned closely after Stalin's, whether by intent or not. It even repeats Stalin's main errors, omitting national consciousness and specifying a common language. The Random House dictionary of 1967 includes national consciousness but omits what we have called "integration." The widely used *Webster's New Collegiate Dictionary* in its 1949 edition even had the nation composed of people who were connected by "supposed ties of blood"—a kind of supertribe. One wonders whether this definition was prepared or reviewed by Hans Kohn, who served as consultant.

It is usual in the United States to include an Indian tribe as one use of the word "nation." This is a perpetuation of some early settlers' vagueness in translation. Whoever called the Iroquois confederation "the six nations" was misusing language. The several Iroquois tribes were not nations, nor were the constituent bodies of other Indian federations. One might equally well refer to the Middle Ages when students at the medieval universities were classified into "nations" according to their countries of provenance.

The best dictionary definition is that of the *Oxford English Dictionary* (1933), according to which the nation is "an extensive aggregation of persons, so closely associated with each other by common descent, language or history, as to form a distinct race or people, usually organized as a separate political state and occupying a definite territory." Even this definition emphasizes kinship and race too much and national consciousness and integration too little.

7. Among them are Hertz, whose discussion shifts back and forth between nation and state (1944:208-23), and Ginsberg, who lists seven ways in which "nations" are formed—but most of the seven refer to the creation of *states* (Ginsberg, 1961:6).

8. We understand that in Hungary István Söter and Aladár Mód believe that national differences should be encouraged in order to avoid the social leveling and equalizing of nations that result from the technological society (King, 1973:254).

9. Joan Robinson recently expressed the opinion that "socialist economies are more nationalistic than capitalist ones," which is no doubt an exaggeration but it illustrates our point (see Robinson and Eatwell, 1974).

10. Kim, long a partisan of national autonomy in Party matters, mentioned in a speech in 1966 the Party's "bitter experience of interference by great-power chauvinists in its internal affairs." No one was in doubt as to who was meant (see Kim, 1969:141-43).

11. Fred Halliday comments: "When the masses rise, revolutionaries support them, as Marx did over the Paris Commune and Lenin did over the July Days" (Halliday, 1971:87).


## CHAPTER 2: THE ETHICS OF NATIONALISM

1. Integration may be cultural or biological, the latter having reference to the unification of the population through the intermarriage of different racial strains. But biological unification may not reduce cultural differentiation, which is frequently not associated with any racial factor at all. Miscegenation also does not involve reducing class or caste differences necessarily (see Petras and Zeitlin, 1968:26f).

2. The passages in question are the following:

> Independent, or but loosely connected provinces, with separate interests, laws, government and systems of taxation, became lumped together into one nation, with one government, one code of laws, one *national* class interest, one frontier and one custom tariff.
>
> At first the contest is carried on by individual laborers, then by the work-people of a factory, then by the operatives

of one trade, in one locality, against the individual bourgeois who directly exploits them ... It was just this contact that was needed to centralize the numerous local struggles, all of the same character, into one *national* struggle between classes. (Marx and Engels, 1949:13, 17-18; emphasis added)

3. This association is overlooked by M. N. Roy, who wrote: "Nationalism is not a democratic force" (Whitaker, 1961:29).

4. But note that this formulation refers to cases of *conflict* of conscience, when the dictates of, say, church and state do not coincide.

5. But before the withdrawal of U.S. troops from Vietnam some hundreds of thousands of GIs had gone AWOL because they were revolted by the war.

6. "The empire was something with which the French people had nothing whatever to do" (Luethy, 1955:205).

7. We cannot do justice to Meinecke's argument within the scope of this book. But one passage will indicate its drift, if not its nuances:

> Machiavellianism came to form an integral part in the complex of an idealist view of the universe, a view which at the same time embraced and confirmed all moral values—whereas in former times Machiavellianism had only been able to exist alongside the moral cosmos that had been built up. What happened now was almost like the legitimization of a bastard. (Meinecke, 1957:350)

The question is, was this bastard ever really legitimized?

8. "Instinctive reactions to concrete situations were sanctified and absolutised in Germany by philosophical reasoning which absolved individual conscience from responsibility" (Kohn, 1954:26).

9. A priceless but little-known satire on the moralizing Liberal statesman is in Chesterton, 1914:Ch. 2.

10. "Every nationalism is guided by the principle, 'My country, right or wrong'" (Braunthal, 1961:192).

11. One hardly knows what any division of the human race should be free to do if not to determine with which of the various collective bodies of human beings they choose to associate themselves. (J. S. Mill, 1861:Ch. 16)

12. He is an Englishman;
    For he himself has said it,
    And it's greatly to his credit

That he is an Englishman.
For he might have been a Rooshian,
A French or Turk or Prooshian,
Or perhaps I-tal-i-an.
But in spite of all temptations
To belong to other nations
He remains an Englishman. (Gilbert, 1878)

13. Published in the United States as *The Psychology of Power*, 1966.
14. Tolstoy's views are given in *Christianity and Politics;* see *The Kingdom of God and Other Essays,* in *World's Classics,* esp. p. 534.
15. Eduard Heimann says that man is the "creative creature." That is why to denounce power as bad, as does pacifism, is to deny man's dignity (Heimann, 1947:326).
16. Fascism is not necessarily nationalistic (on this point see Polanyi, 1944:241).
17. "Patriotism," wrote Thorstein Veblen during World War I, is "a sense of partisan solidarity in respect of prestige. . . . Patriotism finds its full expression in no other outlet than warlike enterprise. . . . Patriotism is useful for breaking the peace, not for keeping it" (Veblen, 1917:31, 33, 78).

    When Richard Nixon described the twenty years of Democratic administration of the U.S. government as "twenty years of treason," President Truman became so incensed that he would not appear on the same platform with Nixon. Yet the latter continued to charge his opponents with treason in a characteristically irresponsible way.
18. "Barefaced covetousness was the moving spirit of civilisation from its first dawn to the present day" (Engels, 1902:215).


CHAPTER 3: THE THEORY OF NATIONALISM:
LUXEMBURG, STALIN, LENIN, AND TROTSKY

1. This is also quoted in Cliffe and Saul (1972:72), but they develop the idea further. Nyerere is no Marxist, but his remarks apply if anything more forcefully to Marxian socialism than to the Nyerere variety.
2. But not any more. See Luxemburg, 1976.

3. The *shlachta,* nobility who for many years were the bearers of Polish nationalism, were, in fact, a quite stratified class and included, besides landowners, a large number of pauperized "nobility."

4. The Maldive Islands, which were admitted to the United Nations in 1965, had at the time a population of under 100,000, and some even smaller units have since been admitted.

5. Actually, as we have seen, Luxemburg did recognize that nationalism has its constructive aspects.

6. The Luxemburgists favored the former Russian Poland (the "Congress Kingdom") becoming part of the Soviet Union. This point of view was advanced also after World War II, but did not prevail.

7. Lenin of course did make this distinction; see his article, "The Question of Nationalities or 'Autonomisation'" (Lenin, CW, XXXVI:607-08).

8. It is most distressing to have Stalin take the position of those who look on ethnic ("race") prejudice as something innate.

9. This definition has been (mis)translated as "stable community of language" and so forth; but while this rendition is unacceptable, the definition as given in the text is also unacceptable (see Pipes, 1954:38).

10. "A nation exists when its component parts believe it to be a nation." This formulation, by Krehbiel, was in use at the time that Stalin was writing his essay. It repeats Renan's idea, and is still current (see Emerson, 1960:102). Others who insist that the "will to be a nation" is fundamental are Chatham House (Carr et al., 1939:259) and Eugen Lemberg (1964).

11. We do not understand how Hélène Carrère d'Encausse can call Stalin non-Leninist on the ground that Stalin put forward psychological factors in his definition (see Carrère d'Encausse, 1971:229).

12. Jean Chesneaux's criticism of the Stalin essay is one of the best we have seen (Chesneaux, 1965:71f.).

13. Stalin fought against anti-Semitism while Lenin lived and did not publicly espouse it until the late 1930s. Deutscher thinks that Stalin encouraged scurrilous sub rosa anti-Semitic attacks on Trotsky as early as 1924, by way of Uglanov. But his public statements at this time were irreproachable. Stalin's protégé, Kaganovich, elevated to the Politburo in 1926, was Jewish.

14. Lenin was equally emphatic on this point. Having in mind the situation in Eastern Europe—not the national liberation movements

in the colonies—Lenin wrote: "Marxism is incompatible with nationalism."

15. It seems that Pipes is somewhat misleading on this point. He says that Lenin disliked the Renner-Bauer plan of "national cultural autonomy" because it "strove artificially to preserve all those ethnic differences which capitalism was already sweeping away" (Pipes, 1954:42). However, Lenin's objection to the Renner-Bauer plan was of a different nature altogether. He thought of it as interfering with *political* integration. Lenin was himself a major defender of ethnic diversity; the survival of the minor languages in the Soviet Union today is due largely to the efforts which he began and which have continued (Lenin, CW, XVIII:191).

16. Stalin also gave lip service to Lenin's concept of a differentiated proletarian culture. In 1925, he wrote:

> Proletarian culture does not preclude, but rather presupposes and fosters national culture, just as national culture does not nullify, but rather supplements and enriches proletarian culture. (Stalin, 1953, II:197)

17. Stalin came out for self-determination of nations, in much the same terms as did Lenin. Curiously, Pipes and Carrère d'Encausse missed this part of Stalin's essay (see Pipes, 1954:40; Carrère d'Encausse, 1971:229; Stalin, 1953, II:321.) We have referred elsewhere to Lenin's analysis, taken over by Stalin, of the responsibility of the bourgeoisie for the nationalist movement.

18. Brandt assumes, but does not specifically show, that the Politburo meeting just after Chiang's coup of March 20, 1926, knew about the coup and chose to disregard it. But Stalin may have been the only one who knew. Later, Trotsky voted to continue cooperation with Chiang, and so the criticism holds (see Brandt, 1938:155-56).

19. By contrast, Christian Rakovsky had said as early as 1929 that the Soviet Union had changed from a proletarian state into a bureaucratic state with residual proletarian elements (Deutscher, 1963:462).

## CHAPTER 4: THE NATIONAL QUESTION IN THE SOVIET UNION

1. Communist party membership on the eve of the October Revolution was as follows, according to the *Great Soviet Encyclopedia:*

200,000 in ethnic Russia; 60,000 in Ukraine, Moldavia, and adjacent war fronts; 20,000 in Caucasus and adjacent war fronts; 10,000 in Central Asia (*Bol'shaia Sovetskaia Entsiklopediia,* 1973: XII:550).

2. The Russian-sponsored government was of course also Ukrainian, and a better interpreter of Ukrainian popular aspirations than the Rada, as the event proved.

3. Lenin had spoken of a "common or international culture of the proletarian movement," though he always coupled this idea with that of tolerance for local or national expressions of culture (Lenin, CW, XX).

4. Skrypnyk's description of official Bolshevik propaganda is not altogether faithful. It would have been more accurate to say that this "line" stressed the "bourgeois nationalism" in the smaller republics, not the "chauvinism of the stateless peoples."

5. The term "proletarian nation" was used by Sultan-Galiev in a sense different from that employed before World War I—for example, by Pascoli and Corradini, who sought to show that Italy was a "proletarian nation" because it did not have as many colonies as the old imperialist powers (see Davis, 1967:116).

6. Bennigsen says that Sultan-Galiev was executed in 1937, but Rodinson finds that he was still alive in 1940 (see Bennigsen, 1957:644; Rodinson, 1972:382). Sultan-Galiev had long since ceased to command a following, owing to the limitations on dissident opinion in the Soviet Union.

7. Islam was not, of course, the only religion whose influence came under Communist attack in the 1920s and 1930s. The established (Greek Orthodox) church was at first strongly opposed to the Russian Revolution—understandably, since one of the first acts of the Bolshevik government was to confiscate the church lands. For two decades the Communists battled to destroy the influence of the conservative clergy. This campaign was carried on both inside and outside the church. Outside, the burden of antireligious propaganda was borne by the League of the Militant Godless, which preached atheism and carried out a frontal assault on religion in general. At the same time, a reformist wing in the church itself was sponsored by the government, and by 1937 it had won control. The League of the Militant Godless was disbanded. During World War II (the "Great Patriotic War" in Soviet Russia) the church

strongly supported the government. In order to solidify the support of backward elements, leading government officials even considered adopting religion themselves, according to General Korneev, the chief of the Soviet mission in Yugoslavia (Djilas, 1962:47-48). There is nothing impossible about this proposition, which illustrates how nationalist considerations had come to override strict Marxist doctrine.

It should not be overlooked that there were in tsarist Russia millions of peasants who were strongly opposed to the Orthodox Church and to the tsar; they were anti-Establishment and anti-nationalist. The "Old Believers," who at the time of the revolution were estimated at one quarter of the Christian population, held strong ideas of social and economic egalitarianism (Wolf, 1969:69-70).

8. Critics of this volte-face by Stalin have usually failed to stress that he had the authority of Engels to back him up. Note especially Engels' retrospective endorsement of the Hapsburgs' effort to annex what is now Switzerland (see Marx and Engels, SW, IV:392).

9. The number of Kazakhs listed in the census decreased from 3,968,000 in 1926 to 3,101,000 in 1939. It has sometimes been rather hastily assumed that this decrease indicated a corresponding loss of life. This interpretation of the figures is subject to qualifications, for the following reasons:

1. The definition of a Kazakh had been changed. Certain smaller tribes that had been included as Kazakhs in 1926 were separated out in 1939 (Bruk, 1972:366).

2. Tens of thousands of Kazakhs had left the area; some turned up in Sinkiang, as had happened with the Kirghiz in 1916.

3. The period in question includes the period of extremely rapid industrialization of the Soviet economy, a time when great numbers of young people were leaving predominantly rural areas, for instance, Kazakhstan, to get jobs in the cities; Kazakhstan had no large cities then.

4. There has always been much inter-republic migration among the nomads in Central Asia, and a period of stress such as the early 1930s in Kazakhstan might find the out-movement exceeding the in-movement.

5. We do not know with certainty whether some Kazakhs changed their nationality and became Russians. We do know that

the number of Russians in Kazakhstan increased appreciably, but that much (probably most) of the increase was caused by immigration of Russians.

10. The source of Smal-Stocki's information was not given. But it is obvious that such figures on the minor nationalities mean little unless accompanied by corresponding figures on the number of Russian defectors, and these Smal-Stocki does not attempt to give.

11. For assistance with this section, I am indebted to Livingston T. Merchant, Jr.

12. The writers cited in this paragraph and those immediately following all contributed articles to *Voprosy Istorii* in 1966.

13. The debate attracted attention abroad. Summaries were published in England (Howard, 1967), in France (Carrère d'Encausse, 1971), in Germany (Meissner, 1976-77), and in the United States.

    It is not possible to classify the various contributors to the discussion in neat camps; the argument ranged widely, back into history, as well as forward into the future. However, in general, the advocates of merging may be said to have included Yevgeni Zhukov, Academic Secretary of the Academy of Sciences, who wrote the original article in *Voprosy Istorii* in 1961; P. G. Semenov in articles in 1961 and later; and especially P. M. Rogachev and M. A. Sverdlin, whose joint article set off the debate in *Voprosy Istorii* in 1966. Champions of the smaller nationalities were M. S. Dzhunusov, M. O. Mnatskanian, T. Yu. Burmistrova, N. A. Tavakalian, and S. T. Kaltakhchyan.

14. This point was made strongly, and repeatedly, by Stalin in his 1913 essay (see Stalin, 1942:46, 63, 65). Of course, the reference there was to capitalist democracy, but is the case so different in a socialist state?

15. The disagreement is *not* over the reliability of Soviet official figures, which are used by all parties. There are still some American scholars, especially in the CIA, who challenge the accuracy of certain official figures, but even they, while rejecting the figures that do not fit their purposes, do use other Russian-compiled figures perforce. In general, Western statisticians some time ago came to the conclusion that Soviet figures are quite reliable, though not always obtainable.

16. It should be borne in mind that the Russian Socialist Federated Soviet Republic (RSFFR) is itself a composite, including some of

the most advanced but also some of the most backward areas of the Soviet Union.

17. Shaheen points out that Jews were recognized as a nationality in the Census and that Jewish schools were opened, although the Jews lacked two of the characteristics a nationality was supposed to have, namely, a common territory and a common economic life (Shaheen, 1956:62).

## CHAPTER 5: SOLVING THE
## NATIONAL QUESTION IN YUGOSLAVIA

1. Andreas Papandreou reported that Yugoslavia had been taken over by NATO and the CIA. According to this authority:

   [Yugoslavia] received $200 million in intelligence funds from the U.S. in 1968 to purchase small arms to organize a guerrilla army for confronting a possible Soviet invasion. It recently received additional money from the U.S. via the Greek Colonels, whom it agreed to live with in the Balkans. Yugoslavia, incidentally, also arrested two freedom fighters very recently who were running resistance material into Greece. (Papandreou, 1972:21)

2. David Horowitz, discussing this point, finds that in Yugoslavia the national orientation of the contending parties was determined by their class character. This rather obscure proposition seems to be a hangover from the days when it was assumed that Marxists had no position on the national question as such—that peoples' attitudes on questions of nationalism could be deduced from their social class. We have already indicated that we believe this point of view is outdated (see Horowitz, 1969:104-105).

3. "[The national question] has been settled, and very well settled, to the satisfaction of all of our peoples . . . on the lines of Lenin's teachings" (Tito, 1963:97-98).

4. In 1968, by contrast, the Soviet occupation of Czechoslovakia was condemned by the Central Committee of the League of Communists (Community Party of Yugoslavia), which said that the occupation resulted from "persistent efforts to solve contradictions and conflicts within socialism . . . by ever more frequent recourse

to the use of force" (resolution adopted August 23, 1968; see Perovic, 1968:78).

5. In 1955 Kosovo-Metohija had been declared in a state of emergency and a "bloody collection of arms" had been made, while in Macedonia there was talk of secession (Shoup, 1968:217-23).

6. On Yugoslavia, see the opinion of W. S. Vucinich: "It seems that the socialist system itself has kept the national question alive" (Vucinich, 1969:260).

7. This point should not be pushed too far. Among the Croatian nationalists, Tripalo and Dapcevic were respected scholars.

## CHAPTER 6:
## NATIONALISM AND THE CHINESE REVOLUTION

1. Those who wish to pursue the matter further may find the following sources helpful: Boersner, 1953; Brandt, 1938; Claudín, 1975; Schram, 1967, among others. The CI itself, in its statement of dissolution, admitted that the task of directing the world revolution from a single center was an impossible one: "Any sort of international center would encounter insuperable obstacles in solving the problems facing the movement in each separate country" (Claudín, 1975:40).

2. On the persistence of militant spirit among the Shanghai workers, see Airey, 1970:122. Rewi Alley has said that the atmosphere in Shanghai in 1933, with its red agitations, was very like that which existed in 1927 before the arrival of the Kuomintang (KMT).

## CHAPTER 7: LATIN AMERICA:
## NATIONALISM OR REVOLUTION?

1. The term "Latin America" will be used, as is customary, but a more inclusive, more accurate, designation for all of the countries south of the Rio Grande would be "America South."

2. Julio Cotler is one who describes the relation of the peasants in Peru to the landowners as "really semifeudal." But even he admits that the peasant is not legally tied to the land (Horowitz, 1970: 415).

3. Of course, it is also true that serfdom in Europe was found in conjunction with production for the market; in fact, it was the desire of the East Prussian junkers to produce grain for the market that led them to reintroduce serfdom in the sixteenth century—they wished to assure themselves of a labor supply (Moore, 1966: 460-62).

4. We pointed out earlier the defects of the analysis which associates nationalism and democracy, as if that were something automatic. But even democracy in the conventional sense—capitalist democracy—has not advanced uniformly in Latin America. As well shown by James Petras, there have been long periods of regression (Petras and Zeitlin, 1968:162-63).

5. But in a statement issued the same year, 1972, Castro joined with the leaders of the Democratic Republic of North Vietnam in a statement deploring the continued antagonism between the two great socialist powers: such antagonism, they said, plays into the hands of the imperialists.

6. It should not be imagined that this policy of the Jesuits in Paraguay was part of a general policy of the Catholic Church. In Mexico, we are told that the uncultured reactionary priests made the practice of writing in native languages a crime punishable by death! (Darcy, 1972:229).

## CHAPTER 8: SOCIAL CLASSES AND THE FORMATION OF NATIONS

1. It is important to note that it is not the common language nor the commonalty of any particular feature of the culture that makes the unity of the tribe. This unity is a moral factor in the consciousness of the members of the tribe, and the cultural symbols of tribalism are "abstractions from cultural reality, not its basic elements" (La Fontaine in Gulliver, 1969:189-90). La Fontaine is here referring to the Gisu, an East African tribe. The same point was made by Minogue regarding the nation.

2. Other African countries that were left with two linguae francae were Somalia (English, Italian, and also French) and South Africa, where the Bantu-speaking population must cope with English and Afrikaans (modified Dutch). In Somalia, Arabic was also an official language.

3. Just how small, it is difficult to judge. Potehkin remarks that the subject has been almost completely disregarded (Potehkin in Wallerstein, 1966:570-71).

4. After the war, Césaire greeted André Malraux on a visit to Martinique with these words: "I salute in your person the great French nation to which we are passionately attached" (Caute, 1970:61).

5. For documentation on the PCF, see Moneta, 1968.

6. Manuel Bridier writes:

> When the working class is integrated into society (as a whole or in one or the other of its factions), when it believes (rightly or wrongly) in the possibility of taking power from within a state, then the problems of decolonization are pushed to the background and subordinated to national strategy. (Bridier, 1968:273)

7. Fanon stated flatly: "Every Frenchman in Algeria is an enemy soldier" (Fanon, 1967b:81).

8. The number of European workers in Algeria was given as 300,000, of whom 35,000 were skilled workers and 55,000 were listed as unskilled. The remainder worked in either administration and management (close to 50,000) or in services of one kind or another (some 160,000) (Wolf, 1969:224). Obviously these workers were an important part of the total picture.

9.     In the colonial countries the peasants alone are revolutionary, for they have nothing to lose and everything to gain. (Fanon, 1966:48)

Fanon's admiration for the positive qualities of the masses of the peasants was no mere romantic sentimentalism. He pointed out very justly that the slowness of the uneducated to grasp the ideas of the educated is frequently the fault of the educated, who use an abstruse vocabulary:

> If you speak the language of every day . . . you will realize that the masses are quick to seize every shade of meaning and to learn all the tricks of the trade . . . Everything can be explained to the people, on the single condition that you really want them to understand. (Ibid.:151)

10. For a Marxist critique of Fanon's concept of alienation, see Zahar, 1974.

11. In China, according to Jack Belden, "guerrilla warfare . . . often brought the Communist cadre into the peasant's hut seeking refuge" (Belden, 1970:83-84).

12. The PAIGC succeeded the Movimento para a Independencia Nacional da Guiné Portuguesa, which had existed between 1954 and 1956 (Gibson, 1972:252).

13. The idea that peasants who have spent some time in the towns and return to the countryside bring with them political sophistication and a sense of nationalist importance is not new, and is not confined to Africa. The same phenomenon was noted in the Ukraine, in a pamphlet published in 1919 (Mazlakh and Shakhrai, 1970:78-79).

14. As Lawrence Kaplan well says:

> By progress Marx meant the expansion of the productive capacity of both society and individual human beings, leading ultimately to greater equality and freedom and to the fulfillment of man's potential. (Kaplan, 1973:xvii)

15. *Wage* earners are probably meant. The original Portuguese, which was not available to us, was undoubtedly *assalariados,* which appears to mean salaried workers, but does not.

16. The Christian unions, which had their own international, also played a role in the French colonies, as did the much smaller Force Ouvrière, whose conservative outlook was comparable to that of the American Federation of Labor.

17. The World Federation of Trade Unions (WFTU) was by this time not advocating social revolution; rather it came out for a middle-of-the-road policy in the Third World, the democratic "noncapitalist road," by way of which it hoped that the countries in question would evolve into socialism (Woddis, 1963; 1967:esp. 124-25; Cox, 1966:Ch.9).

18. Anthony Smith, purportedly basing himself on Robert Davies, gives the impression that certain of the union movements were antinationalist, but that is not what Davies says (see A. Smith, 1971:125; Davies, 1973:97).

## CHAPTER 9: CONCLUSION

1. Rosa Luxemburg had a similar lack of faith in the viability of small nations.

# Bibliography

Abbott, W. M., ed. 1966. *The Documents of Vatican II*. London.

Abdel-Malek, Anouar. 1972. *La Dialectique sociale*. Paris.

Acton, Lord. 1907 (orig. ed. 1862). *The History of Freedom and Other Essays*. London.

Airey, Willis. 1970. *A Learner in China: A Life of Rewi Alley*. Christchurch, New Zealand: Caxton Press and the Monthly Review Society.

Alleg, Henri. 1960. *The Gangrene*. New York.

Allport, Floyd. 1933. *Institutional Behavior*. Chapel Hill, N.C.

Amin, Samir. 1963. "Lutte des classes en Afrique." *Révolution* 1 (Nov.).

Anweiler, Oskar. 1958. *Die Rätebewegung in Russland, 1905–1921*. Leiden.

Armstrong, John A. 1963. *Ukrainian Nationalism*. 2nd ed. New York: Columbia University Press.

Arrighi, Giovanni, and Saul, John S. 1973. *Essays on the Political Economy of Africa*. New York: Monthly Review Press.

Asturias, Miguel Angel. 1968. Interview by Ira Morris. *Monthly Review* 19 (Mar.): 52.

Avtorkhanov, A. 1959. *Stalin and the Soviet Communist Party: A Study in the Technology of Power*. New York.

Balandier, Georges. 1957. *Afrique Ambiguë*. Paris.

Banaji, Jairus. 1974. "Nationalism and Socialism." *Economic and Political Weekly* (Bombay) (Sept.).

Baudin, Louis. 1962. *Une théocratie socialiste: l'état jésuite du Paraguay*. Paris: M.-T. Génin.

Belden, Jack. 1970. *China Shakes the World*. New York: Monthly Review Press. (Orig. ed. 1949.)

Bennigsen, A. 1957. "Sultan-Galiev, l'URSS et la révolution coloniale." *L'Esprit* (April). (Reprinted in W. Z. Laqueur, ed. 1958. *The Middle East in Transition*, pp. 398-414. New York.)

Bennigsen, A., and Lemercier-Quelquejay, C. 1968. *L'Islam en Union Soviétique*. Paris: Payot.

Bennoune, Mahfoud. 1973. "French Counter-Revolutionary Doctrine and the Algerian Peasantry." *Monthly Review* 25 (Dec.).

Berki, R. N. 1971. "On Marxian Thought and the Problem of International Relations." *World Politics* 24 (Oct.)

Boersner, Demetrio. 1953. *The Bolsheviks and the National and Colonial Question, 1917–1928*. Geneva.

Bourdet, Claude. 1971. "Experiments with Liberty." *Nation* (Sept.).

Braden, Thomas W. 1967. "I'm Glad the CIA Is Immoral." *Saturday Evening Post* (May 20).

Brandt, Conrad. 1938. *Stalin's Failure in China*. Cambridge, Mass.

Braunthal, Julius. 1961. In U. G. Whitaker, ed. *Nationalism and International Progress*. San Francisco: Chandler Publishing Company.

Bridier, Manuel. 1968. *International Socialist Journal* 26-27:273.

Bruk, S. I. 1972. "Ethnodemocratic Processes in the USSR." *Soviet Sociology* 10 (Spring).

Burks, R. V. 1961. *The Dynamics of Communism in Eastern Europe*. Princeton, N.J.: Princeton University Press.

Cabral, Amilcar. 1969. *Revolution in Guinea: An African People's Struggle*. London: Stage 1; New York: Monthly Review Press.

———. 1970. *National Liberation and Culture*. Occasional Paper No. 57. Syracuse: Maxwell Graduate School, Syracuse Univ.

Carr, E. H. 1945. *Nationalism and After*. London.

———. 1950a. *Studies in Revolution*. London.

———. 1950b, 1953. *The Bolshevik Revolution 1917–1923*. Vols. 1, 3. London.

———. 1954. *The Interregnum, 1923-24*. London.

———. 1970. *Socialism in One Country*. Baltimore: Penguin.

Carr, E. H., et al. 1939. *Nationalism: A Report by a Study Group of Members of the Royal Institute of International Affairs.* Oxford.

Carrère d'Encausse, Hélène. 1966. *Réforme et révolution chez les musulmans de l'Empire russe, Bukhara, 1867–1924.* Paris: A Colin.

———. 1971. "Unité prolétarienne et diversité nationale: Lénine et la théorie de l'autodétermination." *Revue française de sciences politiques* 21 (April): 221-55.

Castro, Fidel. 1968. *History Will Absolve Me: The Moncada Trial Defence Speech, Santiago de Cuba, October 16th, 1953.* London: Jonathan Cape.

Caute, D. 1970. *Frantz Fanon.* New York: Viking Press.

Chang, C. M. 1950. "Communism and Nationalism in China." *Foreign Affairs* 28: 548-64.

Chesneaux, Jean. 1965. "Le processus de formation des nations en Afrique et en Asie." *La pensée* 119 (Feb.): 71-86.

Chesterton, G. K. 1914. *The Flying Inn.* New York.

Claudín, F. 1975. *The Communist Movement: From Comintern to Cominform.* New York: Monthly Review Press.

Cliffe, Lionel, and Saul, John, eds. 1972. *Socialism in Tanzania: An Interdisciplinary Reader:* Dar es Salaam: East Africa Publishing House.

Cobban, Alfred. 1969. *The Nation State and National Self-Determination.* Rev. ed. London: Collins.

Cohen, Jack, et al. 1975. *Collected Works.* Vol. 4: *Marx and Engels, 1844–1845.* New York: International Publishers.

Cohen, Mortimer T. 1971. Letter in *New York Times* (Dec. 17).

Cohen, R. S., et al., eds. 1974. *For Dirk Struik: Scientific Historical and Political Essays in Honor of Dirk J. Struik.* Boston Studies in the Philosophy of Science, vol. 15. Dordrecht and Boston: D. Reidel Publishing Co.

Coleman, James Smoot. 1958. *Nigeria: Background to Nationalism.* Berkeley: Univ. of California Press.

Cox, Idris. 1966. *Socialist Ideas in Africa.* London: Lawrence and Wishart.

Cranston, Maurice. 1969. "Ideologies, Past and Present." *Survey: A Journal of Soviet and East European Studies* 70-71 (Winter/Spring).

Daniels, R. V. 1960. *The Conscience of the Revolution: Communist Opposition in Soviet Russia.* Cambridge, Mass.: Harvard University Press.

Darcy, Sam. 1971. *Late Afternoon for the Nation-State.* New York.

Davidson, Basil. 1969. *The Liberation of Guiné: Aspects of an African Revolution.* Baltimore: Penguin.

———. 1970. *The Lost Cities of Africa.* Rev. ed. Boston: Little, Brown.

Davidson, Carl. 1975. *Guardian* (March 19).

Davies, Joan. 1966. *African Trade Unions.* Baltimore: Penguin.

Davies, Robert. 1973. "The White Working-Class in South Africa." *New Left Review* 82 (Nov.-Dec.).

Davis, Horace B. 1954. "Conservative Writers on Imperialism." *Science and Society* 18 (Fall): 310-25.

———. 1967. *Nationalism and Socialism.* New York: Monthly Review Press.

Debray, Régis. 1969. Letter in *Sunday Times* (Oct. 12).

Dedijer, Vladimir. 1953. *Tito.* New York.

———. 1971. *The Battle Stalin Lost: Memoirs of Yugoslavia 1948–1953.* New York: Viking Press.

Denich, Bogdan D. 1976. *The Legitimation of a Revolution: The Yugoslav Case.* New Haven: Yale Univ. Press.

Depestre, René. 1965. *Présence africaine* (4th quarter).

Desai, A. R. 1948. *The Social Background of Indian Nationalism.* Oxford.

Deutsch, Karl W. 1953. "The Growth of Nations: Some Recurrent Patterns of Political and Social Integration." *World Politics* 5: 168-95.

———. 1967. *Daedalus* 96 (Summer), special issue, "Toward the Year 2000: Work in Progress."

Deutscher, Isaac. 1949. *Stalin: A Political Biography.* London.

———. 1954. *The Prophet Armed: Trotsky 1879–1921.* London.

———. 1959. *The Prophet Unarmed: Trotsky 1921–1929.* Oxford.

———. 1963. *The Prophet Outcast: Trotsky 1929–1940.* London and New York: Oxford University Press.

———. 1971. *Marxism in Our Time.* Berkeley: Ramparts Press.

———, ed. 1964. *The Age of Permanent Revolution: A Trotsky Anthology.* New York: Dell Publishing.

Diop, Cheik Anta. 1955. *Nations nègres et culture.* Paris.

Djilas, Milovan. 1957. *The New Class: An Analysis of the Communist System.* New York.

———. 1962. *Conversations with Stalin.* New York: Harcourt, Brace and World.

———. 1969. *The Imperfect Society.* New York: Harcourt, Brace, and World.

Drobizheva, L. 1967. "Sociocultural Personality Features and Ethnic Attitudes in the Tatar ASSR." *Sovetskaia etnografia* 3: 3-15.

Dzyuba, Ivan. 1968. *Internationalism or Russification? A Study in the Soviet Nationalities Problem.* London: Weidenfeld and Nicolson.

Elliot Smith, Grafton. 1923. *The Ancient Egyptians and the Origin of Civilization.* Rev. ed. New York.

Emerson, Rupert. 1960. *From Empire to Nation: The Rise to Self-Assertion of Asian and African Peoples.* Cambridge, Mass.: Harvard University Press.

Emmanuel, Arghiri. 1972. *Unequal Exchange.* New York: Monthly Review Press.

——. 1972. "White Settler Colonialism and the Myth of Investment Imperialism." *New Left Review* 73 (May-June).

Engels, Frederick. 1902. *The Origin of the Family, Private Property and the State.* Translated by E. Untermann. Chicago.

Fagen, Richard R. 1972. "Cuban Revolutionary Politics." *Monthly Review* 23 (April): 35.

Fanon, Frantz. 1965. *A Dying Colonialism.* New York: Grove Press.

——. 1966. *The Wretched of the Earth.* New York: Grove Press.

——. 1967a. *Black Skin, White Masks.* New York: Grove Press.

——. 1967b. *Toward the African Revolution.* New York: Grove Press.

Fichte, J. G. 1918. *Nachgelassene Werke.* Edited by Hans Schulz.

Fischer, George. 1952. *Soviet Opposition to Stalin: A Case Study in World War II.* Cambridge, Mass.

Fischer, Louis. 1930. *The Soviets in World Affairs.* 2 vols. London.

Frank, Andre Gunder. 1969. *Latin America: Underdevelopment or Revolution.* New York: Monthly Review Press.

——. 1971. *Capitalism and Underdevelopment in Latin America.* New York: Monthly Review Press.

Friedrich, C. J. 1937. "The Peasant as Evil Genius of Dictatorship." *Yale Review* 4 (June).

Galeano, Eduardo. 1969. "The De-Nationalization of the Brazilian Industry." *Monthly Review* 21 (Dec.): 11-30.

Gankin, O. H., and Fisher, H. H. 1940. *The Bolsheviks and the World War: The Origin of the Third International.* Stanford.

Geertz, Clifford. 1968. *Islam Observed: Religious Development in Morocco and Indonesia.* Chicago: Univ. of Chicago Press.

Geiss, Imanuel. 1965. *Gewerkschaften in Afrika.* Hannover: Verlag für Literatur und Zeitgeschen.

Gellner, Ernest. 1964. *Thought and Change.* London: Weidenfeld and Nicolson.

Gendzier, Irene L. 1973. *Frantz Fanon: A Critical Study.* New York: Pantheon Books.

Gibson, Richard. 1972. *African Liberation Movements: Contemporary Struggles Against White Minority Rule.* London and New York: Oxford University Press.

Gilbert, W. S. 1931. "H.M.S. *Pinafore.*" In *The Complete Plays of Gilbert and Sullivan.* New York. (Orig, written 1878.)

Gillin, Donald G. 1964. Review in *Journal of Asian Studies* 23 (Feb.).

Ginsberg, Morris. 1961. *Nationalism: A Reappraisal.* Leeds: Leeds Univ.

Goldhagen, Erich. 1960. "Communism and Anti-Semitism." *Problems of Communism* 3.

———. 1968. *Ethnic Minorities in the Soviet Union.* New York: Praeger Publishers.

Gott, Richard. 1967. "Guevara, Debray, and the CIA." *Nation* (Nov. 20).

Green, T. H. 1890. *Prolegomena to Ethics.* 3rd ed. Oxford.

Guevara, Che. 1967. *Che Guevara Speaks: Selected Speeches and Writings.* Edited by George Lavan. New York: Merit.

———. 1969. *Che: Selected Works of Ernest Guevara.* Edited by R. E. Bonachea and N. P. Valdes. Cambridge, Mass.: MIT Press.

Gulliver, P. H. 1969. *Tradition and Transition in East Africa: Studies of the Tribal Element in the Modern Era.* Berkeley: Univ. of California Press.

Halliday, Fred. 1971. "The Ceylonese Insurrection." *New Left Review* 69 (Sept.-Oct.): 55-91.

Halperin, Ernst. 1958. *The Triumphant Heretic: Tito's Struggle Against Stalin.* London.

Halperin, Maurice. 1972. *The Rise and Decline of Fidel Castro: An Essay in Contemporary History.* Berkeley: Univ. of California Press.

Handlin, Oscar. 1950. *Race and Nationality in American Life.* New York.

Haupt, Georges, Lowy, Michael, and Weill, Claudie. 1974. *Les marxistes et la question nationale, 1848–1914.* Paris: Maspero.

Heberle, Rudolf. 1970. *From Democracy to Nazism.* New York: Fertig. (Orig. ed. 1945.)

Heimann, Eduard. 1947. *Freedom and Order: Lessons from the War.* New York.

Hentze, J., ed. 1971. *Rosa Luxemburg: Internationalismus und Klassenkampf.* Luchterhand.

Herder, Johann Gottfried. 1909. *Ideen zur Philosophie der Geschichte der Menschheit.* Part 3. Edited by B. Suphan. Berlin.

Herrfahrdt, H. 1950. *Sun Yatsen: Der Vater des neuen China.* Hamburg.

Hertz, Frederick. 1944. *Nationality in History and Politics: A Study of the Psychology and Sociology of National Sentiment and Character.* New York.

Hessel, Arthur R. 1964. "The Bund and Social Democracy, 1903-06." Honors thesis, Harvard Univ.

Hirsch, Fred. 1974. *An Analysis of Our AFL-CIO Role in Latin America, or Under the Covers with the CIA.* San Jose.

*History of the Communist Party of the Soviet Union (Bolshevik): Short Course.* 1939. Moscow.

Hone, Angus. 1973. "The Primary Commodities Boom." *New Left Review* 81: 90.

Horowitz, David. 1969. *Empire and Revolution: A Radical Interpretation of Contemporary History.* New York: Random House.

Horowitz, Irving L., comp. 1970. *Masses in Latin America.* New York: Oxford University Press.

Horowitz, Irving L., de Castro, Josué, and Gerassi, John, eds. 1969. *Latin America Radicalism: A Documentary Report on Left and Nationalist Movements.* New York: Random House.

Howard, Peter. 1967. "The Definition of a Nation: A Discussion in *Voprosy Istorii.*" *Central Asian Review* 15: 27-35.

Hunt, R. N. Carew. 1963. *The Theory and Practice of Communism: An Introduction.* Baltimore: Penguin.

Ianni, Octavio. 1964a. "Political Process and Economic Development in Brazil." Part 1. *New Left Review* 25 (May-June): 39-52.

———. 1964b. "Political Process and Economic Development." Part 2. *New Left Review* 26 (July-Aug.): 50-68.

———, ed. 1965. *Política e revolução social no Brasil.* Rio de Janeiro: Editora Civilização Brasileira.

Irwin, Will. 1921. *The Next War.* New York.

Ivanov, K. 1964. "The National-Liberation Movement and the Non-Capitalist Path of Development." *International Affairs* (Moscow) 9 (Sept.).

Johnson, Chalmers A. 1962. *Peasant Nationalism and Communist Power.* Stanford, Calif.: Stanford Univ. Press.

Johnson, John J., ed. 1962. *The Role of the Military in Underdeveloped Countries.* Princeton: Princeton Univ. Press.

Jončič, Koca. 1969. *Relations Among the Peoples and National Minorities in Yugoslavia.* Belgrade.

Kaltakchyan, S. 1972. "Bilingualism Knits Ties among USSR Nations." *Daily World* (Dec. 8).

Kaplan, Lawrence, and Kaplan, Carol, eds. 1973. *Revolutions: A Comparative Study.* New York: Random House.

Kardelj, Edward [Sperans]. 1958. *Razvoi slovenackog nacionalnog pitania* [The Development of the Slovenian National Question]. 2nd ed. Belgrade.

————. 1960. *Socialism and War: A Survey of Chinese Criticism of the Policy of Coexistence.* Translated by Alec Brown. New York: McGraw-Hill.

Kautsky, John H., ed. 1962. *Political Change in Underdeveloped Countries: Nationalism and Communism.* New York: Wiley.

Kautsky, Karl. 1929. *Die materialistische Geschichtsaffasung.* Vol. 2. Berlin.

Kedourie, Elie. 1960. *Nationalism.* London: Hutchinson.

————, ed. 1970. *Nationalism in Asia and Africa.* New York: Norton.

Kilson, Martin L., Jr. 1958. "Nationalism and Social Classes in British West Africa." *Journal of Politics* (Univ. of Florida) 20 (May).

Kim Il Sung. 1969. *Let Us Promote the World Revolution.* Pyongyang.

King, Robert R. 1973. *Minorities under Communism: Nationalities as a Source of Tension among Balkan Communist States.* Cambridge: Harvard Univ. Press.

Klein, Martin A. 1971. Review in *Science and Society* 35 (Fall): 348-52.

Kohn, Hans. 1929. *A History of Nationalism in the East.* London.

————. 1944. *The Idea of Nationalism.* New York.

————, ed. 1954. *German History: Some New German Views.* Boston.

Kolarz, W. 1956. *Russia and Her Colonies.* 3rd ed. New York.

Krasso, Nicholas. 1967. "Trotsky's Marxism." *New Left Review* 44 (July-Aug.): 64-86.

Kulski, W. W. 1954. *The Soviet Regime.* Syracuse.

Landau, David. 1972. "The Rand Papers." *Ramparts* 11 (Nov.).

Landis, Richard B. 1964. "The Origins of Whampoa Graduates Who Served in the Northern Expedition." *Studies on Asia* (Lincoln, Nebr.).

Laski, Harold J. 1939. "Nationalism and the Future of Civilisation." In *The Danger of Being a Gentleman.* London. (Orig. ed. 1932.)

Lemberg, Eugen. 1964. *Nationalismus.* Vol. 2: *Soziologie und politische Pedagogik.* Hamburg: Rowohlt.

Lendavi, Paul. 1969. *Eagles in Cobwebs: Nationalism and Communism in the Balkans.* Garden City, N.Y.: Doubleday.

————. 1971. *Anti-Semitism Without Jews: Communist Eastern Europe.* Garden City, N.Y.: Doubleday.

Lenin, V. I. 1935–38. *Selected Works.* New York.

————. 1960–75. *Collected Works* (CW). 45 vols. Moscow.

Lepkowski, Tadeusz. 1971. "Socjologiczne in Historyczne Aspekty Teoretycznych Problemow Narodu i Panstwa." *Kwartalnik Historyczny* 78: 94-102.

Lerner, Warren. 1970. *Karl Radek: The Last Internationalist.* Stanford: Stanford Univ. Press.

Lewin, Moshe. 1978. *Lenin's Last Struggle.* New York: Pantheon.

Liu Shao-chi. 1948. *Internationalism and Nationalism.* New York.

Lowy, Michael. 1971. "Rosa Luxemburg et la question nationale." *Partisans* (May-Aug.).

Luethy, Herbert. 1955. *France Against Herself.* New York.

Luxemburg, Rosa [Junius]. 1919. *The Russian Revolution.* Chap. 3: "The Nationalities Question." Translated by Bertram D. Wolfe. New York.

———. 1928. "The Russian Revolution." In *Archiv für die Geschichte des Sozialismus und der Arbeiterbewegung.* Edited by Carl Grünberg. Leipzig.

———. 1969. *The Crisis in the Social Democracy.* New York: Fertig.

———. 1971. *Internationalismus und Klassenkampf.* Translated by J. Hentze. Luchterhand.

———. 1976. *The National Question: Selected Writings.* Edited by Horace B. Davis. New York: Monthly Review Press.

Lynd, G. E. 1968. *The Politics of African Trade Unionism.* New York: Praeger Publishers.

Malloy, J. M. 1970. *Bolivia: The Uncompleted Revolution.* Pittsburgh: Univ. of Pittsburgh Press.

Malloy, James, and Thorne, Richard, eds. 1971. *Beyond the Revolution: Bolivia since 1952.* Pittsburgh: Univ. of Pittsburgh Press.

Mandel, William M. 1974. "Urban Ethnic Minorities in the Soviet Union." Unpublished ms.

Mao Tse-tung. 1954. *Selected Works.* Vol. 5. 1945-1949. New York.

———. 1960. *Selected Works.* 4 vols. Peking: Foreign Languages Press.

———. 1967. *The Thoughts of Chairman Mao Tse-tung.* London: Gibbs.

———. 1977. *A Critique of Soviet Economics.* New York: Monthly Review Press.

Martins, Wilson. 1970. *The Modernist Idea.* New York: New York Univ. Press.

Marx, Karl. 1927. *Gesamtausgabe.*

———. 1936. *Selected Works.* Moscow.

———. 1961. *Economic and Philosophic Manuscripts of 1844.* Moscow: Foreign Languages Publishing House.

———. 1964. *Early Writings.* Translated and edited by T. B. Bottomore. New York: McGraw-Hill.

Marx, Karl, and Engels, Frederick. 1968. *Selected Writings.* New York: International Publishing Co.

Mazlakh, S., and Shakhrai, V. 1970. *On the Current Situation in the Ukraine.* Ann Arbor: Univ. of Michigan Press.

Mboya, Tom. 1963. *Freedom and After.* Boston: Little, Brown.

McDougall, William. 1934. "Ethics of Nationalism." In *Religion and the Sciences of Life.* London.

McNeal, Robert H. 1967. *Stalin's Works,* Vol. 26. Stanford, Ca.: The Hoover Institute.

Medvedyev, Roy A. 1971. "Jews in the USSR: Problems and Prospects." *Survey* 17: 185-200.

————. 1971. *Let History Judge: The Origins and Consequences of Stalinism.* New York: Knopf.

Meinecke, Friedrich. 1957. *Machiavellism: The Doctrine of Raison d'Etat and Its Place in Modern History.* New Haven: Yale Univ. Press.

Meissner, Boris. "The Soviet Concept of Nation and the Right of National Self-Determination." *International Journal of the Canadian Institute of International Affairs* 32, no. 1 (Winter 1976-77).

Memmi, Albert. 1968. *Dominated Man: Notes Toward a Portrait.* New York: Orion Press.

Meszaros, I. 1972. *Marx's Theory of Alienation.* 3rd ed. London: Merlin.

Meyer, Alfred G. 1954. *Marxism: The Unity of Theory and Practice.* Cambridge, Mass.

Mill, John Stuart. 1861. *Considerations on Representative Government.* London.

Miller, Norman, and Aya, Roderick, eds. 1971. *National Liberation: Revolution in the Third World.* New York: Free Press.

Minogue, K. R. 1967. *Nationalism.* London: Batsford.

Moneta, Jakob. 1968. *Die Kolonialpolitik der französischen KP.* Hannover.

Moore, Barrington. 1966. *Social Origins of Dictatorship and Democracy.* Boston: Beacon Press.

More, Carlos. 1965. *Présence africaine* (4th quarter).

Morgenthau, Hans. 1961. "Nationalism: A Dilemma." In U. G. Whitaker, ed. *Nationalism and International Progress.* Rev. ed. San Francisco: Chandler Book Co.

Moseley, George, translator. 1966. *The Party and the National Question in China,* by Chang Chih-i. Cambridge: Massachusetts Institute of Technology.

Mosely, Philip E. 1948. "Aspects of Russian Expansion." *American Slavic and East European Review* 7.

Munger, Edwin S. 1967. *Afrikaner and African Nationalism: South*

*African Parallels and Parameters*. London: Oxford Univ. Press.

Nair, A. S., and Scalabrino, C. 1971. "La question nationale dans la théorie marxiste révolutionnaire." *Partisans* 59-60 (May-Aug.).

Nairn, Tom. 1974. "Scotland and Europe." *New Left Review* 83 (Jan.).

Namier, L. B. 1952. *Avenues of History*. London.

Neal, Fred Warner. 1958. *Titoism in Action: The Reforms in Yugoslavia after 1948*. Berkeley: Univ. of California Press.

North, R. C. 1965. *World Revolutionary Elites*. Cambridge, Mass.

Nyerere, Julius K. 1968. *Freedom and Socialism/Uhuru na Ujamaa: A Selection from Writings and Speeches 1965-1967*. Dar es Salaam: Oxford Univ. Press.

O'Connell, James. 1967. "The Inevitability of Instability." *Journal of Modern African Studies* 5.

O'Connor, James. 1970. *The Origins of Socialism in Cuba*. Syracuse: Cornell Univ. Press.

Ouzegane, Amar. 1962. *Le meilleur combat*. Paris: Julliard.

Ovando, Jorge. 1961. *Sobre el problema nacional y colonial de Bolivia*. Cochabamba.

Owen, Roger, and Sutcliffe, Bob, eds. 1972. *Studies in the Theory of Imperialism*. London: Longman.

Papandreou, Andreas. 1972. "Greece: Neocolonialism and Revolution." *Monthly Review* 24 (Dec.).

Peredo, Inti. 1968. Communication. *New Left Review* 51. *Review* 51.

Perloff, Harvey. 1967. *Daedalus* 96 (Summer), special issue, "Toward the Year 2000: Work in Progress.

Perovic, Punisa. 1968. "Socialism and National Sovereignty." *Socialist Thought and Practice* (Belgrade) 32 (Nov.-Dec.): 78.

Petras, James. 1966. "Coordinated Counter-Revolution: Latin America's New Phase." *New Left Review* 38 (July-Aug.).

———. 1968. "U.S.-Latin American Studies: A Critical Assessment." *Science and Society* 32 (Spring).

Petras, James, and Zeitlin, Maurice, eds. 1968. *Latin America: Reform or Revolution?—A Reader*. Greenwich, Conn.: Fawcett Publications.

Petrovich, Michael B. 1972. "Yugoslavia: Religion and the Tensions of a Multi-National State." *East European Quarterly* (Boulder, Colo.) 6 (Mar.).

Pipes, Richard. 1954. *The Formation of the Soviet Union: Communism and Nationalism 1917-1923*. Cambridge, Mass.

Pokrovsky, M. N. 1968. *Brief History of Russia*. Translated by D. S. Mirsky. 2nd ed. Orono, Me.: University Prints and Reprints.

Polanyi, K. 1944. *The Great Transformation*. Boston.

Potehkin, I. I. 1957–1958. "De quelques problèmes méthodologiques pour l'étude de la formation des nations en Afrique au sud du Sahara." *Présence africaine* 17 (Dec.-Jan.): 60-73.

———. 1964. *Africa: Ways of Development.* Moscow.

Prado, Caio, Jr. 1966. *A revolução Brasileira.* São Paulo: Editora Brasiliense.

Quíjano, Aníbal. 1971. "Nationalism and Capitalism in Peru: A Study in Neo-Imperialism." *Monthly Review* 23 (July-Aug.).

Rakic, Vojo. 1968. "Economic Relations in the Yugoslav Multinational Community." *Socialist Thought and Practice* (Belgrade) 29.

Raymond, Ellsworth Lester. 1968. *The Soviet State.* New York: Macmillan.

Reddaway, Peter. 1974. Review in *New York Review of Books* (Dec. 12).

Renan, Ernest. 1882. *Qu'est-ce qu'une nation?* Paris.

Robert, Paul. 1958. *Dictionnaire alphabétique et analytique de la langue française.* Paris.

Robinson, Joan, and Eatwell, John. 1973. *An Introduction to Modern Economics.* New York: McGraw-Hill.

Rodinson, Maxime. 1966. Preface to *Réforme et révolution chez les musulmans de l'Empire russe, Bukhara, 1867–1924* by Hélène Carrère d'Encausse. Paris: A. Colin.

———. 1968. "Le marxisme et la nation." *L'homme et la Société* 7 (Jan.-March).

———. 1972. *Marxisme et monde musulman.* Paris: Editions du Seuil.

———. 1973. *Islam and Capitalism.* New York: Pantheon.

Rosdolsky, Roman. 1965. Note in *Science and Society* (Summer): 330-37.

Royce, Josiah. 1908. *The Philosophy of Loyalty.* New York.

Salov. 1972. *International Affairs* (Moscow) (Aug.).

Sampson, R. V. 1965. *Equality and Power.* London: Heinemann. (Published in the United States as *The Psychology of Power.* New York: Pantheon, 1966.)

Schapiro, Leonard. 1970. *The Communist Party of the Soviet Union.* 2nd ed. London: Eyre and Spottiswoode.

Schirmer, Daniel Boone. 1972. *Republic or Empire: American Resistance to the Philippine War.* Cambridge, Mass.: Schenkman.

Schram, Stuart R. 1967. *Mao Tse-tung.* New York: Simon and Schuster.

Schroeder, Gertrude E. 1973. "Soviet Wage and Income Policies in Regional Perspective." Mimeographed. (Revision of article in J. N. Bandera and Z. Lew Melnyk, eds. 1973. *The Soviet Economy in Regional Perspective.* New York: Praeger Publishers.)

Schuman, Frederick L. 1976. "More on the Nature of Soviet Society." *Monthly Review* 27 (Mar.).

Seidman, Ann, and Green, Reginald. 1968. *Unity or Poverty?* Baltimore: Penguin.

Selden, Mark. 1969. "People's War and Transformation of Peasant Society: China and Vietnam." In Edward Friedman and Mark Selden, eds. *America's Asia: Dissenting Essays on Asian-American Relations.* New York: Pantheon.

Shaheen, Samad. 1956. *The Communist (Bolshevik) Theory of National Self-Determination: Its Historical Evolution up to the October Revolution.* The Hague-Bandung.

Sheehy, Ann. 1969. *Mizan* (London) 11 (Sept.-Oct.): 271-83.

Shoup, Paul. 1968. *Communism and the Yugoslav National Question.* New York: Columbia Univ. Press.

Sigmund, Paul E., ed. 1972. *The Ideologies of the Developing Nations.* 2nd ed. New York: Praeger Publishers.

Silvert, K. H. 1966. *The Conflict Society: Reaction and Revolution in Latin America.* Rev. ed. New York: American Universities Field Staff.

———, ed. 1963. *Expectant Peoples: Nationalism and Development.* New York: Random House.

Sklar, Richard L. 1967. "Political Science and Radical Integration: A Radical Approach." *Journal of Modern African Studies* 5.

Smal-Stocki, Roman. 1960. *The Captive Nations: Nationalism of the Non-Russian Nations in the Soviet Union.* New York: Bookman Associates.

Smith, Anthony D. 1971. *Theories of Nationalism.* London: Duckworth.

Solchanyk, Roman. 1968. "The 'Sophistication' of Soviet Nationality Policy in the Ukraine." *Ukrainian Quarterly* 24 (Winter).

Souvarine, Boris. 1939. *Stalin: A Critical Survey of Bolshevism.* New York.

*Soviet Union, 50 Years Statistical Returns.* 1969. Moscow: Progress Publishers.

Stalin, Joseph. 1942. *Marxism and the National Question: Selected Writings and Speeches.* New York.

———. 1952–1955. *Works.* Vols. 1-13. Moscow.

Stavis, Ben. 1974. "China's Green Revolution." *Monthly Review* 26 (Oct.).

Steenberg, Sven. 1970. *Vlasov.* New York: Knopf.

Sterling, Richard W. 1958. *Ethics in a World of Power: The Political Ideas of Friedrich Meinecke.* Princeton.

Stoianovich, Traian. 1974. Review in *Political Science Quarterly* 89.

Sulzbach, Walter. 1943. *National Consciousness*. Washington, D.C.

Symmons-Somonolewicz, K. 1968. *Modern Nationalism: Towards a Consensus Theory*. New York: Polish-Institute of Arts and Sciences of America.

———. 1970. *Nationalist Movements: A Comparative View*. Meadville, Pa.: Maplewood.

Tito. Josip Broz. 1963. *Selected Speeches and Articles 1941-1961*. Zagreb: Naprijed.

Tobias, Henry J. 1972. *The Jewish Bund in Russia from Its Origins to 1905*. Stanford: Stanford University Press.

Tomasic, Dinko. 1946. "Nationality Problems in Partisan Yugoslavia." *Journal of Central European Affairs* 6(July).

———. 1960. "The New Class and Nationalism." *Journal of Croatian Studies* 1.

Toynbee, Arnold. 1939. *A Study of History*. Vol. 4. London.

Trotsky (Trotskii), Leon. 1947. *Stalin: An Appraisal of the Man and His Influence*. London.

———. 1970. 1916 letter to Henriette Roland Holst in *Spokesman* 4 (June): 25.

———. 1973. *Writings of Leon Trotsky* [1930–1931]. New York: Merit.

Tucker, Robert C. 1973. *Stalin as Revolutionary, 1879-1929: A Study in History and Personality*. New York: Norton.

Ulam, Adam B. 1973. *Stalin: The Man and His Era*. New York: Viking.

Vasilev, Kiro Hadzi. 1961. "Internationalism and the Unity of Socialist Forces." *Socialist Thought and Practice* (Belgrade) 4 (Dec.).

Veblen, Thorstein. 1917. *An Inquiry into the Nature of Peace and the Terms of Its Perpetuation*. New York.

Véliz, Claudio. 1968. "Centralism and Nationalism in Latin America." *Foreign Affairs* 47 (Oct.).

Vincent, Theodore G. 1972. *Black Power and the Garvey Movement*. Berkeley, Ca.: Ramparts Press.

Vlahovic, Veljko. 1964. "National Relations." *Socialist Thought and Practice* (Belgrade) 16.

Von Rauch, Georg. 1959. *A History of Soviet Russia*. Rev. ed. New York.

Vratusa, Antun. 1971. "Yugoslavia 1971." *Foreign Affairs* 50 (October).

Vucinich, W. S., ed. 1969. *Contemporary Yugoslavia: Twenty Years of Socialist Experiment*. Berkeley, Ca.: Univ. of California Press.

Wales, Nym [Helen Snow]. 1939. *Inside Red China*. New York.

———. 1945. *The Chinese Labor Movement*. New York.

Wallerstein, Immanuel, ed. 1966. *Social Change: The Colonial Situation.* New York: Wiley.

Ward, Barbara. 1966. *Nationalism and Ideology.* New York: Norton.

Warren, Bill. 1973. "Imperialism and Capitalist Industrialisation." *New Left Review* 81 (Sept.-Oct.): 3-45.

Whitaker, U. G., ed. 1961. *Nationalism and International Progress.* Rev. ed. San Francisco: Chandler Publishing Co.

Wiatr, Jerzy J. 1969. *Narod i panstwo* [Nationality and State]. 2nd ed. Warsaw: Ksiaźka i Wiedza.

————, ed. 1971. *The State of Sociology in Eastern Europe Today.* Carbondale, Ill.: Southern Illinois Univ. Press.

Wilber, Charles K. 1969. *The Soviet Model and Underdeveloped Countries.* Chapel Hill, N.C.: Univ. of North Carolina Press.

Woddis, Jack. 1963. *Africa: The Way Ahead.* London: Lawrence and Wishart.

————. 1967. *An Introduction to Neo-Colonialism.* London: Lawrence and Wishart.

Wolf, Eric. 1969. *Peasant Wars in the Twentieth Century: Class Basis of Peasant Revolution.* New York: Harper and Row.

Worsley, Peter. 1972. "Frantz Fanon and the 'Lumpenproletariat.' " *Socialist Register 1972.* New York: Monthly Review Press.

Zahar, Renate. 1975. *Frantz Fanon: Colonialism and Alienation.* New York: Monthly Review Press.

Znaniecki, Florian. 1952. *Modern Nationalities: A Sociological Study.* Urbana, Ill.

# Index

Abdel-Malek, Anouar, 170
Acton, Lord, 40-41, 43, 245
African culture: Fanon and, 217-18
African nations: attitudes of
    unions toward national libera-
    tion in, 235-38; Cabral's theory
    of national liberation for,
    220-28; colonialism and building
    of, 202-8; Fanon's theory of
    national liberation for, 209-20;
    nationalism and democracy in,
    33; as neither historically evolved
    nor stable, 72; pan-Africanism,
    231-38; See also specific African
    nations
Afro-Cubans, 194
Agricultural development, see
    Development
Albania, 137-39
Alexander the Great, 39
Aleksandr I (King of Yugoslavia),
    140
Algerian War of Independence:
    Césaire and, 212-13; Fanon and,
    209, 211, 213-15, 219-20;
    French Communist Party and,

212; leadership in, 228; measur-
    ing Algerian nationalism during,
    15-16, 36; rise of nationalist
    movement and, 9-10; white
    Algerian workers opposed to,
    229
Altai nationality, 110
Altai-Saian nationality, 110
Amangeldi, Iman-Suli, 95
Amaru, Túpac, 196
Amin, Samir, 205
Anarchist view of nationalism,
    39-40
Angola, 219, 227, 234
Anguilla, 7
Anticolonialism: formation of
    nations as result of, 9; nation-
    alism in, 5; See also African
    nations; Latin America; and
    specific Latin American
    countries
Anti-Semitism, 74, 128-34
Argentina, 183, 197, 243
Aristocracy: landed, as social basis
    of nationalism, 76
Armenia (S.S.R.), 66, 69, 74, 90,